MATTHEW 23-25
A LITERARY, HISTORICAL, AND
THEOLOGICAL COMMENTARY

Other books by James B. Jordan

The Law of the Covenant

Judges: God's War Against Humanism

Through New Eyes Christendom and the Nations

Creation in Six Days

The Handwriting on the Wall

Primeval Saints

The Vindication of Jesus Christ

The Liturgy Trap

Crisis, Opportunity, and the Christian Future

Covenant Sequence in Leviticus and Deuteronomy

MATTHEW
23-25

A LITERARY, HISTORICAL, AND THEOLOGICAL COMMENTARY

—∞∞∞—

JAMES B. JORDAN

American Vision
Powder Springs, Georgia

Published by:
The American Vision, Inc.
3150 Florence Road
Powder Springs, Georgia 30127-5385
www.AmericanVision.org

Cover art: Enrique Simonet, *Flevit super illam* (1892)
Design and typesetting: Michael Bull

Produced in the United States of America.
ISBN: 978-0-9826105-8-9

TABLE OF CONTENTS

Table of Contents

FOREWORD

JERRY BOWYER

It's pretty unlikely you have already read the middle of this book. People generally don't start at the middle of a book and then move to the Foreword or introduction. They almost always look at the cover first, which is why we have an aphorism warning us not to judge a book by its cover and none that warn us not to judge a book by its center. Books are physically structured so that the first thing we see is the outside.

But before books, we had scrolls and scrolls don't start in the beginning; they start in the middle. As one starts to unroll a scroll, the middle is exposed first. My wife and I once visited a Christian television network, and they had a Torah scroll as a kind of background prop. We wanted to read the opening chapter of Genesis, a favorite and familiar passage, but at first, only the middle was exposed. We had to roll the scroll back to the beginning, which took about twenty minutes. A rolled-up scroll starts in the middle, while a book starts with the beginning.

My point is that the mode of ancient publishing, the scroll, is inherently conducive to chiastic content, which typically emphasizes what is in the middle of a book or passage. Books, modern ones like the one you're holding now, start with a hook in the beginning and then move towards some sort of climax towards the end.

For this and other reasons, we modern readers, when we read ancient literature, have to consciously readjust our style of thinking in a way that doesn't feel natural.

In this book, James Jordan brilliantly unlocks the chiastic structure, not just of the title passage but of the whole book of Matthew. He shows how the central hinge on which the book is structured is the decision by the Pharisees in Matthew 12:14 to kill Jesus—the center through which all the themes cross is the decision to send Jesus to the cross. The cross is the crux of the book.

On the surface level, Jordan's book is a defense of what is sometimes called "partial preterism," which is an interpretive approach for dealing with eschatological sections of the Bible. This approach sees many of the texts which in the past century have been interpreted as predictions of the end of the world, as being in reality about the end of Jerusalem, the Temple, and the Old Covenant. But partial preterism stands not just in contrast to futurism (e.g., the Left Behind series, microchips, global government under the anti-Christ, etc.) but also in contrast to "full preterism," also known as "consistent preterism" which denies a yet second coming altogether. Jordan's view is that the Olivet Discourse (which is the main topic of this book) is mainly focused on the Fall of Jerusalem, but that some of the later passages are about the second coming.

So, Jordan clearly believes in the second coming. This is important to emphasize because the futurist interpretation has become so deeply engrained in the evangelical mind, at least since the 1970s, that it is often thought of as the only orthodox view. This is simply wrong. During the Patristic era, it was commonly believed that passages such as Matthew 24 were about the Fall of Jerusalem in AD 70, not about the end of the world. Early commentaries identified Nero Caesar as the "beast" mentioned in Revelation. So, the AD 70 fulfillment has a long pedigree among orthodox Christians.

It's the modern approach of pop evangelicalism that is doctrinally suspect. For example, the earliest creed of the church says that Jesus "ascended into heaven and sits at the right hand of the Father from whence He shall come to judge the living and the dead." Let me repeat, "from whence he shall come to judge." The early church did not believe that Jesus would come halfway down, trigger a rapture of the church, resurrect some, then leave for 1,000 years and then come back down when the 1,000 years were over and then after that judge the living and the dead. No, He just comes from the right hand to judge. It's Left Behindism that is on dubious ground in terms of orthodoxy.

With the publication of this book, the ball is now in the court of the futurists. Jordan's meticulous, detailed treatment of these passages requires either an equally detailed rebuttal or else acceptance.

As an aside, I really don't like the label "preterism" because "isms" can be off-putting and because saying that one holds to "partial preterism" and opposes the heretical "full preterism" sounds a little bit like one is halfway towards heresy. I prefer to call this approach "historical fulfillment." There's nothing odd in thinking that books written in the First Century are mainly about things that happened in the First Century. And there is certainly nothing odd in believing that a Jesus who repeatedly warned about "this generation" and its uniquely evil ways was issuing warnings about things that would happen within a generation.

But Jordan goes much deeper here than just issuing the definitive defense of an AD 70 fulfillment for Matthew 24. He goes on to unpack in fascinating ways deeper aspects of the text. Those who are committed to hermeneutical minimalism will, of course, scoff. And maybe they'll be right too in some cases. He may go too far into what he likes to call "the deep weird," but as long as we hold loosely to speculative interpretations, it's worth stretching outside of our comfort zone, otherwise there is no chance for theological advancement.

In hypothesis testing, there are two types of error. Type I error refers to accepting a hypothesis that in reality is wrong. One might notice a pattern or a correlation and consider one's favorite theory confirmed. But sometimes these are false positives. Sometimes the evidence is overread.

On the other hand, there is Type II error, rejecting a true theory. Type I is excess credulity. Type II is excess skepticism. Often conservative evangelical and especially classic reformed exegesis seems worried only about excess credulity and not about excess skepticism. But both types of errors are, well, errors. Jordan's gift to the church is to press us into thinking hard about how to uncover the insights more deeply hidden in the Bible and not just rush on to "Move along, there's nothing to see here" hermeneutics. There's a lot to see here.

One aspect of the book I found myself pushing back against was how Jordan uses the phrase "the Jews." It's not always clear who that refers to. To his credit, he rightly condemns the idea that no wrongdoing from previous generations, including one almost 2,000 years ago, carries forward throughout history resting on the Jewish people even to the present day. But I still found myself wondering whether Jordan has read the case made by N.T. Wright (whom Jordan cites respectfully on another matter in this book) that the default translation of the Greek *iudaios* in the context of the Gospels should probably be something more like "Judeans" than "Jews" generally. Personally, I've concluded that the Gospel accounts recognize a clear distinction between the capitol region of Judea and other regions such as Galilee. The issue is complex and the word is used differently in different historical contexts and Wright (and I) could be wrong. But this issue should not be glossed over in favor of always defaulting to "the Jews." I think this is doubly needed in that there is going to be a certain tendency for some unsavory elements to drift into the outer penumbra of various preterist circles and caution is called for in not inadvertently giving cover to extremist anti-Semitic factions.

But that quibble aside, I urge readers to set aside newspaper exegesis and read this book to help you read The Book through ancient eyes so you can read it again through new eyes.

Jerry Bowyer, STL Magna Cum Laude, is an economist, author, and ordained deacon. He is a fellow with the Center for Cultural Leadership and with The Discovery Institute's Center on Wealth & Poverty and is a member of the advisory board of Theopolis Institute. Jerry is the author of *The Maker Versus the Takers: What Jesus Really Said About Social Justice and Economics* and writes for The Christian Post's Business page and *World Magazine*'s Opinion page.

INTRODUCTION

GARY DeMar

Every Bible commentary on Matthew, Mark, and Luke includes an exposition of the Olivet Discourse. Individual books that deal with prophecy often incorporate a commentary on the Olivet Discourse.[1] There are several approaches to explain what events Jesus was describing and when they would occur. The most popular interpretation argues that Jesus was outlining events in the lead up to the rise and rule of the antichrist, the impact of the great tribulation, and great signs in the physical heavens. The claim is made that use of "this generation" in Matthew 24:34 refers to a future generation that sees all the signs Jesus mentions fulfilled at that time. Verse 34 is read this way: "The generation **that sees these signs** will not pass away until all these things take place." The near demonstrative "this" must be removed and "that sees these signs" must be added to make the passage read that way. Jesus was very clear which generation would see all these signs: "even so **you** too, when **you** see all these signs, recognize that it is near, at the door" (v. 33). The "you" refers to those of that generation.

Others argue that the Greek word *genea* can be translated as "race," that is, the Jewish race will not pass away until all the events listed by Jesus pass away. *Genea* means "generation" (Matt. 1:17) while *genos* means "race." Jesus uses *genea*. In addition, there is a logical problem in that when all the events described by Jesus take place, the Jewish race passes away. This makes no sense since those who advocate for this view

---

1. For example, see Sam Storms, *Kingdom Come: The Amillennial Alternative* (Scotland: Mentor, 2013), 229–281 and Gary DeMar, *Last Days Madness: Obsession of the Modern Church,* 4th ed. (Powder Springs, GA: The American Vision [1999] 2019).

believe that Israel will be physically restored to the land forever after the events described by Jesus in the Olivet Discourse.

Some claim that Jesus meant that "this kind of generation" would not pass away until all these things take place. To get this interpretation to work, the word "kind" or "type of" must be added to what Jesus said. Jesus does not say "this kind of generation will not pass away." He says "this generation," the same phrase that is used in Matthew 23:36 which even futurists teach refers to the lead up to the destruction of the temple that took place in AD 70 at the hands of the Romans. For example, Thomas Ice agrees that Matthew 23:36 "is an undisputed reference to AD 70."[2]

While the distant futurist view is popular, the most striking problem is that the use of "this generation" always refers to the generation to whom Jesus was speaking (Mt. 11:16; 12:41, 45; 23:36; 24:34; Mark 8:12 [twice], 8:38; 13:30 Luke 7:31; 11:29 [in sentence form]; 11:30, 31, 32, 50, 51, 17:25; 21:32).

Another interpretation argues for a mixed approach. Some events are said to refer to the destruction of the temple, an event that took place in AD 70, while other prophetic markers refer to events in the distant future yet to be fulfilled.

Throughout the discourse, Jesus continually uses the second-person plural (Matt. 24:2, 6, 9, 19, 23, 25, 26, 33, 34). In fact, He begins by identifying the audience as far back as Matthew 21:16. The religious leaders understood that Jesus "was speaking about them" (21:45), not some distant group of people. Tim LaHaye's *Prophecy Study Bible* argues that the word "'you' must be taken generically as 'you of the Jewish nation'"[3] beginning with Matthew 24:9. There is nothing that indicates that a shift in the audience takes place.

---

2. Thomas Ice, "The Great Tribulation is Past: Rebuttal," *The Great Tribulation: Past or Future?—Two Evangelicals Debate the Question* (Grand Rapids, MI: Kregel, 1999), 103–104.

3. Tim LaHaye, ed. *Prophecy Study Bible* (Chattanooga, TN: AMG Publishers, 2000), 1038, note on Matthew 24:15.)

John Murray, a non-dispensationalist, similarly argues that there are divisions in the Olivet Discourse that address different periods of prophetic time. For example, he claims that "[i]n verses 4-14 Jesus deals with certain outstanding features of the interadventual period,"[4] that is, the time between Jesus' first coming and His physical Second Coming, an event that is still in our future. For Murray, "the end" (Matt. 24:3, 6, 13, 14) is a yet future end that will commence with these similar prophetic events and the return of Jesus in glory. The thing of it is, everything before verse 35 was to have taken place before that generation passed away. "This generation will not pass away **until all these things take place**" (24:34).

Still, others see a double fulfillment. Yes, Jesus was describing events that affected that first-century generation, but these events would occur again before either the "rapture of the church" or the Second Coming of Jesus. The disciples ask about the temple, the temple that Jesus said would be left to them desolate (Matt. 23:38). They were surprised by this statement. Jesus confirmed His judgment language with the following:

> Jesus left the temple and was going away when His disciples came up to point out the temple buildings to Him. But He responded and said to them, "Do you not see all these things? Truly I say to you, not one stone here will be left upon another, which will not be torn down" (24:1-2).

Jesus made it very clear: "not one stone here will be left upon another." It was the temple that was standing in their day, completed in AD 64, and finally destroyed six years later that would be torn down before their generation passed away, not a future rebuilt temple. The New Testament does not say anything about a rebuilt temple. If there is a double fulfillment, could there not be triple or quadruple fulfillment? If this is true of the Olivet Discourse, then what about other prophetic passages? Another Messiah born of a virgin?

---

4. John Murray, "The Interadventual Period and the Advent: Matthew 24 and 25," *Collected Writings of John Murray (2): Select Lectures in Systematic Theology* (Carlisle, PA: The Banner of Truth Trust, 1977), 2:388.

The preterist approach to Matthew 24 argues that Jesus was referring to the generation of His day (Matt. 24:34), not a distant generation. From our point in history, the events described by Jesus have been fulfilled. The fulfillment is in the past (the definition of preterist). The preterist approach has a long and distinguished interpretive history going back centuries. There is nothing novel about it.

What makes James Jordan's commentary on Matthew 23–25 different? While many commentators argue in terms of historical fulfillment by appealing to sources like *The Jewish War* by Flavius Josephus (c. 37–100) (not in itself wrong),[5] an eyewitness to the destruction of the temple and judgment on Jerusalem in AD 70, Jordan concentrates on the biblical literary connections. He does this by putting Matthew 23–25 in the full context of Matthew's gospel and the rest of the Bible. This way, the forest can be seen within the context of the trees. The Olivet Discourse is not a tacked-on discourse by Jesus. It serves as a necessary conclusion to His ministry and warning to Israel and the prelude to the Passion Narratives that follow.

Those who first read Matthew's gospel only would have had as an interpretive reference what we describe as the Old Testament. They were living the history that Jesus said would take place before their generation passed away. They would have immediately noted the Old Testament parallels with the abomination of desolation (Matt. 24:15; Dan. 9:27), the judgment on Sodom and fleeing to the mountains to escape the coming conflagration (Matt. 24:16; Gen. 19:17), false prophets (Matt. 24:24; Jer. 14:14), signs in the sun, moon, and stars (Matt. 24:29; Isa. 3:10; 24:33; Ezek. 32:7; Amos 5:2; 8:9; etc.), the Son of Man coming on the clouds of heaven (Matt. 24:30; Dan. 7:13), and so much more.

Jordan's *Matthew 23–25: A Literary, Historical, and Theological Commentary* is truly a biblical-theological approach to interpretation, using the Bible to interpret the Bible, and in doing so, shows that the Bible is the best interpreter of itself.

---

5. John L. Bray, *Matthew 24 Fulfilled* (Powder Springs, GA: American Vision, [1996] 2008.

OVERVIEW

A.

THE STRUCTURE OF
MATTHEW'S GOSPEL

Since many of the books of the Bible are structured in a chiastic fashion (also called introversion or palistrophe),[1] I am persuaded that Matthew is no exception. I have come to the conclusion that Matthew is indeed chiastically organized. Ethelbert Bullinger[2] and John Breck[3] point out many smaller chiasms in particular paragraphs in Matthew's Gospel. Our concern here is with the book as a whole.

A chiastic structure has the form A B C B' A'. It can be brief or can extend over a whole book or even set of books. Chiasm differs from "inverted parallelism" by having a central pivot-point that in some way is the most important aspect of the structure. Inverted parallelism, consisting of ABBA, may not have such a central point (unless BB is also a pivot or the more important aspect of the overall section). In this book, I use the word "chiasm" to cover both of these patterns. As we shall see, the central or pivot point of Matthew seems to be the decision of the Pharisees to kill the innocent Servant of the Lord (12:14-21).

Chiasms can overlap in various ways. Large chiastic structures can include several smaller ones. The end of one chiasm can form the beginning of another. One section of a chiasm (usually the first or last) can be a smaller version of a larger chiasm of which it is a part. And so

---

1. See David A. Dorsey, *The Literary Structure of the Old Testament: A Commentary on Genesis–Malachi* (Grand Rapids: Baker, 1999).

2. Ethelbert Bullinger, *The Companion Bible* (London, 1910; reprint, Grand Rapids: Kregel, 1990).

3. John Breck, *The Shape of Biblical Language: Chiasmus in the Scriptures and Beyond* (Crestwood, NY: St. Vladimir's, 1994).

forth. This is not a problem, since chiastic structures are by their nature rather tightly constructed. Either a chiasm is present or it is not. There are not many ambiguous cases. Of course, nothing prohibits a writer from composing an incomplete chiasm.

It is possible, in an excess of enthusiasm and by forcing the text, to "discover" chiasms where none are present. At the same time, the abuse of a practice does not negate its proper use. Chiasms are arguably the most common literary structures in the Bible,[4] and so we will not go wrong by looking to find them in Matthew, provided we do not abuse the text.

In a chiastic structure, the recurrence of A at the end, and of B at B', and of C at C', and so on, involves some kind of intensification of the original statement. What was said the first time at B is said again at B', but in a new way because of what has happened in the meantime—and especially because of what happened at the central pivot. As we shall see, in Matthew 2:13-21, Jesus departs the "Egypt" of Bethlehem, where Pharaoh Herod is killing Hebrew babies.[5] This brief passage is answered by Matthew 21:1-27:56, where Jesus enters the "Egypt" of Jerusalem and heads for His death, but in the midst thereof pronounces doom upon the Jews (ch. 23–25).

This example displays the value of chiastic reading. Jesus' departure from spiritual Egypt for protection in literal Egypt has a direct relationship to His departure from Jerusalem in Matthew 24 and following, though in this second case, He leaves "Egypt" for crucifixion, not protection. The martyrdom of the little children is prophetically related to the coming destruction of Jerusalem. Apart from a chiastic reading, we probably would not make these connections. But Matthew's literary structure has placed these connections there, and in this way

---

4. See Dorsey and Breck.

5. Matthew 2:15 puts the phrase, "Out of Egypt did I call My son," not at the point where the child Jesus leaves Egypt and goes to Nazareth (after v. 20), but at the point where the infant Jesus leaves Bethlehem. Herod's land is the true Egypt. Like Moses, Jesus was hidden from the Egyptians in Egypt!

Matthew can make the theological point that Jesus' death is a departure from Egypt into the wilderness, and His resurrection is a new conquest of Canaan.

With this in mind, let us turn to a consideration of the book of Matthew.

Matthew is traditionally the first of the Gospels. In my opinion, as I argue below, the tradition is correct. Matthew was one of the disciples and was a man of letters. Who better to take notes during Jesus' lifetime?

Moreover, immediately after Pentecost there would have been a demand for a book containing the teaching and works of Jesus. The Jews were a people of the book. Each time God did a great work, a new part of Scripture was written to tell about it. The three thousand converts on the day of Pentecost would have expected such a book, and it is entirely possible that Matthew sat right down to write it. Doubtless he spoke with the other disciples, and perhaps Matthew's Gospel is to some extent a joint work. It is perfectly reasonable to suppose that within a month after Pentecost copies of Matthew's Gospel were in circulation.

Apart from the demand of the Jewish converts, there is another reason why Matthew's Gospel needed to be written right away, namely that most of what Jesus said and did was said and done privately. Jesus was mysterious. When He taught the multitudes, He used parables. When He healed, He told people to keep it secret. Thus, there were lots of rumors about Jesus, but not many hard facts. Matthew explains all this. The messages recorded in Matthew were given to the disciples, though sometimes other people around the periphery listened in.[6] Matthew tells us that it was Jesus who commanded that His miracles be kept under wraps. Now that Jesus had been raised, however, the secrets were to be revealed: The mystery of the kingdom was to be published.

---

6. How many of the multitude could have actually heard the Sermon on the Mount, delivered while Jesus was *seated* with His disciples around Him (Matt. 5:1-2)? Some did hear (7:28), but how many? Note also that the great Cost of Discipleship sermon in chapter 10 was heard only by the disciples. And as Nelson Kloosterman has pointed out to me, after the Pharisees determine to kill Jesus (12:14), Jesus never taught the multitudes again except in parables (13:34).

The idea that the disciples waited fifteen or twenty years before getting the story of Jesus into written form is a notion that strains credulity.

The alternative is to believe that for over a decade hundreds of Christian communities came into existence with nothing but rumors and stories to go on. In such a situation error would have abounded. The disciples would have had to spend all their time putting out fires. In no time at all, they would have realized the need to produce a writing that could be used by the Christian leaders to teach their people. Are we to believe that they allowed such a chaotic situation to continue for years, with the Christians scattered from Jerusalem and new churches springing up all over Judea, Samaria, and in Gentile lands?[7]

As Matthew was written first, it is also the case that Matthew (whose name was Levi) presents Jesus as a new priestly Moses (a Levite, of course), as Mark presents Him as a new David,[8] and Luke as a new prophet.[9] The early chapters of Matthew recapitulate the history of the Pentateuch and set the theme, to wit:

---

7. For those who want "all the arguments," John Wenham has recently made a full case for the primacy of Matthew, though he believes that there was a period of oral tradition and learning by rote for several years after Pentecost before Matthew wrote. Perhaps. But I find this rather unlikely, especially since the Jews were people of a book of books, and they believed that men like Jeremiah and Daniel had published their books while they were still alive (Jer. 36; Dan. 4, 7) and that the other prophets had their memoirs published immediately after their deaths. They would have expected a book that they could study in their new Christian synagogues. They would have clamored for it. What reason would the disciples have had for delaying such a writing?

The idea that Matthew wrote first in Hebrew or Aramaic does not square with the day of Pentecost, which meant that the Jews would be evangelized in other tongues and not in Hebrew/Aramaic. Perhaps there was a Hebrew translation, but the first version would have been in Greek. On all the ins and outs, see Wenham, *Redating Matthew, Mark, and Luke: A Fresh Assault on the Synoptic Problem* (Downers Grove, IL: InterVarsity Press, 1992).

8. With Herod as Saul, and Jesus as largely the suffering David of the psalter. The opening of Mark presents Jesus as king, "son of God," a kingly title (cf. Ps. 2). See Mark Horne, *The Victory according to Mark: An Exposition of the Second Gospel* (Moscow, ID: Canon, 2003).

9. With, for example, Jesus and John as Samuel, then John as Elijah and Jesus as Elisha; many Gentiles; much attention to Jesus' travels.

1:1-17	genealogies; Genesis
1:18-25	birth of Jesus; birth of Moses
2:1-23	wealth; departure from and return to "Egypt" (Herod's land)
3:1-17	baptism of Jesus; Red Sea crossing
4:1-11	forty days wrestling in wilderness; forty years in wilderness
4:12-25	initial ministry; initial conquests in Numbers
5–7	Sermon on the Mount; Deuteronomy

The rest of Matthew does not continue this history, nor does it apparently move over the Pentateuchal history a second time in more detail. Egyptian-Pentateuchal themes do, however, continue to be important. At the center of the book, as we shall see, we find the Pharisees as new Egyptians denying the sabbath to the people, with Jesus as new Moses granting them sabbath. The entire movement of the book of Exodus is from slavery to sabbath, and we find that theme at the heart of Matthew.

Also, where the other Gospels will have Jesus healing one person or being witnessed by one person, Matthew will very often have two. The legal (i.e., Mosaic) theme of a testimony of two witnesses is being carried forth by Matthew in this respect.

It cannot be my purpose in this book to argue further for this paradigm. Even if you, courteous reader, are dubious about this schema, at least you are aware of how I am approaching the text.

Here is the overall structure of Matthew, as I see it:

A. Genealogy (past), 1:1-17

  B. First Mary and Jesus' birth, 1:18-25

    C. Gifts of wealth at birth, 2:1-12

      D. Descent into Egypt; murder of children, 2:13-21

        E. Judea avoided, 2:22-23

          F. Baptism of Jesus, 3:1–8:23

            G. Crossing the sea, 8:24–11:1

              H. John's ministry, 11:2-19

                I. Rejection of Jesus, 11:20-24

                  J. Gifts for the new children, 11:25-30

                    K. Attack of Pharisees, 12:1-13

                      L. Pharisees determine to kill the innocent Servant, 12:14-21

                    K' Condemnation of Pharisees, 12:22-45

                  J' Gifts for the new children, 12:46–13:52

                I' Rejection of Jesus, 13:53-58

              H' John's death, 14:1-12

            G' Crossing the sea, 14:13–16:12

          F' Transfiguration of Jesus, 16:13–18:35

        E' Judean ministry, 19:1–20:34

      D' Ascent into Jerusalem; judgment on Jews, 21:1–27:56

    C' Gift of wealth at death, 27:57-66

  B' Last Marys and Jesus' resurrection, 28:1-15

A' Commission (future), 28:16-20

A. Past and Future

The genealogy of Jesus in 1:1-17 brings us up from the past, while the commission in 28:16-20 moves us into the future. The commission should probably be compared to the commissioning of Joshua to take the promised land toward the end of Deuteronomy.

B. The Marys

The birth narrative of 1:18-25 can be analyzed as having three parts: Mary is presented, an angel appears with a message, and Jesus is born. In the same way, the resurrection narrative of 28:1-10 presents two Marys, an angel appears with a message, and then Jesus appears in His resurrected body. (John 1:1-18 presents only one Mary, the Magdalene.)

Section B' has appended to it the story of the Jewish leaders putting out lies about the resurrection, 28:11-15. This is an inversion of the Messianic secret: Now that the hidden mystery is to be published, men seek to hide it.

C. Rich Gifts

The story of the magi in 2:1-12 also involves Herod's thwarted desire to kill Jesus. In terms of the chiasm of Matthew, the first point to notice is the rich gifts given to Jesus, which will sustain the family while in Egypt. Similarly, the wealthy Joseph of Arimathaea provides a rich tomb for Jesus while He is in the Egypt of the grave (27:57-61). Second, notice that the Jews prevailed on Pilate to guard the grave of Jesus (27:62-66). As Herod sought to prevent Jesus' birth, the Jews seek to prevent reports of His resurrection, His new transfigured birth.

D. Egypt and Crucifixion

The first D section is short, while the second is the longest section of Matthew.

In 2:13-21, we find a second Joseph taking his family down into Egypt to hide from Herod. This is because the real Egypt is Judea, where

Herod is Pharaoh. Herod slaughters the boy children, as Pharaoh did in Exodus 1. Matthew quotes Jeremiah 31:15, a lamentation over the destruction of Jerusalem in the days of Nebuchadnezzar. This is relevant, because the parallel is to Matthew 23–25, the prediction of the coming destruction of Jerusalem under Vespasian and Titus. Moreover, Jeremiah identifies Jerusalem with Egypt, especially in Jeremiah 34.[10] Matthew 24:19 recalls Matthew 2:18 by saying "Woe to those who are with child or who nurse babes in those days!"

The parallel D' section runs from the triumphal entry to the death of Jesus. This is the greater entry into Egypt, the real Egypt of Jerusalem. Just as the destruction of Jewish babies is sandwiched into the account of Jesus' sojourn in Egypt, so Jesus' announcement of the destruction of Jerusalem is found in the middle of His sojourn in the real Egypt. Section D' looks like this:

I. **David's Son:** Here Jesus comes as king-to-be, as a new Solomon, whose wisdom confounds all questioners. At a deeper level in Matthew, Jesus arrives in Egypt as a returning Moses to confound the Egyptian prophets.

    1. David's Son enters Jerusalem, 21:1-11
    2. Cleansing the Temple, 21:12-17
    3. The Barren Fig Tree, 21:18-22
    4. Priests' question, 21:23-27
    5. Parable of Two Sons, 21:28-32
    6. Parable of Vineyard, 21:33-46
    7. Parable of Wedding Feast, 22:1-14
    8. Pharisees' question, 22:15-22
    9. Sadducees' question, 22:23-33
    10. Lawyer's question, 22:34-40
    11. David's Son answers Pharisees, 22:41-45

---

10. For more, see Peter J. Leithart, *A House for My Name: A Survey of the Old Testament* (Moscow: Canon, 2000), 202ff.

II. **Judgment on Jews:** I will discuss the large chiasm of this section below (B). Here I provide only a brief outline. At a deep level in Matthew, Jesus announces the destruction of Egypt, the equivalent of the final plague against the firstborn and the devastation of Egypt that followed. Jesus' departure from Jerusalem we should link back to Joseph's departure from the "Egypt" of Herod in 2:13-15, and the prophesied destruction of Jerusalem we should link back to the martyrdom of the innocents in 2:16-18.

1. Warnings against Pharisees, 23:1-12
2. Octave of Woes against Jewish leaders, 23:13-31
3. Sentence of death against Pharisees, 23:32-36
4. Lamentation over Jerusalem, 23:37-39
5. Judgment on Jerusalem (and world), 24:1–25:46

III. **Death of God's Firstborn:** The martyrdom of the children of Bethlehem and the death of the firstborn in Egypt are here applied a second time, this time to Jesus Himself rather than to Egypt/Jerusalem. The destruction of Jerusalem falls upon Jesus as He takes the punishment that His faithful people deserve.

   a. Passover and crucifixion, 26:1-2
     b. Priests plot, 26:3-5
       c. Jesus anointed for burial, 26:6-13
         d. Preparations: Judas enlisted, 26:14-16; Passover prepared, 26:17-19
           e. Judas exposed, 26:20-25
              f. Lord's Supper inaugurated, 26:26-28
                g. Nazirite vow, 26:29
                  h. Removal to Olivet, 26:30
                    i. Denial predicted, 26:31-35
                      j. Agony, 26:36-46
                        k. Judas betrays Jesus, 26:47-56
                          l. Trial before Sanhedrin, 26:57-68
                            m. Denial of Peter, 26:69-75
                        l' Sanhedrin delivers Jesus to Pilate, 27:1-2
                      k' Judas hangs himself, 27:3-10
                    j' Trial before Pilate; Passover release, 27:11-26
                  i' Mockery, 27:27-31
                h' Removal to Golgotha, 27:32-33
              g' Nazirite vow, 27:34
           f' Crucifixion, 27:35-44; Death, 27:45-50
         e' Temple exposed, 27:51
       d' Aftermath, 27:52-56
     [c' Burial, 27:57-61
   [b' Priests plot, 27:62-66
 [a' Passover resurrection, 28:1-10

This huge chiasm has as its center the betrayal of Peter, as the leader of the disciples himself rejects Jesus. Peter holds an official position as high priest among the disciples of the incarnate Lord. His rejection of Jesus is the turning point. Jesus is now forsaken of men.

The chiasm overlaps the sections that follow our section D', but that is not a problem. Jesus' anointing for burial is found in paragraphs c and c'. The crucifixion scene is parallel to the Passover and Last Supper (d-g & g'-d'). The exposure of Judas at the Passover meal is parallel to the exposure of the temple at the crucifixion, for the temple had hired Judas (e & e'). The inauguration of the Lord's Supper as memorial of the crucifixion and death of Jesus is parallel to His crucifixion and death (g & g'). The agony of Jesus, when He asks the Father if He might be released from His coming doom, is answered by the trial of Jesus before Pilate, when Pilate chooses not to release Him (j & j'). Judas's betrayal is answered by Judas's suicide (k & k').

The interplay of "Egypt" and "Wilderness" runs throughout this section. Jesus defeats the Jews in Matthew 21–23 and leaves "Egypt" for the Mount of Olives. He returns to Egypt-Jerusalem for Passover and then leaves again for Olivet. He is brought back again, is beaten by the priests and the Romans as the Passover Lamb is slain, and then is taken out of Egypt to be crucified in the "Wilderness," again probably Olivet (since only from Olivet could the centurion have seen the temple veil rent and the aftermath in the temple courtyard).

IV. **Galilee:** Following out Matthew's typological progression, we find in 2:20-23 that after the martyrdom of the innocents while Jesus was in physical Egypt, Joseph took Jesus to Galilee. In the same way, after the murder of the Innocent Jesus, Jesus met His disciples in Galilee (28:10, 16). Joseph did not return to Bethlehem, and Jesus did not return to Jerusalem. They went to a new place. Similarly, having left Egypt and delivered his people from there, Moses did not return to Egypt again, but took the people to a new place.

E. JUDEA

Joseph decided not to go into Judea, because it was clear that there was a threat against Jesus there (2:22-23). The complementary E' section concerns Jesus' ministry in Judea, where the threats against Him mounted swiftly. While we know from John's Gospel that Jesus did make forays into Judea to attend the feasts, Matthew says nothing about these. Jesus does not enter Judea until chapter 19 of Matthew, after His transfiguration, after He set His face to the cross. Joseph's fears were, thus, quite apt: Judea was a great threat to Jesus.

The E' section of the Judean Ministry can be outlined thus:

1. Healings in Judea, 19:1-2
2. Discussion about divorce, 19:3-12
3. Blessing on children, 19:13-14
4. The rich young man, 19:15-22
5. Perils of riches, rewards of service, 19:23-30
6. Parable of the Laborers, 20:1-16
7. Jesus predicts His death, 20:17-19
8. The request of the wife of Zebedee, 20:20-28
9. Two blind men of Jericho healed, 20:29-34

Though the healings in Judea and Jericho form an inclusio for this section, the section does not seem to have a chiastic internal structure. Notice that Matthew has two blind men healed at Jericho; the other Gospels have only one (Mark 10:46; Luke 18:45).

F. BAPTISM AND TRANSFIGURATION

Both F sections are fairly long. Each begins with a revelation of Jesus as God's honored Son, followed by a series of events that bring out what those revelations entail. The implications of Jesus' baptism occupy much more text, since they include the Sermon on the Mount. In a larger sense, the implications of Jesus' baptism extend all the way to the transfiguration, and indeed to the end of the book. The transfiguration, which focuses Jesus on His coming death, is followed by a shorter section, which leads into the Judean ministry and then to the events in Jerusalem.

The two F sections are, however, parallel in a number of significant regards. The first F section looks like this:

1. Preliminary setting: John's witness, 3:1-12
2. Revelation of the Son, 3:13-17
3. Wrestling with Satan, 4:1-11
4. Removal to Capernaum, 4:12-16
5. Repent, 4:17
6. Call of disciples, 4:18-22
7. Mission begins, 4:23-25

8. Sermon on the Mount, 5:1-8:1
9. Leper and Messianic secret, 8:2-4
10. Centurion and great Gentile faith, 8:5-13
11. Peter's mother-in-law, 8:14-17
12. Reluctant disciples, 8:18-23

The F' section looks like this:

1. Preliminary setting: Peter's witness, 16:13-28
2. Revelation of the Son, 17:1-8
   – reference back to John, 17:9-13
3. Satan cast out, 17:14-23
4. Removal to Capernaum, 17:24-27
5. Disciples: Sermon on Discipleship, ch. 18
   – references back to Sermon on the Mount

A comparison of the two sections reveals their parallels. Both begin with the witness of a chief servant of Jesus. Next comes a revelation of the Son and the voice of the Father. Wrestling with Satan and his demons comes next in both cases, followed by a removal to Capernaum. In F:6-12 we have the calling of the disciples, a sermon delivered to their ears (5:1-2), ministry to a disciple's family, and two cases of reluctant disciples. In F':5 we have a sermon delivered to the disciples on discipleship. The only elements that are not parallel are the healing of the leper and of the centurion's servant.

G. CROSSING THE SEA

As with the F sections, the G sections begin with a similar event (crossing the sea), followed up by parallel events that should be seen as flowing from the initial event.

Crossing the sea should be seen in terms of the exodus from Egypt and the entrance through the Jordan into the promised land. Alternatively it can be seen as Jonah's passage from Israel to Assyria, anticipating the "sign of Jonah." In both cases, the sea crossing is followed by a conquest.

In the G section, we have a double crossing. First, Jesus crosses eastward to Gentile territory, where He heals two Gadarene demoniacs. Notice that Matthew has two; the others Gospels have only one (Mark 5:1, Luke 8:26). Like Jonah, Jesus is asleep on the boat during a storm. Then Jesus crosses back into Galilee, and begins a conquest.

1. Crossing the sea, 8:24-27
2. Gadarene demoniacs, 8:28-34
3. Crossing the sea, 9:1
4. Paralytic healed, 9:2-8
5. Conflict with Pharisees, 9:9-13
6. Question from John's disciples, 9:14-17
7. Jairus's daughter and the daughter of Israel, 9:18-26
8. Two blind men, 9:27-31
9. Dumb man demon possessed, 9:32-34
10. Jesus heals, moved with compassion, 9:35-38
11. Therefore, He sends the disciples to heal, 10:1–11:1

In the G' section, we have again two sea crossings that are contextualized with Jesus' feeding of the people. It is not hard to see G and G' as concerned with Word and Sacrament. The movement in this section is the reverse of the G section: Jesus crosses the sea into Israelite territory, and then goes back across eastward, toward Caesarea Philippi (16:13).

1. Many compassionate healings, 14:13-14
2. Disciples sent to feed, 14:15-21
3. Crossing the sea, 14:22-33
4. Gennesaret healings, 14:34-36
5. Conflict with Pharisees, 15:1-20
6. Canaanite woman's daughter healed (dogs eat bread), 15:21-28
7. Many compassionate healings, 15:29-31
8. Disciples sent to feed, 15:32-38
9. Crossing the sea, 15:39
10. Conflict with Pharisees, 16:1-4
11. Discussion with disciples about bread, 16:5-12

I have tried to make clear the structure of the passage, which is about bread for the most part. In paragraph 2, the disciples feed 5000. In paragraph 5, the Pharisees argue about eating. In paragraph 6, the Canaanite woman says that even the dogs eat the children's bread. In paragraph 8, the disciples feed 4000. In paragraph 11, Jesus warns against the leaven of the Pharisees.

Events within the passage are duplicated. Twice Jesus heals, sends disciples to feed, crosses the sea, enters into conflict with the Pharisees, and has a discussion about bread.

Parallel to the G section, Jesus crosses the sea and heals people, is attacked by the Pharisees, and heals daughters.

H. JOHN'S MINISTRY

The H and H' sections have to do with the Forerunner. Jesus describes John's work in H, and John's death is described in H' (11:2-9; 14:1-12). John's ministry and death are prophetic types of Jesus' own.

I. JESUS' REJECTION

The I sections have to do with the rejection of Jesus. In the I section, Jesus condemns the cities that did not listen to John and Himself (11:20-24). In the I' section, Jesus is rejected at Nazareth (13:53-58). Both sections stress miracles.

J. GIFTS FOR THE CHILDREN

The J sections have to do with the blessings and gifts God gives to His true children and stand in contrast to the K section, which pronounces judgment upon those who have Satan for their father.

In the J section (11:25-30), Jesus praises the Father for revealing His truth to the babes, who are the disciples.

In the J' section (13:1-52), Jesus reveals truth to the disciples. The J' section (the parables) seems to have a chiastic structure, which overlaps with the preceding and following sections of Matthew as we have outlined it:

[Jesus' mother and brothers, 12:46-50]
1. Sower, 13:1-9
2. Hidden mysteries, 13:10-17
3. Sower explanation, 13:18-23
4. Tares, 13:24-30
5. Mustard, 13:31-32
6. Leaven, 13:33
7. Parables only, 13:34-35
8. Tares explained, 13:36-43
9. Treasure, 13:44
10. Pearl, 13:45-46
11. Dragnet, 13:47-50
[Jesus' mother and brothers, 13:51-58]

The Sower who gathers a mixed harvest is parallel to the Fisherman who gets a mixed catch. The hidden mysteries are parallel to the Pearl of great price. The explanation of the Sower parable is parallel to the treasure found in a *field*. The Tares parable is parallel to its explanation. At the center is the parable of the Leaven, which concerns the insertion of the Holy Spirit into the bread of humanity.

We can also note a movement from Jew to Gentile as we move from field parables to the pearl and finally to the dragnet: from land to sea.

K. CONDEMNATION OF THE PHARISEES
L. INNOCENCE OF THE SERVANT

This is the central section of Matthew, and at its center is a revelation of Jesus Christ.

K.1. Sabbath eating argument with Pharisees, 12:1-8

   K.2. Sabbath healing argument with Pharisees, 12:9-13

      L.3. Pharisees determine to kill Jesus, 12:14

      L.4. Innocence of Jesus, 12:15-21

   K'5. Healing; Pharisees condemned as Satanists, 12:22-37 (blasphemy)

   K'6. Pharisees condemned as demonic, 12:38-45 (false household);

      Jesus' mothers and brothers, 12:46-50 (true household)

The Egyptian theme is pregnant here. The Egyptians denied any sabbath rest to the Hebrews, but Yahweh delivered them into sabbath. The Pharisees deny the sabbath, while affirming it hollowly. Jesus says that they are sons of snakes, of Satan, and then says that their house is inhabited by demons, reversing the tabernacle built at the exodus, which was filled with God's glory. During His discourse on the demonic house, Jesus comments that the members of His household are those who trust and obey His Father.

Paragraphs 1 and 6 both have to do with houses of God: the temple of David's day and the demonic temple under the Pharisees. Paragraphs 2 and 5 both have to do with healing, the restoration of persons to God's house in terms of the Levitical law.

At the center of this section, and at the center of Matthew, is the decision of the Pharisees to kill Jesus. Following this is a quotation from Isaiah 42, indicating that Jesus is God's Servant and that He will deliver the Gentiles. In other words, Jesus is innocent of wrongdoing and has done only right. The Pharisees only doom themselves by seeking His doom.

B.
THE STRUCTURE OF
MATTHEW 23–25

Matthew 23–25 is structured chiastically. The "proof" of the presence of a chiastic structure consists of laying it out and inviting the reader to see for himself that it is there, and this is the first thing we need to do. If indeed Matthew 23–25 is a chiasm, then we can compare the beginning and end, take note of the central point, and reflect on how these govern the passage. We can also compare matching sections and see how these relate one to another.

One thing that seems to emerge from the unity of the passage is that all of it is concerned with the events leading down to AD 70, though I shall argue that the last part of the passage (25:14-46), through some shifts in language, pushes us to realize that a final coming and final judgment are also to come. This last judgment of the New Creation will bear a general, but not a specific, analogy to the last judgment of the Old Creation. Of course, the reality of the future coming of Jesus to judge the living and the dead is not at issue, since other places in the Bible clearly teach this. The only question before us is what Matthew 23–25 is concerned with.

As we have seen, Matthew 2:13-21 chiastically matches 21:1–27:56. Within these sections, 2:16-18 parallels chapters 23–25—that is, the Jeremiah quotation in chapter 2 parallels Jesus' prophetic condemnation of Jerusalem. As we discussed in the preceding section of this chapter, in 2:13-21 we find a second Joseph taking his family down into Egypt to hide from Herod. The old geographical Egypt is a "wilderness" Egypt, to which the infant Jesus goes to escape the "spiritual" Egypt of Judea.

The section parallel to Matthew 2:13-21 runs from the triumphal entry to the death of Jesus (21:1–27:56). This is the greater descent into and exodus from Egypt, the real Egypt of Jerusalem (cp. Rev. 11:8), as we have seen above. Just as the destruction of Jewish babies is sandwiched into Jesus' sojourn in the literal "wilderness" Egypt away from "spiritual Egypt," so Jesus' announcement of the destruction of Jerusalem is given on the "wilderness" Mount of Olives after He leaves the Jerusalem "Egypt."

The overall structure is this:

> A. Seat of Moses (23:1-12)
> > B. Eight Woes (23:13-32)
> > > C. Full Judgment (23:33-35)
> > > > D. All in This Generation (23:36)
> > > > > **Middle (23:37–24:31)**
> > > > D' All in This Generation (24:32-36)
> > > C' Full Judgment (24:37-44)
> > B' Three Parables (24:45–25:30)
> A' Seat of Jesus (25:31-45)

While the B and C sections may not obviously be parallel, the parallel between the seat of Moses and the seat of Jesus is clear enough to provide the outer boundaries of the passage. Moreover, the two D sections are obviously parallel. The question now concerns the middle section. If that section is chiastic, then we can be pretty sure that Matthew and the Spirit intend us to read the entire passage chiastically.

The following is the structure of the middle section:

D. This Generation (23:36)

   E. Gathering (23:37)

      F. The Temple (23:38–24:2)

         G. Jesus' Arrival (24:3)

           H. False Prophets (24:4-5)

              I. Wars (24:6a)

                J. End (24:6b)

                   K. Nations (24:7)

                      L. Birth (24:8)

                         M. Persecution (24:9-10)

           H' False Prophets (24:11)

                        M' Lawlessness (24:12)

                      L' End (24:13)

                   K' Nations (24:14a)

                J' End (24:14b)

              I' War (24:15-21)

           H" False Prophets (24:22-24)

         G' Jesus' Arrival (24:25-27)

      F' Corpse (24:28)

   E' Gathering (24:29-31)

D' This Generation (24:32-36)

A glance at the structure will reveal that this section is clearly chiastic, and since it is the middle of the overall passage (Matt. 23–25), we are confirmed in our suspicion that the passage as a whole is chiastic.

Another line of confirmation comes from the central point, which is a warning against false prophets. That warning is also found in the middle of the central section on both sides. It is also the fundamental point of the first section of the passage, which begins with the scribes and Pharisees in Moses' seat. With this point in mind, we can see that the passage as a whole is very concerned with false prophets: the eight woes against the Pharisees and two of the matching parables, that of the unfaithful servant (24:45-51) and that of the men left with talents (25:14-30). The other parable, of the virgins, concerns the question of who has the Spirit, another deeply prophetic concern. This discourse on false prophets plays into the identity and role of the False Prophet in Revelation and also invites our study of the role of false prophets in the first destruction of Jerusalem in the days of Jeremiah.

C.
TRANSLATION

The following translation is designed to be read aloud. It is very literal, following as closely as possible the word order of the original Greek text. The reader will see and hear a series of sentences and clauses linked with "and," which provides the "sing-song" rhythm and flow of the text. This style of writing follows from the pattern of Hebrew in the Hebrew Scriptures (the Old Testament). All of the Bible was written to be heard, to be read aloud and heard by others. There is a kind of "chanted" or "intoned" rhythm in the text that is not quite prose, but not quite poetry. It is sometimes called "prosody." The rhythm is provided by the series of "ands" and other connectives. Thus, the goal of this translation is not to provide "smooth English prose" according to modern standards, but to preserve the shape and form of the Word of God so that it can shape and form how we hear that Word.

The reader will see that I have usually identified the specific Greek word that underlies the word "and." The particle *de* is a general connective. It is not a strong contrastive "but" and can be translated "and" just as readily, according to context. I shall translate it "and" throughout this book, letting the context indicate whether some degree of contrast is in view. The word *kai* is a connective conjunction, almost always translated "and," occasionally "also."

I urge the user of this commentary to read this whole passage aloud from time to time, slightly pausing at the end of each line and skipping the italicized words in parentheses, so as to get a sense of how it is to be heard, exposing himself or herself to the flow, shape, and rhythm of the Word of God.[11]

23 [1]At that time Jesus spoke to the multitudes and to His disciples,

[2]saying, "Upon the seat of Moses have sat down the scribes and the Pharisees.

[3]Therefore, all they tell you, keep doing and keep guarding.

And (*de*) according to their works, do not do,

for they speak,

and (*kai*) do not do.

[4]And (*de*) they bind heavy burdens,

and (*kai*) lay them on the shoulders of men,

and (*de*) with their own finger they will not move them.

[5]And (*de*) all their works they do in order to be noticed by men:

for they broaden their charm boxes,

and (*kai*) magnify the tassels,

[6]and (*de*) they love the first places at the feasts,

and (*kai*) the first seats in the synagogues,

[7]and (*kai*) the respectful greetings in the markets,

and (*kai*) to be called by men, 'Master Teacher (Rabbi).'

[8]And (*de*) you do not be called 'Master Teacher,'

for One is your Teacher,

and (*de*) all of you are brothers.

[9]And (*kai*) 'Father' do not you call anyone on the earth,

for One is your Father,

the heavenly one.

[10]And (*de*) do not be called 'Leaders,'

because your Leader is One,

the Christ.

[11]And (*de*) the greatest among you must be your servant.

[12]And (*de*) whoever will exalt himself will be humbled.

And (*de*) whoever will humble himself will be exalted.

---

11. In the following translation, brackets "[ ]" sometimes mark textual variants, sometimes explanatory expansions of the text. The bracketed phrases are discussed in detail in the commentary.

¹³And (*de*) woe to you, scribes and Pharisees, hypocrites!
Because you shut off the kingdom of heaven in front of men,
For you do not enter in,
nor those entering in do you permit to enter in.
¹⁴Woe to you, scribes and Pharisees, hypocrites!
Because you devour the houses of widows
and (*kai*) for appearance's sake praying at length.
Because of this you will receive more abundant judgment.

¹⁵Woe to you, scribes and Pharisees, hypocrites!
Because you roam around the sea and the withered-up places to make one proselyte,
and (*kai*) when he has become such, you make him a son of Gehenna twice yourselves.

¹⁶Woe to you, blind guides who say, 'Whoever swears by the sanctuary, it is nothing,
and (*de*) whoever swears by the gold of the sanctuary is obligated.'
¹⁷Fools and blind men!
Which is greater: the gold?
Or the sanctuary that sanctifies the gold?

¹⁸And (*kai*): 'Whoever swears by the altar, it is nothing,
and (*de*) whoever swears by the gift that is upon it is obligated.'
¹⁹[Fools and] blind men!
For which is greater: the gift?
Or the altar that sanctifies the gift?
²⁰He therefore who swears by the altar
swears by it and by all the things on it.
²¹And (*kai*) he who swears by the sanctuary
swears by it and by all the things in it.
²²And (*kai*) he who swears by heaven
swears by the throne of God and by Him who sits on it.

²³Woe to you, scribes and Pharisees, hypocrites!
Because you are tithing mint and dill and cumin,
and (*kai*) you dismissed the weightier parts of the law:
the justice and the mercy and the faith.
These you should have done,
without dismissing the others.
²⁴Blind guides! Who filter out the gnat while gulping down the camel!

²⁵Woe to you, scribes and Pharisees, hypocrites!
Because you clean the outside of the cup and of the dish,
and (*de*) inside they are full of rapacity and self-indulgence.

²⁶Blind Pharisee!

Clean first the inside of the cup and
    of the dish,

so that also the outside of it may be
    clean.

²⁷Woe to you, scribes and Pharisees,
    hypocrites!

Because you resemble whitewashed
    tombs,

which outwardly on the one hand
    appear beautiful,

and (*de*) inwardly on the other hand
    are full of dead bones and all
    uncleanness.

²⁸Thus also (*kai*) you outwardly on
    the one hand appear righteous to
    men,

and (*de*) inwardly on the other hand
    are full of hypocrisy and
    lawlessness.

²⁹Woe to you, scribes and Pharisees,
    hypocrites!

Because you build the tombs of the
    prophets,

and (*kai*) decorate the memorials of
    the righteous,

³⁰and (*kai*) say, 'If we had lived in the
    days of the fathers,

we would not have been partners
    with them in the blood of the
    prophets.'

³¹Just so you witness against
    yourselves that you are the sons
    of the murderers of the prophets.

Yes, you!

³²Fill up the measure of your fathers!

³³Serpents!

Offspring of vipers!

How shall you escape the judgment
    of Gehenna?

³⁴Therefore, behold! I Myself am
    sending you prophets and wise
    men and scribes.

Some of them you will kill
    and (*kai*) crucify.

And (*kai*) some of them you will
    scourge in your synagogues

and (*kai*) persecute from city to city;

³⁵that upon you may fall all the
    righteous blood shed on the
    earth,

from the blood of righteous Abel

to the blood of Zechariah the son of
    Berechiah,

whom you murdered between the
    sanctuary and the altar.

³⁶Amen I say to you, all these things
    shall come upon this generation.

³⁷Jerusalem!

Jerusalem!

who kills the prophets

and (*kai*) stones those sent to her,

how often I willed to have gathered
    your children,

in the way a hen gathers her brood
    under her wings,

and (*kai*) you willed not.

³⁸Behold, your house is left to you
    desolate.

³⁹For I say to you, in no way will you
see Me again until you say,
'Blessed is the one coming
(*erchomai*) in the Lord's name.'"

———

24 ¹And (*kai*) going forth, Jesus
went away from the temple.
And (*kai*) His disciples came to point
out to Him the buildings of the
temple.
²And (*de*) Jesus said to them, "Do
you not see all these things?
Amen I say to you, not at all shall be
left here stone upon stone that
shall not be thrown down."

³And (*de*) as He was sitting on the
Mount of Olives, the disciples
came to Him apart, saying,
"Tell us when these things will be,
and (*kai*) what is the sign of Your
manifestation (*parousia*),
and (*kai*) of the consummation of
the age."

⁴And (*kai*) answering, Jesus said to
them,
"Discern, lest anyone mislead you.
⁵For many will come in My name,
saying, 'I myself am the Messiah,'
and (*kai*) many they will mislead.

⁶And (*de*) you will be hearing of wars
and rumors of wars.
Watch carefully so that you are not
startled,

for it is necessary for this to happen;
but (*alla*) not yet is the end.
⁷For nation will rise up against
nation,
and (*kai*) kingdom against kingdom.

And (*kai*) there will be famines and
earthquakes in various places.
⁸And (*de*) all these are a beginning of
birthpangs.
⁹At that time they will deliver you up
to tribulation,
and (*kai*) will kill you,
and (*kai*) you will be hated by all
nations on account of My name.
¹⁰And (*kai*) at that time many will be
scandalized,
and (*kai*) they will betray one another,
and (*kai*) hate one another.

¹¹And (*kai*) many false prophets will
arise,
and (*kai*) will mislead many.

¹²And (*kai*) because lawlessness has
been multiplied,
the love of the many will grow cold.
¹³And (*de*) the one enduring to the
end,
that one will be saved.

¹⁴And (*kai*) this gospel of the
kingdom will be proclaimed in
the whole Oikumene,
for a witness to all the nations,
and (*kai*) at that time the end will
come.

¹⁵When, therefore, you see the
abomination of desolation,
which is spoken of through Daniel
the prophet,
standing in the holy place
(he who reads should
understand/interpret),
¹⁶at that time let those who are in
Judea flee into the mountains.
¹⁷The one who is on the housetop,
let him not go down to take anything
out of his house.
¹⁸And (*kai*) the one who is in the
field,
let him not turn back to get his cloak.
¹⁹And (*de*) woe to those who are with
child
and (*kai*) to those who nurse babes
in those days!
²⁰And (*de*) pray that your flight may
not be in the winter,
or on a sabbath.
²¹For at that time there will be a great
tribulation,
such as has not occurred since the
beginning of the world until now,
nor ever shall be.
²²And (*kai*) unless those days had
been cut short,
no flesh would have been saved.
And (*de*) for the sake of the elect
those days will be cut short.

²³At that time if anyone says to you,
'Behold, here is the Messiah!,'
or, 'Here!,'
do not believe it.

²⁴For there will arise false messiahs
and false prophets,
and (*kai*) will give great signs and
wonders,
so as to mislead, if possible, even the
elect.
²⁵Behold, I have foretold you.
²⁶If therefore they say to you,
'Behold, in the wilderness he is!,'
go not forth;
'Behold, in the inner chambers!,'
believe it not.
²⁷For just as the lightning comes
(*erchomai*) forth from east,
and (*kai*) appears as far as west,
so will be the manifestation
(*parousia*) of the Son of Man.
²⁸For wherever will be the corpse,
there will be gathered the eagles.

²⁹And (*de*) immediately after the
tribulation of those days
the sun will be darkened,
and (*kai*) the moon will not give her
light,
and (*kai*) the stars will fall from the
heaven,
and (*kai*) the powers of the heavens
will be shaken.
³⁰And (*kai*) at that time will appear
the sign of the Son of Man in
heaven;
and (*kai*) at that time will mourn all
the tribes of the land,
and (*kai*) they will see the Son of
Man coming (*erchomai*) on the
clouds of the heaven with power
and great glory.

³¹And (*kai*) He will send His angels
with a great trumpet sound,
and (*kai*) they will gather together
His elect from the four winds,
from [one] ends of heavens to
[other] ends of them.

³²And (*de*) from the fig tree learn the
parable:
When already its branch has become
tender,
and (*kai*) it is putting forth leaves,
you know that the summer is near.
³³Thus also you,
when you see all these things,
know that it is near,
at the doors.
³⁴Amen I say to you,
certainly this generation will not
have passed away
until all these things shall have taken
place.

³⁵The heaven and the earth will pass
away,
and (*de*) My words certainly will not
pass away.
³⁶And (*de*) concerning that day and
hour:
no one knows,
not even the angels of the heavens,
[nor the Son,]
but My Father only.

³⁷And (*de*) just as the days of Noah,
so will be the manifestation
(*parousia*) of the Son of Man.

³⁸For just as they were in the days
before the Flood,
eating and drinking,
marrying and giving in marriage,
until the day when Noah entered
into the ark,
³⁹and (*kai*) they did not know until
the Flood came
and (*kai*) took away all,
so also will be the manifestation
(*parousia*) of the Son of Man.

⁴⁰At that time two will be in the field:
One is taken and one is left.
⁴¹Two [women] will be grinding in
the mill:
One is taken and one is left.
⁴²Be watching, therefore, for you do
not know what day your Lord
comes (*erchomai*).

⁴³And (*de*) know this,
that if the master of the house had
known in what watch the thief
comes (*erchomai*),
he would have watched,
and (*kai*) not have allowed his house
to be dug through [broken into].
⁴⁴Therefore also (*kai*) you, be ready,
for you do not know what hour the
Son of Man comes (*erchomai*).
⁴⁵Who then (*ara*) is the faithful and
prudent slave,
whom the master has set over his
household,
that he give to them food at the
proper time?

30

⁴⁶Blessed is that slave, who, his master having come, will be found thus doing. ⁴⁷Amen I say to you, that over all his property he will set him.

⁴⁸And (*de*) if that evil slave should say in his heart,
'Delays my master,'
⁴⁹and (*kai*) should begin to beat the fellow-slaves,
and (*de*) eat and drink with the drunkards,
⁵⁰he will come, the master of that slave,
in a day that he does not expect,
and (*kai*) in a hour that he does not know,
⁵¹and (*kai*) will cut him in two,
and (*kai*) his portion with the hypocrites will appoint;
in that place will be the weeping and the gnashing of the teeth.

——— ❧ ———

2 5 ¹At that time the kingdom of heaven will be like ten virgins,
who, having taken their lamps,
went forth to meet the bridegroom.
²And (*de*) five of them were foolish
and (*kai*) five prudent:
³for they who were foolish,
having taken their lamps,
did not take oil with themselves,
⁴and (*de*) those who were prudent
took oil in their vessels
with their lamps.

⁵And (*de*) with the delaying of the bridegroom,
they all became drowsy and slept.
⁶And (*de*) in the middle of the night there was a cry,
'Behold! The bridegroom comes!
Go forth to meet him!'
⁷At that time all those virgins arose
and (*kai*) trimmed their lamps.

⁸And (*de*) the foolish to the prudent said,
'Give us of your oil,
because our lamps are going out.'
⁹And (*de*) the prudent answered, saying,
'There may not suffice for us and you.
Rather go to the sellers
and (*kai*) buy for yourselves.'
¹⁰And (*de*) as they went away to buy,
the bridegroom came,
and (*kai*) those ready entered with him to the wedding feast,
and (*kai*) the door was shut.
¹¹And (*de*) afterwards came also (*kai*) the other virgins, saying,
'Master, Master, open to us.'
¹²And (*de*) he answering said,
'Amen I say to you: I do not know you.'
¹³Watch, therefore,
because you do not know
the day or the hour
in which the Son of Man comes (*erchomai*).

¹⁴For [it is] just like [this:]
A man going on a journey
called his own slaves,
and (*kai*) delivered to them his
	property;
¹⁵and (*kai*) to one he gave five talents,
and (*de*) to another two,
and (*de*) to another one,
each according to his own ability;
and (*kai*) went on the journey.
Immediately ¹⁶he who received the
	five talents worked with them
and (*kai*) gained another five talents.
¹⁷In like manner he of the two gained
	also another two,
¹⁸and (*de*) he who received the one,
having gone away,
dug earth and hid the money of his
	master.
¹⁹And (*de*) after a long time comes
	the master of those slaves
and (*kai*) settles account with them.
²⁰And (*kai*) having come forward,
he who had received the five talents
	brought another five talents,
saying, 'Master, five talents to me you
	delivered.
Behold, another five talents have I
	gained besides them.'
²¹His master said to him,
'Well done, good and faithful slave.
Over a few things you were faithful;
over many things will I set you.
Enter into the joy of your master.'
²²And also (*de kai*) having come
	forward, he of the two talents
	said,

'Master, two talents to me you
	delivered.
Behold, another two talents have I
	gained besides them.'
²³His master said to him,
'Well done, good and faithful slave.
Over a few things you were faithful;
over many things will I set you.
Enter into the joy of your master.'
²⁴And also (*de kai*) having come
	forward,
he who had received [and still
	retained] the one talent said,
'Master, I knew [full well] that you
	[of all people] are a hard man,
reaping where you did not sow
and (*kai*) gathering whence you did
	not scatter,
²⁵And (*kai*) being afraid,
having gone away I hid your talent in
	the earth.
Behold, you have your own.'
²⁶And (*de*) answering, his master said
	to him,
'Wicked slave, and slothful!
Did you know [have information]
	that I reap where I sowed not
and (*kai*) gather whence I scattered
	not?
²⁷You were obligated therefore to put
	my money with the bankers,
and (*kai*) coming I should have
	received my own with interest.
²⁸Take therefore from him the talent,
and (*kai*) give to him who has the ten
	talents.

²⁹For to everyone one who has will be given,
and (*kai*) he will be in abundance,
and (*de*) the one who has not,
even what he has will be taken from him.
³⁰And (*kai*) the useless slave, cast out into the outer darkness.
In that place will be the weeping and the gnashing of the teeth.'

³¹And (*de*) when the Son of Man comes (*erchomai*) in His glory,
and (*kai*) all the angels with Him,
at that time will He sit on the throne of His glory,
³²and (*kai*) before Him will be gathered all the nations.
And (*kai*) He will separate them from one another,
as the shepherd separates the sheep from the goats.
³³And (*kai*) He will set the sheep at His right hand,
and (*de*) the goats at the left.

³⁴At that time will the King say to them at His right hand,
'Come, blessed ones of My Father,
inherit the kingdom prepared for you from the foundation of the world
³⁵for I hungered, and you gave Me to eat;
I thirsted, and you gave Me drink;
a stranger I was, and you took Me in;
³⁶naked, and you clothed Me;

I became ill, and you looked after Me;
in prison I was, and you came to Me.'

³⁷At that time will the righteous answer Him, saying,
'Lord, when did we see You hungry, and fed You?
or thirsty, and gave You drink?
³⁸And (*de*) when did we see You a stranger, and took You in?
or naked, and clothed You?
³⁹And (*de*) when did we see You ill, or in prison, and came to You?'
⁴⁰And (*kai*) answering the King will say to them,
'Amen I say to you,
inasmuch as you did it to one of these least of My brethren,
you did it to Me.'

⁴¹At that time will He say also (*kai*) to them at the left hand,
'Depart from Me, cursed ones,
into the everlasting fire which is prepared for the devil and his angels:
⁴²for I hungered, and you did not give Me to eat;
I thirsted, and you gave Me no drink;
⁴³a stranger I was, and you took Me not in;
naked, and you clothed Me not;
ill, and in prison, and you did not look after Me.'

⁴⁴At that time they also will answer, saying,

'Lord, when did we see You
hungry,
or athirst,
or a stranger,
or naked,
or ill,
or in prison,
and did not minister to You?'

[45]At that time will He answer them,
    saying,
'Amen I say to you,
inasmuch as you did it not to one of
    these least,
you did it not to Me.'
[46]And (*kai*) these will go away into
    everlasting punishment,
and (*de*) the righteous into
    everlasting life."

COMMENTARY

1
THE SEAT OF MOSES
(23:1-12)

¹At that time Jesus spoke to the multitudes and to His disciples,

T he discourse begins with Jesus speaking to the multitudes and to His disciples (23:1), and then moves in 24:3 to a continuation given only to the disciples. The sentence that Jesus pronounces upon the scribes and Pharisees needs to be heard by all, while the detailed warnings need to be heard by the disciples only. Why is this?

The answer, I believe, is that the multitudes and the disciples needed to be presented with a clear and unmistakable choice between the Jewish leaders on the one hand and Jesus on the other. They needed to be presented with that choice before Jesus' arrest and trial because they would be called upon to act in terms of it. The other information became relevant only after Pentecost, so only the disciples were told it; they would pass it on later.

Matthew follows this theme by showing that the multitude decided to choose against Jesus, as did the disciples. First, Judas betrayed Him (Matt. 26:14-16). Then a "multitude" joined with Judas to arrest Him (26:47, 55). Then the disciples fled (26:56). Then Peter changed sides (26:69-75). Then the chief priests and elders persuaded the multitude to call for Jesus' death (27:20-25).

All of this highlights the immediate relevance of Jesus' public ministry in Jerusalem, which climaxed with His condemnation of the Pharisees. The multitudes initially welcomed Him as the son of David (Matt. 21:8-11). Then Jesus publicly defeated the chief priests and elders in the temple (21:23ff.), and then publicly defeated the Herodians, Sadducees,

Lawyers, and Pharisees (22:16-46, note v. 33). Having been welcomed by the multitude as King and having defeated all His enemies, Jesus passed judgment on these enemies in chapter 23. This was done in the hearing of the multitude, and thus the multitude was made accountable.

A. THE SEATS

[2] saying, "Upon the seat of Moses have sat down the scribes and the Pharisees."

The first and last passages in our section are closely related, as is evident from a comparison of their wording. Matthew 23:2 reads, "Upon the seat *(kathedra)* of Moses have sat down *(kathizo)* the scribes and the Pharisees." Matthew 25:31 reads, "...then [the Son of Man] will sit *(kathizo)* upon His glorious throne *(thronos)*." At first the scribes and Pharisees are sitting and ruling among the people; but at the last Jesus will sit and judge among the people.

The contrasts between these two sections might seem to indicate that they are not designed as parallels, but in fact the contrasts bring out the parallelism. The scribes and Pharisees are sitting at the present time. They are ruling, not passing final judgments. The emphasis is on their teaching: "all that they tell you, do and observe" (v. 3). By way of contrast, Jesus does not sit down at the end to teach but to judge. History is over.

Teaching begins things; judgments end them and start new beginnings. Moses was a definitive beginning point in the history of the Old Creation. The history preceding Sinai leads to Sinai, and the subsequent history follows from it. Sinai is the great revelation of the Old Creation. Sinai is the place where the history of the Old Creation was initiated in a definitive way (though the history had begun with Adam). The seat of Moses, therefore, has to do with beginnings. The ongoing teaching of the scribes and Pharisees keeps this history going by renewing it constantly.

The reiterated teachings continue to direct the future, but they also have the effect of preventing a genuinely new future from arriving. The Old Creation Law tended to become an end in itself through constant reiteration, and thereby was perverted so that the New Creation Gospel could not be heard. For the time being, the Law was still to be followed, but not forever, because a transfigured version of the Law was coming in the New Creation.

Thus, the first A section concerns those who give direction and impetus to history, while the last A section concerns Him who will end and judge history. In this way, it is clear that the contrasts between the two A sections only highlight their relationship and clearly mark out the beginning and end of the discourse.

There are other contrasts also. Moses' seat is only a ruling chair, while Jesus' seat is a royal throne. The first seat is that of Moses, the type, while the final seat is that of the Greater Moses, the antitype.

Our passage has more to say about seats of authority. First of all, Jesus tells the disciples not to imitate the ways of the scribes and Pharisees (23:3-12). This clearly means that they will become rulers and sit on chairs, and in fact Jesus' words have to do with the character and quality of their coming rule. They will be the teachers who through the Spirit initiate the New Creation after Jesus' departure.[12]

Second, Jesus Himself sits to teach at the beginning of the second part of the discourse. Matthew 24:3 reads, "And as [Jesus] was sitting (*kathemai*) upon the Mount of Olives…." What Jesus teaches the disciples here is, as we have seen, what they will teach later on. Thus, there is a new beginning. There is a chair of Jesus, which the disciples will occupy when He is gone. For a brief time the chair of Jesus will operate simultaneously with the chair of Moses, but in AD 70 the chair of Moses will be removed.

While the chair of Moses remained, however, it was to be accorded respect. Jesus was not a revolutionary but sought transformation. He taught respect for existing authority, paying both the temple tax and the taxes due to Caesar. Thus, His word to the disciples was this: "As long as the Pharisees are ruling the religious life of the true Jewish church, you should go along with what they teach and prescribe. Don't create a

---

12. Compare Genesis 1:2 and Numbers 11:16-17, as well as Genesis 2:7 and Exodus 31:1-5.

ruckus by revolting against them. They'll soon be gone." It was important for Jesus to establish this point, because the condemnation He was about to pronounce might cause His disciples and the multitude to draw the wrong conclusions.

B. THE SCRIBES AND PHARISEES

We notice that Jesus directs the disciples to listen to the scribes and Pharisees. He grants that they have the chair of Moses. It is important to realize that by no means did everyone agree with this. There were three other denominations operating in the Jewish ecclesiastical scene: the Essenes, the Zealots, and the Sadducees.

The Essenes were a drop-out sect, like the Anabaptists before and after the Protestant Reformation. For them, the main problem of humanity was worldly existence. Neither Jesus nor any other person in the New Testament even so much as mentions them. It seems that when people choose to drop out of history and society, they drop from God's view and concern also, for God is very much concerned with His world.

The Zealots were political revolutionaries who sought the overthrow of Rome. For them, the main problem was political. The New Testament mentions them only occasionally. Their mindset was so far removed from what Jesus was doing that they did not interact with Him very much.

The Sadducees were liberals, who tended to discount the miraculous, rejected a physical resurrection, and had adopted the mindset of Greek philosophy to a great extent. The priests were mainly Sadducees. Jesus has little to do with them either. Though the priests also claimed to occupy Moses' chair, Jesus does not recognize their claim. Mainly they were Jerusalem aristocrats who had little to say to the common people.

Finally, the Pharisees. The Pharisees were the evangelicals. They took the Bible very seriously, and many of them learned to read and write (rare in the pre-Gutenberg world), so that many were "scribes." The particular "scribes" in the New Testament were experts in Biblical interpretation and instruction. The scribes and Pharisees held to the Bible and the Messianic promise and obeyed the Law. They worked among the poor and common people and came up with discipleship formulas to help people live better lives. Jesus interacts with them constantly. Of course, for many their evangelical faith had degenerated into a legalistic religion, and this form of demonic religion blinded them to the reality of the Messiah when He arrived in their midst. Still, most of the Jews who converted to Jesus were from the Pharisaical party.

So, we notice that before He condemns them, Jesus authorizes the Pharisees to occupy the Mosaic teaching position. They are the true heirs of Moses and of the earlier faith. When they expound the Law of Moses, they should be heard and obeyed.

Sadly, this is not all that they do. They have also come to believe that their traditions are almost as spiritually important as God's own laws. These traditions are heavy burdens that they lay on men's shoulders (23:5). Throughout His ministry, Jesus made it clear that His disciples did not have to listen to such teachings, though for the sake of peace, they should try to go along with them where possible.

The Pharisees were the best of the Jews, who were the chosen people. Jesus' condemnation of the Pharisees was the condemnation of the best of Jewry. Those Jews who knew the Bible the best and had the most truth hated Jesus the most and came under the sharpest condemnation. In this we see in a very focused way the condemnation of all Adamic humanity apart from Christ.

C. THE STRUCTURE OF THE PASSAGE

> a. In Moses' seat the Pharisees rule, 2-3a
> > b. What they say is hypocritical, 3b
> > > c. What they do is tyrannical, 4
> > > > d. What they are is vainglorious, 5-7
> > > > d' Do not seek glory, 8-10
> > > c' Do not be tyrants, 11-12
> > b' Octave of woes against hypocrisy, 13-31
> a' Fill up the measure of your guilt then, 32

We notice first of all that this chiasm occupies both the A and B sections of our original analysis. Similarly, B' concerns parables of the coming of

Christ to judge, while A' presents the judgment. Thus, the two B sections present dramatic pictures related to the theme of the two A sections.

Second, we can notice the relationship between the two "a" subsections in our passage. If we put them together, we get a coherent statement: "Upon the seat of Moses have sat down the scribes and the Pharisees… And you [scribes and Pharisees] fill up the measure of your fathers." In other words, they have assumed the seat of Moses, so they will be judged by that standard and condemned by it.

Third, we notice that three general charges are brought against the Pharisees and that these are dealt with one way or another in reverse order.

D. COMMENTARY

[3]Therefore, all they *tell* you, do and keep guarding;
> and/but (*de*) according to their *works*, do not do,
for they *speak*,
> and (*kai*) do not *do*.

Jesus says that the hypocritical Pharisees could do a good job of preaching Moses, but that their practice was significantly out of accord with their preaching. The "seat of Moses" refers to teaching the whole Bible and everything in it. In this, the Pharisees were hypocrites.[13]

Moses was the meekest of men (Num. 12:3), and evidently such meekness was preached by the Pharisees. They did not, however, practice it. That meekness and humility are specifically in view emerges from what follows. Jesus tells the disciples to be (like Moses) humble and

---

13. We should note in passing that the fact that these men were hypocrites means that they taught the truth, for the most part, though they did not live according to their own teachings. The notion that the Pharisees had bad theology, that they taught "salvation by meritorious works," is questionable. The Protestant Reformers saw in the Pharisees people much like the merit-centered Roman Church of their day, but the Reformers were probably mainly wrong in this. To be sure, salvation by meritorious works is wrong, and the Roman Church in Luther's day was wrong, but modern scholars have disputed whether the Jews of Jesus' day really believed such a notion. What Jesus says here certainly adds weight to the modern view. The Pharisees had correct doctrine (to a considerable extent), but hypocritically failed to live by it.

unassuming. Part of their meekness and humility must be to obey the Pharisees, even though they know that the Pharisees are wicked men.

Jesus' charge that the Pharisees preach humility but practice pride is followed up by His repeated accusation: "Hypocrites!" throughout verses 13-31. In that octave of woes, Jesus exposes eight ways in which the Pharisees contradict their own teaching of Moses. At the outset, however, Jesus points to pride and vainglory as the root of all their other sins.

> ⁴And/but (*de*) they bind heavy *burdens,*
>> and (*kai*) lay them on the *shoulders* of men,
>> and/but (*de*) with their own *finger*
> they will not move them.

This charge of tyranny is laid out in inverse parallelism: burdens, body, body, burdens. The text behind the AV reads, "For they bind" rather than "And they bind," thus implying that verse 4 explains or expands upon verse 3cd. This is unlikely, both from the standpoint of the flow of argument and from the standpoint of textual witnesses. The charge in verse 3cd is hypocrisy, while the charge in verse 4 is tyranny. Tyranny does not seem to be a subset of hypocrisy. It seems rather clear that Jesus is adding a second charge here. Moreover, the textual evidence evidently is clearly in favor of "and" here.

Now, what is it that the Pharisees do? They add to the law God gave to Moses. They use Moses' seat to impose rules upon the people that God did not give. If this sounds like the typical sin of evangelical Christianity, that is because the Pharisees were the evangelicals of their day. The rules added by the Pharisees are of the same sort as the "no smoke, no drink" rules added by evangelicalism. (Though we must bear in mind that some Pharisees, like some evangelicals, were not guilty of such legalism.)[14]

---

14. As noted above, the Pharisees don't seem to have taught a religion of "meriting" God's favor by "good works." The additional rules that they added were not for earning salvation but for earning status as super-believers, as those who "seek God's best," perhaps as a way of earning greater rewards in the life to come.

The notion of heavy loads that weigh men down contrasts with the picture of spirited dancing that sometimes accompanied the singing of the Psalms. The joyful man leaps against gravity, while the depressed man is pulled down by it. Thus has God designed the world.

It is unclear if "move with the finger" means that the Pharisees will not even lift a finger to help other men weighed down by such burdens or if it means that the Pharisees do not themselves take up the burdens they put on others—so that while other men carry heavy loads on their shoulders, the Pharisee won't even carry a feather on his own finger.

Peter Leithart, reading this manuscript for me, pointed out that this may well be another reference to Egypt. The Pharaoh tied burdens onto the Hebrews (Exod. 1:11; 2:11; 5:4-5; 6:6-7), while it was the finger of God that delivered them (8:19; and cf. Deut. 9:10). The Pharisees, claiming to be agents of God, were acting as Egyptian slavemasters.

One final point is that the Pharisees were not only hypocritical as regards the actual teachings of the Bible, but also as regards their own added teachings. They did not do the true things that they taught and doubtless they did not always do the false things that they had invented. They were like an evangelical preacher who teaches against adultery (true teaching) and alcohol (false teaching), but secretly indulges in both.

> [5]And/but (*de*) all their works they do
> in order to be noticed by men:
> for they broaden their charm boxes,
> and (*kai*) magnify the tassels;
> [6]and/but (*de*) they love the first places at the banquets,
> and (*kai*) the first seats in the synagogues,
> [7]and (*kai*) the respectful greetings in the markets,
> and (*kai*) to be called by men, "My Master Teacher (Rabbi)."

Jesus now adds a third charge, vainglory, which is then illustrated by six statements that follow. There is no need for Jesus to state that His disciples should want to be noticed by God, for the point is obvious. The two different Greek words for "and" structure the passage for us.

The two separate descriptions point in different directions. First, the Pharisees expanded the size of parts of their garments. (Perhaps there is an ironic allusion to the great burdens they lay on other men.) The charm boxes or "phylacteries" were small leather cases that contained parts of the Scriptures, which were worn on forehead and wrist in a mistaken literal application of Deuteronomy 6:8. The Jews did not call these items "magic charms" but *tefillin;* apparently Jesus is insulting them here. The tassels, four of them, were worn at the corners (literally "wings") of garments (Num. 15:37-41).

The Pharisees enlarged these in order to make a show before men, but ironically it only added to their offensiveness to God. The command in Deuteronomy 6:8 meant that the Law of God was to be bound on the forehead and hand in such a way that the inner thoughts and outer actions of the Godly person were governed by God's will. This corresponds with the words and works of the Pharisees already in view in this passage (v. 3). The large phylacteries of the Pharisees only highlighted their hypocrisy. The False Prophet Pharisees are pictured the same way in Revelation 13:16-17.

The tassels prescribed by God in Numbers 15 were put on the four wings of the Israelite garment. The four wings made each person a human cherub, a guardian of God's holiness. In each tassel of linen was a single blue thread of wool, creating a small piece of holy, mixed cloth. The tassel of holiness was to be worn as a visible reminder of the "commandments of Yahweh," so that they would remember to obey Yahweh and be a holy people. Unlike the command of Deuteronomy 6:8, this order was supposed to be carried out literally; but by enlarging their tassels the Pharisees were preaching loudly to everyone around them. They sported large tassels to remind other people of the Law of God. They themselves, however, did not truly respect God's law, and thus their tassels only added to their offense before Him.

Jesus' second unflattering description of the scribes and Pharisees is that they seek places of honor. Actually, He says that they "love" these things. The Pharisees were ordinarily too subtle to demand them, but it was obvious that they coveted them. Four types of honor are mentioned.

First, they loved the most honorable reclining places at banquets—literally, "the banquets," which might imply the feasts of Israel as well as other special dinners.

Second, they loved the chief seats in the synagogues. Sacramental worship was not conducted at the synagogue meetings, which were services of Scripture and prayer. The exposition of the Scripture was conducted from a seated position (compare "the seat of Moses").

Third, they loved being honored publicly in the marketplaces. They wanted all men to speak well of them, something Jesus warns us about (Luke 6:26). We move here from the context of worship and semi-worship occasions to the common life of man in the world.

Finally, they loved being called Rabbi, which means "My Master Teacher." Compare the expression in English, "My Lord."

The structure of these descriptions seems to be this:

1. Honor at special community events.
2. Honor at special teaching events.
3. Honor in general community life.
4. Honor as teacher in general.

The Christian Church has been most careful to insist that the special position of the minister of the Word in the worship service, his position as viceroy at the Lord's Table, and the honor shown him in common life, all flow from his being but a symbol of Jesus Christ. His "slave collar" reminds him and us that he is a servant. Sadly, it is not unusual to see a pastor who "loves" the honors associated with his office.

a.   ⁸And/but (*de*) you do not be called "Master Teacher," for

  b.   One

    c.   is your Teacher,

      d.   and/but (*de*) all of you are brothers.

        e.   ⁹And (*kai*) "Father" do not you call anyone on the earth, for

          f.   One

          f'   is your Father,

        e'   the heavenly one.

      d'   ¹⁰And/but (*de*) do not be called "Leaders,"

    c'   because your Leader is

  b'   One,

a'   the Christ.

We now begin to move back outward in the chiasm of this passage. The word "Rabbi" with which verse 7 ends becomes the first topic addressed in verse 8.

Though not apparent at first glance, and not apparent in English translations, verses 8-10 are a chiasm. At first glance, these verses look like three parallel statements, but the phrase "for One is your Teacher" is matched with "because your Leader is One," which reverses the order. Also, around the central focus, the Father, is the pair "earth and heaven."

This beautifully constructed passage brings out much that a chiasm is capable of showing. First of all, we have a movement from Christ to the Father and back to Christ. Then we have at the center a movement from earth to heaven. Putting these together, we have Christ as Teacher taking us from earth to heaven, to the Father, and then descending again to be the Leader and Messiah of His people on earth.

Second, the chiasm brings into association elements that we would not associate if we only laid out the passage in a parallelistic fashion. A parallelistic outline, following the larger connective word *de* is:

Not Rabbi	One Teacher	You are brothers
Not Father	One Father	The Heavenly One
Not Leaders	One Leader	The Anointed One

Such a parallelistic outline shows us, in the third column, that we are brothers because we have God as our Father, and because we are led by the Messiah.

The chiastic outline brings out other features, equally valid. The a & a' association brings out that the true Master Teacher is the Anointed Messiah. The c & c' association brings out that the Teacher is the Leader. These are different associations from those the parallelistic outline provided. Also, the chiastic outline associates the phrase "all of you are brothers" with "do not be called leaders." Finally, the chiasm puts the Father in the center even more obviously than the parallelism does.

One would not need this literary structure in order to make these points, with one exception: The chiasm brings out the notion of ascent from earth to heaven in a way that reading the passage only in a parallelistic fashion does not.

Clearly this teaching of Jesus does not contradict the many places in the Bible that teach that we should honor those put over us in all areas of life, including the Church. The prophets were called "father" (2 Kgs. 13:14), and many parts of the Church have employed this terminology for ministers (1 Cor. 4:15; Phil 2:22). Rather, Jesus' point here is that no Christian should seek such honors. All Christians should be wholly content as brethren in Christ under the Father.

[11]And/but (*de*) the greatest among you must be your servant.
    [12]And/but (*de*) whoever will exalt
        himself
            will be humbled.
            And/but (*de*) whoever will humble
        himself
    will be exalted.

Having discussed the honors associated with special names, Jesus turns to the second sin of the Pharisees: tyranny. He makes two statements. The first is that it is through service rather than through domination that honor is acquired in the Kingdom. The second is that God will reverse the deeds and desires of men, as the inverted structure indicates.

This brings us to the Octave of Woes pronounced against the Pharisees for their hypocrisy.

2
THE OCTAVE OF WOES
(23:13-32)

A. STRUCTURE OF THE PASSAGE

The eight woes of Matthew 23 correspond to the eight beatitudes of Matthew 5. This may not seem immediately apparent, especially if we count seven woes and nine beatitudes. A comparison of the two sections, however, will display numerous parallels.

Blessings and curses are linked in Leviticus 26 and Deuteronomy 28. As Jesus expounds the Law, He sets forth both blessings and woes (curses) together in Luke 6, a sermon that parallels the Sermon on the Mount of Matthew 5–7.[15] If the woes in Matthew 23 correspond to the blessings of Matthew 5, then we find Matthew making the same point as Luke, but doing so in a different way.

One problem with Matthew 23 is that the second woe (v. 14) does not appear in the ancient Greek texts that are commonly thought best at the present time. If the parallel between Matthew 5 and Matthew 23 stands up, it may shed light on this textual problem.

A second question about the Matthew 23 woes is whether they are chiastically arranged. Some who have sought to find such an arrangement have done so only by changing the order of the woes. The parallels with the beatitudes will help us deal with this matter also.

---

15. This may or may not be the same occasion. If it is the same, we have to bear in mind that both Matthew and Luke are condensing what Jesus said, since He doubtless spoke at length. Matthew stresses some things and Luke others. On the other hand, this might be basically the same sermon delivered on another occasion around the same time.

Thus, our first order of business is to show that indeed the eight woes specifically correspond to the eight beatitudes (Matt. 5:1-12).

The first woe of Matthew 23 (v. 13) condemns the Pharisees because they "shut off the kingdom of heaven from men." This agrees with the first beatitude, which blesses the poor in spirit, "for theirs is the kingdom of heaven."

The second (and textually disputed) woe of Matthew 23 (v. 14) condemns the Pharisees because they "devour widows' houses." This agrees with the second beatitude, which blesses "those who mourn."

The third woe of Matthew 23 (v. 15) condemns the Pharisees because they "travel about on sea and land to make one convert," but then "make him twice as much a son of Gehenna as yourselves." This agrees with the third beatitude, which blesses the meek, "for they shall inherit the earth."

The fourth woe of Matthew 23 (vv. 16-22) condemns the Pharisees for inventing ways to get around promises made to God. This does not seem to go with the fourth beatitude, which blesses "those who hunger and thirst for righteousness." Since the rest do correspond, however, we shall have to explore possible connections here as well.

The fifth woe of Matthew 23 (vv. 23-24) condemns the Pharisees for ignoring "justice and mercy and faith." This agrees with the fifth beatitude, which blesses "those who are merciful, for they shall obtain mercy."

The sixth woe of Matthew 23 (vv. 25-26) condemns the Pharisees for being concerned with externals more than with the heart. They "clean the outside of the cup and of the dish, but inside they are full of robbery and self-indulgence." This agrees with the sixth beatitude, which blesses "the pure in heart."

The seventh woe of Matthew 23 (vv. 27-28) condemns the Pharisees because, though they are outwardly honorable to men, inside they are dead and "full of dead men's bones and all uncleanness." This seems to agree with the seventh beatitude, which blesses peacemakers as genuine "sons of God," righteous both inwardly and outwardly.

Finally, the eighth and climactic woe of Matthew 23 (vv. 29-31) condemns the Pharisees because they persecuted and killed the prophets. This agrees with the eighth beatitude, which blesses "those who have been persecuted for the sake of righteousness," and which goes on to bless those who, like the prophets, are reviled, persecuted, and lied about for the sake of the Kingdom.

The reward of the eighth beatitude (5:10, 12) is to receive the Kingdom of heaven. Opposite this, the judgment on the Pharisees is the destruction of Jerusalem, which was "their" kingdom.

Turning now to the questions we mentioned above: First, if Matthew 23:14 is removed from the series, the correlations shift and become inexact; therefore, it may well be that Matthew 23:14 is to be regarded as a genuine part of Matthew's Gospel. At the same time, at present there is not much "good" manuscript evidence for it, and currently few scholars believe it is genuine. They believe it was added in later on, based on Mark 12:40 and Luke 20:47. If that should prove to be the case, we have uncovered the reason why it was inserted here: to create a clearer parallel with Matthew 5. Since I am personally inclined to accept verse 14 as genuine, I have been proceeding on that assumption.

Second, we see that we can rightly regard the beatitudes as eight in number. The ninth beatitude in Matthew 5:11 expands the eighth (and in fact is chiastically structured with it, as we will see below). The eighth woe focuses on the murder of the prophets, and the second part of the eighth beatitude mentions the persecution of the prophets. (The beatitudes can also be counted as nine, however, and we shall take that up later.)

This brings us to the suggestion that the woes are arranged chiastically. As mentioned above, those who have sought to make such an arrangement have resorted to altering the text in order to make it come out right. I suggest that there is a chiastic order in the text as it stands.

To start with, we notice that the two central woes (4 & 5) both uniquely accuse the Pharisees of being blind guides (23:16, 24). Moreover, these two woes are themselves chiastically arranged:

a. Blind guides, v. 16a

    b. Sin of false swearing, vv. 16b-22

    b' Sin of stealing, v. 23

a' Blind guides, v. 24

This is the center of the octave of woes. The two sins here are that of twisting and negating the oaths men swear to God and that of robbing from God what He desires in the way of tithes.

This pair of sins is distinctively highlighted in the Oikumenical era. We find it first in Zechariah 5:1-4, where God's Law strikes with leprosy any house wherein people swear falsely or steal. What is true of the ordinary home is true of the house of God, the temple. Thus, Jesus comes to the temple and says that it should be a house of prayer (true swearing of allegiance to God) but has become a den of thieves. By doing so, He acted as a priest to inspect the house for leprosy, and His cleansing of the temple should be taken as a fulfillment of the laws of house leprosy in Leviticus 14. (We shall take this up when we get to Matthew 24:2.) Moreover, Matthew 23–25 focuses, as we have seen and shall see again, on false prophets. The False Prophet or Land Beast in Revelation 13 enforces false worship and wicked trade (Rev. 13:15-17). Thus, it is significant that these two "benchmark sins" are found at the center of the octave of woes.

At the same time, the other woes don't seem to be chiastically related. We can get a bit of help by looking back at the beatitudes. If we count the beatitudes as eight, then the first and last both promise the kingdom of heaven. This forms an inclusio, but the other beatitudes are not chiastically arranged (though see below). Yet this does indicate that, since the woes correspond with the beatitudes, the first and eighth are linked conceptually. In the first woe, the Pharisees shut off the kingdom of heaven from men and do not enter themselves. The last woe introduces the full judgment upon the Jews, which continues all the way to the end of Matthew 25 and which has as its climax the exclusion of the wicked from the kingdom of heaven.

At this point, I think we are in a position to see a general, though not a highly specific, chiastic structure in the woes:

a. Woe 1: Pharisees shut up kingdom of heaven.

  b. Woes 2–3: Sins against others.

    c. Woe 4: Sin against God: blasphemy.

    c′ Woe 5: Sin against God: theft.

  b′ Woes 6–7: Sin inside themselves.

a′ Woe 8: Pharisees shut out of kingdom of heaven.

There is an inward motion from the sin of shutting off heaven through sins against others to the sin of blasphemy. Then there is an outward motion from the sin of selfishness through internal sins to being cut off from the kingdom of heaven. Thus, the first four woes can be connected together as one chain, and the latter four as another.

For completeness's sake, I must mention that it is also proper to count the beatitudes as nine in number, and that if this is done, the beatitudes form a chiasm:

1. Poor in spirit, kingdom of heaven.

  2. Mourning, comfort

    3. Meekness, inherit earth.

      4. Pursuit of righteousness, satisfied.

        5. Mercy, receive mercy.

      6. Purity of heart, see God.

    7. Peacemaking, sons of God (rulers).

  8. Persecution, kingdom of heaven.

9. Persecution, reward in heaven.

Not much needs to be said about this. "Sons of God" (7) is the designation of rulers in the Bible, and goes with "inherit the earth" (3). The "satisfaction" found in 4 is clearly the presence of God (6). It is most noteworthy that free salvation—mercy—is highlighted at the center.

Finally, let me display the chiastic structure of the eighth and ninth beatitudes, which show that these two are also one:

   a. Blessed are they that have been *persecuted* for righteousness sake,

     b. for theirs is the kingdom of *heaven*.

       c. *Blessed* are you,

         d. when they *reproach* you,

a' and *persecute* you,

         d' and *say all manner of evil* against you falsely for My sake.

       c' *Rejoice* and be exceeding *glad,*

     b' for great is your reward in *heaven,*

a" for thus they *persecuted* the prophets that were before you.

B.   THE FIRST THREE WOES (23:13-15)

[13]And/but (*de*) woe to you, scribes and Pharisees, hypocrites!
Because you shut off the kingdom of heaven in front of men.
For you do not enter in,
nor those entering in do you permit to enter in.

The word "hypocrite" comes from the theater and refers to someone who wears a mask. In the Jewish context it came to mean someone who pretended to be righteous but was not so.

The language here is a bit more picturesque than may appear in many translations. People are seeking to enter the kingdom of heaven. They are on their way in, becoming followers of Jesus. Then the Pharisees slam the door shut right in their faces.

According to the first beatitude, those seeking to enter are the poor in spirit. They are near death (Gen. 2:7; Eccl. 12:7). They seek life and the new life of the Spirit, which Jesus possesses. The Pharisees should have been foremost among these, and should have been leading others to Christ.

[14]Woe to you, scribes and Pharisees, hypocrites!
Because you devour the houses of widows
and/while (*kai*) for appearance's sake praying at length.
because of this you will receive more abundant judgment.

I have translated *kai* ("and") as "while," because this use of *kai* is to link the two statements as parts of one whole.

The second beatitude promises comfort to mourners. Here the Pharisees come to comfort widows, praying with them at length, but all the while only seeking their inheritance. The pathetically grateful widow would transfer assets to the Pharisees (cf. Mark 12:41-44; Luke 21:1-4).

In terms of God's perfect "eye for eye" justice, those who pray greater hypocritical prayers will receive greater judgment.

> [15]Woe to you, scribes and Pharisees, hypocrites!
> Because you roam around the sea and the withered-up places to make one proselyte,
> and (*kai*) when he has become such,
> you make him a son of Gehenna twice yourselves.

The Oikumenical Era was a great time of missionary outreach for the Jews. Positioned within the great empires, they traveled the seas and went to foreign lands ("withered places" outside the "garden land" of Israel), bringing the good news that God had not abandoned humanity and that a Messiah would come to save us all.

This wonderful missionary project could be perverted, however. As the Pharisees moved away from a true interpretation of the word of God and increasingly came up with new doctrines of their own, their converts were being brought not to the truth but to a lie from the pit. With the zeal of converts, they were twice as bad as the Pharisees themselves. It appears from what Jesus says here, however, that the Pharisees were not often successful in bringing Gentile converts into their own extreme customs.

Gehenna, the continually-burning garbage pit below Jerusalem, was a symbol of hell. The irony is that in Biblical symbolism, the mountainous land of Israel was raised up above the sea and other "withered" lands. Thus, true conversion was to be lifted out of low-lying places. The Pharisees, however, were simply delivering their converts into the lowest places of all, the "deep" of hades, the "withered land" of hell. The Pharisees insisted that Gentile converts become super-Jews, even more anti-Christian than Jews themselves.

C. THE FOURTH WOE (23:16-22)

[16] Woe to you, blind guides who say:

A. a. "Whoever swears by the sanctuary, it is nothing,
     b. and/but (*de*) whoever swears by the gold of the sanctuary is obligated."
        c. [17] Fools and blind men!
     b' Which is greater: the gold?
    a' Or the sanctuary that sanctifies the gold?

B. d. [18] And (*kai*): "Whoever swears by the altar, it is nothing,
     e. and/but (*de*) whoever swears by the gift that is upon it is obligated."
        f. [19] [Fools and] blind men!
     e' For which is greater: the gift?
    d' Or the altar that sanctifies the gift?

B' [20] He therefore who swears by the altar
swears by it and by all the things on it.

A' [21] And (*kai*) he who swears by the sanctuary
swears by it and by all the things in it.

A" [22] And (*kai*) he who swears by heaven
swears by the throne of God and by Him who sits on it.

This woe is unique in that the scribes and Pharisees are not called hypocrites and in that it does not have an obvious link with the fourth beatitude. Also, in verse 19 is it not clear from the manuscript evidence whether we should read "fools and blind men" or simply "blind men"; though the parallel indicates that "fools and blind men" is probably correct.

As can be seen, this woe has a generally chiastic structure. To be complete, it would have to begin with something like "Whoever swears by heaven, it is nothing; but whoever swears by the throne of heaven is obligated." This, however, is not something the Pharisees could have done, since "heaven" was a way of saying "God" among the superstitious

Jews. Thus, what we have is a chiasm of sanctuary—altar—altar—sanctuary, followed by a climactic application to heaven itself. Altar and sanctuary were each symbols of heavenly realities.

Some translations speak here of the "temple," but I have translated the word as "sanctuary," since the word refers not to the entire temple building but to the "temple proper," the Holy of Holies and the Holy Place.

There is apparently no information from Jewish sources about this business of swearing by the sanctuary versus swearing by its gold, and so forth. We must seek to uncover the reasoning of the Pharisees from the Bible itself. If we look back at 1 Kings 6, which provides the instructions for the first temple—and thus the theology of it—we find the following sequence of events:

1. The house itself is built of stone, vv. 2-14.
2. The inside of the house of paneled with cedar, vv. 15-18.
3. The inside of the house is filled with gold, vv. 19-36.

Gold represents glory, because gold (which can be considered "solid light," as oil is "liquid light") is glorious. Filling the house with gold is related to God's entering the house to dwell there. The Pharisees may have reasoned that it was the gold that sanctified the house, analogous to God's sanctifying it by His presence.

Similarly, there were a series of altars in use during the Patriarchal era. On the altar was the sacrifice that represented God's acceptance of the worshiper. It would seem that what was on the altar was more important than the altar itself. After all, we might reason, which is more important: the cross or Jesus on the cross?

Jesus seems to reverse this line of reasoning, and it is curious, perhaps even paradoxical, that He does so. A similar curiosity is found in Matthew 15:11, where Jesus says, "Not what enters into the mouth defiles the man, but what proceeds out of the mouth, this defiles the man." Now, anyone familiar with Leviticus 11 knows that eating carrion or the flesh of unclean animals caused ceremonial defilement. Jesus seems to be directly contradicting what He Himself, as Yahweh, had told Moses in Leviticus 11.

If we look for a full explanation of this apparent contradiction we shall be disappointed. Jesus does, however, indicate what He means in Matthew 15:17-18: "Do you not understand that everything that goes into the mouth passes into the belly and is cast out into the latrine? But the things that proceed out of the mouth come from the heart, and those defile the man."

By saying this, Jesus points to two levels of meaning. The first is symbolic, the level at which the food laws of Leviticus operated. In terms of that symbolism, eating forbidden food is like committing the sin of Adam, and eating such animals is like taking the serpent into your heart. Jesus is not, however, engaged in a discussion at this level. At the second level, food is just food. It cannot affect us morally and spiritually one way or another. At this moral/spiritual level, it is what comes out of our hearts through our mouths that makes us truly unclean in God's sight. Compare Psalm 5:9.

Now, with this "two level" understanding in mind, I think we can come to grips with what Jesus says in Matthew 23:16-22. The clue is in what Jesus adds at the end about heaven and the throne of God. The sanctuary was a symbol of the firmament heavens (holy place) and the highest heavens (holy of holies). God is present in the heavens. True, as an earthly building, the stone is less glorious than the gold; but as a sanctuary, it is a place where God is present. At that level of discourse, it is God who sanctifies the gold. Similarly, as a pile of stones, an altar is inferior to the sacrifice placed on it. But the fire on the altar signifies God's glory-presence consuming the sacrifice, and it is His presence that sanctifies the sacrifice.

What makes a stone building a sanctuary is not gold but God's presence. What makes a pile of stones an altar is not a sacrifice but God's presence. This is precisely the point Jesus makes in the last three statements. "All the things" on the altar and in the sanctuary include the presence of God. This is made clear by the third statement, where it is God's presence in heaven that makes heaven holy.

It is precisely "God" whom the Pharisees avoided mentioning. They were too superstitious to say the name of God for fear of taking it in vain. Thus, they came up with circumlocutions. Instead of swearing an oath "as God is my witness," they would swear by the sanctuary or by its gold, by the altar or its gift. Instead of saying "God" they would say "heaven."

Jesus sweeps all this away. Which is greater: the gold or the sanctuary? Neither, perhaps. If you are referring to God by using these circumlocutions, you might as well say "God," because He is not fooled. If you swear by heaven—if you even swear by the throne of God—you are swearing by God Himself. Thus, all these clever distinctions mean nothing. You can say that the altar is greater, or you can say that the gift is greater, depending on your perspective. So what? You can say that heaven is greater, or that the throne is greater. So what? Your intention is to swear by God's name, or to pretend to do so, and He knows it. He is not fooled. He takes it seriously. If you swear such an oath, you'd better take it seriously also.

By means of their distinctions, though, the Pharisees sought to distinguish between serious and non-serious oaths. If they swore a promise by the sanctuary, they felt free to break it. They were men who swore falsely, and their houses—both their own and the temple—would be cursed with leprosy and be destroyed (Zech. 5:4).

D. The Fifth Woe (23:23-24)

[23]Woe to you, scribes and Pharisees, hypocrites!
a. Because you are tithing mint and dill and cumin,
    b. and/while (*kai*) you dismissed the weightier parts of the law:
    the justice and the mercy and the faith.
a' These you should have done,
    b' without dismissing the others.
[24]Blind guides! Who filter out the gnat while gulping down the camel!

The Pharisees are meticulous about tithing on their herb gardens but have dropped the serious parts of the law. Jesus says that they are right to be careful about tithing, but they should not have dismissed the serious matters. The triad of herbs is matched by the triad of serious virtues.

Should we read "the faith" or "faithfulness"? The answer seems to be the former, because Jesus seems to be alluding directly to Micah 6:8b. Micah 6:6-8 as a whole is parallel to Matthew 23:23-24. Micah 6:6-7 asks the question what a man should bring as a gift to Yahweh. The answer, in verse 8b, is to "do justice, love mercy, and walk humbly with your God." The last phrase speaks of the walk of personal faith, not the faithfulness of obedience (though these are hardly separable). Moreover, "justice and mercy" already cover the notion of "faithfulness."

"Justice" in the Bible means "social justice" in the sense of equity, giving each his due. "Mercy" is the outreach to those in need. "Faith" is the trusting relationship with God.

I have remarked above that this woe accuses the Pharisees of theft and brings upon them the other half of the curse of Zechariah 5:4:

> "I will make it go forth," declares the Lord of hosts, "and it will enter the house of the thief and the house of the one who swears falsely by My name; and it will spend the night within that house and consume it with its timber and stones."

The way to understand this is the same way as with the preceding curse. The Pharisees maintain that they swear truly, but Jesus says they swear falsely. The Pharisees maintain that they give to God, but Jesus says that they steal honor from Him. Consider that Jesus might have said, "For you attend synagogue twice each sabbath, but dismissed the weightier matters." That is not the point He made, however. By using a monetary reference and doing so right after discussing false swearing, Jesus appears to be referencing the dual sin of Zechariah 5:4. Thus, once again the Pharisees are bringing leprosy upon their own houses and upon the temple they profess as their own larger house. This matter of house leprosy will be very important for what Jesus will have to say later on.

Why does Jesus specifically mention mint, dill, and cumin? We do not find much about these spices in the Bible, but in the modern diet they are associated with different meats: mint with lamb, dill with beef, cumin with mutton (?). Perhaps the spices are somehow the "clothing" of sacrificial meats. I cannot prove this, but perhaps this suggestion will help some reader to make a better guess.

E. THE LAST THREE WOES (23:25-31)

²⁵Woe to you, scribes and Pharisees, hypocrites!
a. Because you clean the outside of the cup and of the dish,
    b. and/but (*de*) inside they are full of rapacity and self-indulgence.
        c. ²⁶Blind Pharisee!
    b' Clean first the inside of the cup and of the dish,
a' so that also the outside of it may be clean.

Jesus speaks metaphorically here. Doubtless the Pharisees did clean the inside of their dishes. Jesus says that what is inside their dishes is rapacity (in Greek, a word related to "harpy") and self-indulgence. That is, the contents of their wine glasses and the fine food on their dishes had been acquired by oppression and for the purpose of sensuality. Both culinary and sexual sensuality can be implied in the term here, which literally means "lack of self-restraint." In contrast to the sixth beatitude, the Pharisees were not pure in heart.

Throughout the Bible, plates, bowls, and cups represent people (e.g., 2 Tim 2:20). The Pharisees wanted the cups and plates of their lives to appear clean. Jesus says that if we want to be clean on the outside, we have to be clean on the inside (pure of heart). The only way for the Pharisees to be really clean on the outside, and not just hypocritically so, is to repent and change their ways.

²⁷Woe to you, scribes and Pharisees, hypocrites!
Because you resemble whitewashed tombs,
a. which outwardly on the one hand appear beautiful,
    b. and/but (*de*) inwardly on the other hand are full of dead bones and all uncleanness.
a' ²⁸Thus also (*kai*) you outwardly on the one hand appear righteous to men,
    b' and/but (*de*) inwardly on the other hand are full of hypocrisy and lawlessness.

Tombs were whitewashed, especially just before Passover, so that no Jew would by mistake come in contact with them and thereby become unclean (Num. 19:16). As in the last woe, Jesus rebukes the Pharisees for glorifying the outer man without cleansing the inner man.

The comparison of inward and outward cleanness is very similar to the preceding woe, except that this time it is the moral character rather than the behavior of the Pharisees that is in view. Their character is dead. Jesus associates hypocrisy and lawlessness with literal and symbolic death (uncleanness). The person wearing a mask to appear righteous does so because he is dead, lifeless inside. The person who lives lawlessly does not have the Spirit-quickened law of God written on his heart. Such dead men are the opposite of the "sons of God" of the seventh beatitude.

> [29]Woe to you, scribes and Pharisees, hypocrites!
> Because you build the tombs of the prophets,
> and (*kai*) decorate the memorials of the righteous;
> a. [30]and (*kai*) say, "If we had lived in the days of the fathers,
>> b. We would not have been partners with them in the blood of the prophets."
>> b' [31]Just so you witness against yourselves that you are the sons of the murderers of the prophets. Yes, you!
> a' [32]Fill up the measure of your fathers!

The meaning of this woe is pretty clear. The Pharisees were so blind that they thought that if they had lived in the days of the prophets, they would have supported them. Any true believer should know better. All of us abandoned Jesus, and all of us would have abandoned the prophets also, and for the same basic reason. Only the special operations of God's grace enabled anyone to support the prophets during their lives.

As mentioned above, the final phrase completes the section that begins with the scribes and Pharisees sitting in Moses' seat. They have assumed the responsibility of this position, and so they must be judged in terms of it.

The final phrase is a summation of the preceding condemnations, which leads to the judgments pronounced in the following verses, to which we now turn.

Before doing so, however, there is an interesting sub-textual progression in the last four woes. The fifth uses an analogy to garden herbs, calling to mind the Garden of Eden. The sixth deals with food, the desire for food, acquiring food unlawfully. This alludes to the sin of Adam and Eve in the Garden of Eden. The seventh woe deals with death, which was the sentence on Adam and Eve for their sin. Awareness of this death caused them to cover themselves with leaves, analogous to the whited tombs. Finally, the eighth woe deals with the murder of the prophets and the righteous. Abel was the righteous man who was murdered by Cain, and in v. 35 Jesus specifically refers to Abel and all those murdered after him. In this way, the last four woes lead forward to the sentence that follows them. The Pharisees have simply carried forward the original sin of humanity and have brought it to a point of fullness. They will fill it up over the next thirty-five or so years, after which will come the Flood, the destruction of the Old Creation.

Note also that the second and third woes deal with widows and strangers. Repeatedly (ten times) in Deuteronomy, Moses said not to oppress widows, fatherless, and strangers (10:18-19; 14:29; 16:11, 14; 24:19-21 [3x]; 26:12-13 [2x]; 27:19). This triad is here condensed into a pair of "two witnesses" against the scribes and Pharisees. They sit in Moses' seat, but oppress widows and make strangers into sons of hell.

Additionally, the sixth and seventh woes both deal with vessels containing unclean things: cups and graves. This is also a matching pair forming a testimony of two witnesses (a common theme in Matthew).

Also, chiastically the seventh woe (graves) is matched with the second (widows). The scribes and Pharisees were supposed to act as husbands for the widows, as God's husbandly representatives. But, like the original husbands of these widows, the scribes and Pharisees were dead, though theirs was the much more serious death of inner depravity.

Finally, this leaves only the third woe (strangers) and the sixth woe (cups) as not having an apparent chiastic match. Since all the others do match, we are invited to consider what might correspond here. I suggest that glorious Jerusalem with dark Gehenna as the pit beside it corresponds to a beautiful cup with uncleanness within. The temple is a grave, beautiful on the outside but full of dead men. By converting Gentiles, the Pharisees only pollute them.

3.
THE JUDGMENT OF THE OLD CREATION
(23:33-36)

Here we are concerned with sections C and D of our overall chiastic outline. The C section delineates the final condemnation of the Pharisees and their followers, while the statement in D both ends this first major part of the passage and introduces the next part, forming an inclusio with Matthew 24:34.

1. [33]Serpents!
2. Offspring of vipers!
3. How shall you escape the judgment of Gehenna?

4. [34]Therefore, behold! I Myself am sending you prophets and wise men and scribes.
5. Some of them you will kill and crucify.
6. And (*kai*) some of them you will scourge in your synagogues and (*kai*) persecute from city to city;

7. [35]That upon you may fall all the righteous blood shed on the earth,
8. from the blood of righteous Abel
9. to the blood of Zechariah the son of Berechiah, whom you murdered between the sanctuary and the altar.

10. [36]Amen I say to you, all these things shall come upon this generation.

This passage does not have a chiastic or parallelistic structure, but it does have a definite triple rhythm. Jesus' woes are like ten hammer blows, as He pronounces doom upon the final generation of the Old Creation.

1. "Serpents" Jesus calls them, a direct and unmistakable allusion to the original serpent of Genesis 3. As angels were the tutors of humanity during our minority, Lucifer was Chief Tutor.[16] Now the Pharisees sit in Moses' seat, and like Lucifer, they choose to mislead humanity. As Lucifer used the serpent, the wisest of beasts, as his agent, so Satan now uses the wise Pharisees as his tempting serpents (Gen. 3:1; Matt. 10:16). The poison of Pharisaical doctrine, in its Judaizing form, is referred to in Revelation 12:14-15.

2. "Offspring of vipers," adds Jesus. They are children of their father, the devil (John 8:44). The viper that attacked Paul in Acts 28:3 came out of the fire and was thus a "fiery serpent" like those that attacked Israel in the wilderness. Paul was not affected by the viper's bite, for he trusted in Jesus, who was the true Bronze Serpent (Num. 21). The Pharisees not only mislead men, but they also attack them and poison them.

3. The judgment of being cast into Gehenna is inevitable, because they are united to Satan and that is his destiny (Rev. 20:10). The judgment of false Judaism is pictured in Revelation 19:20 as the immediate consequence of the fall of Jerusalem-Babylon:[17]

    a. And the Beast was seized,
    a. and with him the False Prophet, who performed the signs in his presence,
        b. by which he deceived those who had received the mark of the beast [to buy and sell: theft motif (Rev. 13:17)],
        b. and those who worshiped his image [false swearing motif];
    a' these two were thrown alive [like Korah, Dathan, and Abiram] into the lake of fire,
    a' which burns with brimstone.

---

16. Acts 7:53; Galatians 3:19, 23-25; 4:1ff.; Hebrews 2:2. See John Barach, "The Glory of the Son of Man: An Exposition of Psalm 8," in Peter J. Leithart and John Barach, eds., *The Glory of Kings: A Festschrift in Honor of James B. Jordan* (Eugene, OR: Wipf & Stock, 2011), 3-34.

17. Babylon is not physical Jerusalem, though that is included, but the spiritual counterfeit of the "Jerusalem without walls" of Zechariah 2:4, the spiritual Jerusalem

4. Jesus has told them to fill up the cup of their judgment (Matt. 23:32). He now explains how this will happen. He will send them prophets, just like those they have been killing for generations. He will send them wise men, true serpents, to counteract their poisonous teaching. He will send them true scribes, to counter their false scribes. These will form a testimony of "two or three witnesses" against them.

5. Some will be killed and crucified. The added thought of crucifixion links the death of Jesus' servants with His own. Jesus had already declared that He would be crucified, in Matthew 20:19. His servants must take up their own crosses and follow Him.

6. Others will not be killed, but will be scourged and persecuted. Matthew 20:19 also refers to Jesus' scourging, and so once again the servants are united to their Master. Jesus had linked scourging in the synagogues and being persecuted from city to city in His commissioning of the disciples in Matthew 10:16-23. This passage has the same eschatological horizon as Matthew 23–25, for Jesus states in 10:23, "Amen I say to you, you shall not finish the cities of Israel before the Son of Man comes," a reference to the events surrounding the destruction of Jerusalem.

7. Now we come to the climax. Jesus tells the Pharisees, and all the impenitent Jews with them, that all the blood of the righteous slain from the beginning of the world will come upon them. This is an extremely significant statement. We might expect the Jews to pay for all the blood spilled from Mount Sinai forward, or from the call of Abram forward, but Jesus says that they will pay for all the blood from Abel forward. It is the entire Old Creation, the entire First History, that is being brought to an end and judged in the final events of Jesus' first coming, which events took place down to AD 70.

Blood calls forth the Avenger of Blood. If the blood is concealed, the Avenger waits. The Egyptians, for instance, made the Nile red

---

after the return from exile, which includes all the Jews wherever they are in the Oikumene. Zechariah 5:5-11 displays the formation of the counterfeit spiritual Jerusalem at the same time and provides most of the imagery later used in Revelation 17.

with the blood of Hebrew babies, but it was eighty years later when the Nile was bloodied again by Aaron's rod and the Avenger moved against Egypt. Similarly, the destruction of Jerusalem-Babylon in Revelation 16–19 is called forth by the blood of the martyrs who died outside the city in Revelation 14 and whose blood covers the land. The bowls of Revelation 16 pour that blood upon the city, and then the Avenger destroys it.

Was it right to punish the Jews of that generation for the blood of all the righteous of all the world? Yes, and for this reason: Israel was established as the priest of the nations. That was her call and privilege, which she accepted. The Jews of Jesus' day were sinfully proud of that privilege. The sacrifices offered by Israel were offered for the whole world.

As Kiuchi has shown, the blood rites of the Purification Offering in particular had the effect of rolling the guilt off of the people onto the priests and eventually onto the high priest, who dealt with all of it on the Day of Coverings.[18] In this way, Israel bore the sins of the world, which she was then to transfer to the goats of Covering. Rejecting Jesus as Covering, the Jews were left with the sins on themselves.

Yet, if the Day of Coverings put the sins on the high priest, then why were all the apostate Jews judged? Why not just the high priest? The answer, I suggest, is that after the days of the Maccabees there was never a true, legitimate, Zadokite high priest operating in Israel. Thus, there was never a legitimate Day of Coverings ceremony. The sins of the world piled up on the Jews and were neither symbolically removed by the Day of Coverings nor really removed by the death of Christ.

All men benefit from the death of Christ in the sense that their bloodguilt is temporarily removed and hidden. Those who accept

---

18. Not "Day of Atonement." The Hebrew word means "covering," and providing clean garments is essential to the rite; cf. Genesis 3:21. On the rite as a whole, see N. Kiuchi, *The Purification Offering in the Priestly Literature: Its Meaning and Function*, Journal for the Study of the Old Testament Supplement Series 56 (Sheffield, England: Sheffield Academic Press, 1987).

Christ have their bloodguilt permanently removed. Those who won't accept Him will have their bloodguilt returned upon their heads at the end and will have to answer for it. This will happen at the end of the New Creation, as Revelation 20 shows us. It also happened at the end of the Old Creation, as we are seeing.

The massacre of the 144,000 faithful in Revelation 14 fills the land with blood. Because this number is symbolic, we don't know how many faithful Jews actually died in the Great Tribulation at the hands of the wicked Jews. The blood that fills the land comes not only from them, but also from all the righteous of the entire history of the Old Creation.

Let us be clear about this: The destruction of the temple and of Jerusalem was not merely the end of the Hebrew-Israelite-Jewish period of history that began with Abraham. It was the end of the entire Old Creation from Adam forward. The Church is the replacement not merely of Israel, but also of the older and larger Gentile world that began with Adam and continued through the Noahic covenant. The Kingdom of Jesus is a wholly New Creation, and nothing less.

8. The history of bloodguilt begins with Abel, whose blood cried from the ground. God did not kill Cain but sent him into exile. Exile, thus, is a kind of death penalty. The apostate Jews who are not killed by the Romans will be exiled, like Cain, and become wanderers.

   Cain murdered his brother, which is exactly what the Pharisees will do to Jesus and to Jesus' disciples. Jew will kill Jew.

   Moreover, Cain went out and built a city based on that murder. The true city of God is built on the blood of Jesus, but the false Babylon-Jerusalem is built on the blood of the saints. The filling of the land with blood in Revelation 14 is followed in Revelation 17 with a vision of the wicked city perched on mountains, above that blood. The blood of the martyrs is the foundation of the wicked city.

9. Now we come to one of the really difficult places in the Gospels. Jesus mentions the blood of Zechariah the son of Berechiah. The martyr Zechariah was the son of Jehoiada (2 Chr. 24:20-22). On the

other hand, Zechariah the son of Berechiah was the author of the book of Zechariah, and another person altogether (Zech. 1:1). So, how are we to understand this?

One suggestion is that we have a copyist's error here, though there is no manuscript evidence to support that notion. Another is that Jesus deliberately conflates the two Zechariahs because the prophecies in Zechariah 11:12-13 about the "field of blood" link with the general concept. I admit that this may be a possibility, but there is another that seems better.

The older and still most common view is that Berechiah is another name for Jehoiada. It is generally assumed that this identification is correct, though devoid of any textual support. There is, however, a line of argument for it that is worth rehearsing because it is usually overlooked. The great Puritan scholar John Lightfoot provides a fairly compelling argument for this view.[19] He calls attention to Isaiah 8:1-2: "Then Yahweh said to me, 'Take for yourself a large tablet and write on it with ordinary letters: TO HASTEN THE SPOIL, HE HASTENS THE PREY. And I will take for Myself faithful witnesses for testimony: Uriah the priest, and Zechariah the son of Jeberechiah.'"

Who are these two witnesses, and what is their function? Generally it is assumed that they bear witness that Isaiah actually wrote the words on the tablet. If such were the case, however, the text should read, "You take for yourself these two faithful witnesses …" In other words, just as Isaiah was to write the words, so he was to get two men to notarize the document. That is not, however, what is stated. It is only stated that God will raise up two faithful witnesses.

Now, Uriah cannot be linked with the high priest Uriah, who served Ahaz in the days of Isaiah (Isa. 7:1; 2 Kgs. 16:10-16), for he was not a faithful witness but very shortly cooperated with Ahaz's establishment of false worship in the temple precincts.

---

19. John Lightfoot, *Commentary on the New Testament from the Talmud and Hebraica* (original Latin, 1658–74; English trans. 1859; reprint, Peabody, MA: Hendrickson, 1989).

Is there a Uriah whose witness relates to Isaiah's words and who seems to fulfill the stipulations? Yes, there is: Uriah the son of Shemaiah of Kiriath-Jearim, a prophet who stood with Jeremiah against King Jehoiakim and who was slain for doing so (Jer. 26:20-24). But was this Uriah a priest? We cannot know for certain, but we do know that for many years the Ark of the Covenant was located at Kiriath-Jearim (1 Sam. 7:1-2; 1 Chr. 13:5-6; 2 Chr. 1:4). There were probably families of priests still living there. Also, the name Shemaiah is used for twenty-six different men in the Bible.[20] Ten of these were Levites, and six more were priests. Three more were prophets or false prophets, and prophets were usually taken from the Levitical or priestly families. Thus, Shemaiah is a name common in Levitical and priestly families, which greatly heightens the likelihood that Uriah the son of Shemaiah was a priest.

Was Uriah a faithful witness? Yes. Did he bring forward and apply the words of Isaiah? Yes.

With this in mind, Lightfoot suggests, the other faithful witness (and martyr) is Zechariah the son of Jehoiada. For Jehoiada to have another name, Jeberechiah or Berechiah, is not unusual. The three names have closely related meanings:

Jeho-Yada means Yah Knows.
Berech-Yah means Yah Blesses.
Yberech-Yah means May Yah Bless.

As Lightfoot points out, these two martyrs are the first and last of the first temple era. Why, then, does Jesus refer to Zechariah rather than Uriah? I think Lightfoot has it right in pointing out that only in the two instances of Abel and Zechariah do we have a cry for vengeance (2 Chr. 24:22). This particular point is expanded by H. G. L. Peels,

---

20. John N. Oswalt, "Shemaiah," *The International Standard Bible Encyclopedia* (Grand Rapids: Eerdmans, 1988), 470-471.

In short, in Abel and Zechariah the text is referring to two figures who over a span of centuries portray the entire tragedy of the murder of God's servants. Both of them working in the service of God, killed for that very reason, and crying out for God's justice. Abel was murdered in secret, in the field, far away from the altar, and without witnesses. Zechariah was openly murdered at the altar, in public, on orders from the chief justice. Abel was killed abroad, at an unknown location in God's wide world; Zechariah at the heart of Israel, the place where God caused his name to dwell, in Jerusalem.[21]

To be sure, Lightfoot's interpretation of Isaiah 8:2 is exceptional, and perhaps cannot stand, in which case we are left with the sheer supposition that Jehoiada was also known as Berechiah, or some other explanation of Matthew 23:35.[22]

10. All these disasters were to come upon the generation to which Jesus was speaking. The notion that "generation" means "race" and that this prophecy is to be extended into the far future is totally devoid of foundation and has to be rejected as a ridiculous and appalling case of special pleading. In Matthew, "this generation" always means the present generation, not "this race" or any notion of an extended

---

21. H. G. L. Peels, "The Blood 'from Abel to Zechariah' (Matt. 23,35; Luke 11,50f.) and the Canon of the Old Testament," *Zeitschrift für die Alttestamentliche Wissenschaft* 113 (2001): 599.

22. Editor's note: A better solution is to take Jesus at His word. There were those in Jesus' audience who killed someone named Zechariah son of Berechiah. Berechiah, like Zechariah, a name that appears 30 times in the Old Testament, is also a common name (1 Chron. 3:20; 6:39; 9:16; 15:17; 15:23; 2 Chron. 28:12; Neh. 3:4, 30). Jesus says that it was this Zechariah son of Berechiah who was murdered by some of those who were standing before Him. James Burton Coffman takes the most logical and straightforward view that some see as a well-known difficulty. "The difficulty disappears," Coffman argues, "if we trust the text. It is obvious that Christ here referred to some secret murder perpetrated, not by the ancestors of those men, but 'by them. Whom ye slew!' This could not be an indictment of their ancestors but plainly refers to a murder those wicked men had committed themselves." For a comprehensive study of this topic, see Gary DeMar, *Wars and Rumors of Wars* (Powder Springs, GA: American Vision, 2017), 18-27.

series of offspring (Matt. 11:26; 12:39-45; 16:4; 17:17). As far as the Old Creation was concerned, Jesus' hearers were the "Terminal Generation."

I should note that anyone wishing to extend the judgment upon the Jews beyond the first century is violating the law of God, which says that God's wrath extends only to the third and fourth generation (Exod. 20:5). The true and proper application of Jesus' threats against the Pharisees is to the Church, as Revelation 2–3 show us.

4
REJECTION AND DESOLATION
(23:37–24:3)

The two paragraphs considered here cover sections E, F, and G of our overall chiastic outline:

> E. Gathering (23:37)
>> F. The Temple (23:38–24:2)
>>> G. Jesus' Arrival (24:3)
>>> G' Jesus' Arrival (24:27)
>> F' The Corpse (24:28)
> E' Gathering (24:29-31)

In 23:37, Jesus laments that Jerusalem's people refused to be gathered by Him, while in 24:29-31, Jesus' messengers gather His elect. The temple, said to be emptied and soon to be destroyed in 23:38–24:2, is called a corpse in 24:28, following on Haggai 2 (and cf. Matt. 23:37). Jesus arrives on the Mount of Olives to pronounce judgment in 24:3, and arrives to bring judgment in 24:27.

A. THE DESOLATION OF JERUSALEM

a. ³⁷Jerusalem!

a. Jerusalem!

a. Who kills the prophets

a. and *(kai)* stones those sent to her,

   b. how often I willed

      c. to have gathered your children,

         d. in the way a hen

      c' gathers her brood under her wings,

   b' and *(kai)* you willed not.

a' ³⁸Behold, your house is left to you desolate.

We may be stretching matters to see a chiastic structure in this paragraph, but Jesus' willing in b is matched by Jerusalem's unwillingness in b'. Moreover, b-c-d-c-b is a separate thought from a & a', which more closely match one another. Thus, I tend to think a chiastic structure is indeed intended here.

Jerusalem has heaped up a double witness against herself by killing and stoning the prophets. Stoning was often used because Leviticus 24:16 commanded that those who blaspheme the Name of Yahweh be stoned, and that is what the Godly prophets were accused of doing, as in John 10:31 and Acts 7:58-59 and 14:19.

In the Scriptures, Yahweh is not infrequently portrayed as a bird sheltering His people under His wings (Deut. 32:11; Ruth 2:12; Ps. 17:8; 61:4; Isa. 31:5). The analogy of a hen and her chicks is not found in the older Scriptures, however. Matthew introduces it here without any particular context, but Luke explains the analogy further and sheds light back on Matthew's usage. In Luke 13:31–14:1, we read this sequence:

Herod wants to *kill* Jesus.

Jesus calls Herod a *fox.*

Jerusalem *kills* the prophets.

Jesus is a *hen* gathering chicks.

Jerusalem's *house* is desolated.

Jesus enters *house* of a Sanhedrin member.

Luke is describing a different occasion, an occasion when Jesus used the same metaphor. Luke's presentation suggests that Jesus is a hen because His enemies are foxes. With this in mind, when we re-read Matthew we see that the scribes and Pharisees are foxes who are attacking the chicks that Jesus wishes to protect.

In the incident Luke records, the "house" that is desolated represents apostate Jewry, as the following events in Luke 14 serve to indicate. In Matthew's context, Jesus seems to be referring directly to the temple. This emerges from several considerations. In Matthew 21:13, Jesus had referred to the temple as God's house of prayer. In Matthew 24:1, immediately after saying that the house would be emptied, the Messiah leaves the temple and then pronounces its destruction.

Jesus' departure from the temple is the reverse of His arrival. As we shall see, the same scripture is quoted on both occasions (Matt. 21:9; 23:39; cf. Psa. 118:26). Jesus' ministry in the temple has now been rejected by everyone, and so He leaves it. This is the essential act of desolating the temple, for Yahweh Incarnate has abandoned it. Therefore, the temple is now "your" house and is left "to you." Jesus says, "You want the temple? Okay, it's yours! I'm leaving."

The word "desolate" is not in some manuscripts of Matthew but is regarded as authentic by virtually all commentators. This term immediately calls to mind the "abomination of desolation," which will be the focus of Jesus' attention in 24:15 and which we shall address more fully when we arrive at that statement. For now, we should notice that the abomination that causes Jesus to desolate the temple consists of the murder of the prophets. The preceding context from 23:39 onwards makes this clear, as does the chiastic structure of the present paragraph. Note that the "abomination of desolation" has nothing to do with the Roman Army or its banners and ensigns.

B. JESUS' DEPARTURE

a.   ³⁹For I say to you, in no way will you see Me again until you say,
  "Blessed is the one coming (*erchomai*) in the Lord's name."
  b.   ²⁴:¹And (*kai*) going forth, Jesus went away from the temple.
    c.   And (*kai*) His disciples came to point out to Him the buildings
      of the temple.
    c' ²And/but (*de*) Jesus said to them, "Do you not see all these things?
  b' Amen I say to you, not at all shall be left here stone upon stone that
      shall not be thrown down."
a' ³And/but (*de*) as He was sitting on the Mount of Olives, the disciples
    came to Him apart, saying,
"Tell us when these things will be,
and (*kai*) what is the sign of Your manifestation,
and (*kai*) of the consummation of the age."

I have set these verses out to show a possible hint of chiasm in their order. In a & a' we find the matter of seeing Jesus and of His appearing. In b & b' we find Jesus leaving the temple and then stating that it will be torn down, the two stages of desolation. Finally, c & c' seem matched by the disciples asking Jesus to look at the temple and His asking them to look at it.

When Jesus entered Jerusalem in Matthew 21:9, the people shouted, "Blessed is the One coming in the Lord's name," and they saw Jesus daily in the temple until they had rejected Him. Now, leaving the temple and the city, Jesus states that they will not see Him again until they reaffirm what they said when He first arrived.

It is clear that "The One Coming in Yahweh's Name" is the Messiah. The quotation is from Psalm 118:26. This same Person has been identified as "Yahweh's Right Hand" (vv. 15-16) and as the "Chief Cornerstone" (v. 22). Jerusalem will not see Jesus again until they again affirm that He is the promised Messiah. Their temple will not stand unless Jesus is the Chief Corner.

This "seeing" will not, however, be a seeing with the eye. As in English, "seeing" means "discerning"—if you see what I mean! It can also mean "take care," as in Matthew 24:4, "See that no one misleads you." There can also be the idea of presence. To see someone is to be present with him, even if you don't see him visually. As we shall see below, when the disciples ask Jesus about His "appearing," the same kind of mental and relational sight is meant.

Jesus' departure from the temple fulfills the numerous departures of Yahweh from the sanctuary in the preceding history. In Exodus 32–34, after the golden calf incident, Yahweh pitched His tent away from the people and did not return to their midst until the tabernacle had been set up. In 1 Samuel 1–4, Yahweh departed from the sanctuary, went into Philistia, and allowed the sanctuary to be taken apart; the Ark and Altar were not put back together until the building of Solomon's temple. In Ezekiel 8–11, Yahweh is seen leaving the temple in Jerusalem and going with the exiles to Babylon; shortly thereafter the temple is destroyed.

In a parallel way, Jesus' departure from the temple is the departure of the righteous from the wicked city. In Matthew 10:14–15, Jesus had told the disciples to kick the dust off their feet as they leave a city that rejects the gospel. He compared such a city to Sodom. Only after Lot and his family left Sodom was Sodom destroyed. After the Israelites left Egypt, we find the Amalekites moving in to destroy it, and Egypt does not figure in Biblical history for several centuries thereafter. Jesus and His disciples are God's faithful, who are leaving behind the city of destruction. In Matthew 24:15–20, Jesus informs the disciples that this sequence of events will be repeated again and that they are to leave Sodom-Jerusalem when they see the "abomination of desolation."[23] The Lord is with His people. When they leave, He leaves, whether in the days of Ezekiel or in the days of the Great Tribulation.

The disciples followed Jesus and caught up with Him. They knew that He had pronounced doom upon the temple, but Herod's temple was so massive and magnificent that they had a hard time believing it could really happen. Jesus assures them that it will.

---

23. On Jerusalem as Sodom and Egypt, see Revelation 11:8.

C. The "Leprous House"

Jesus' statement that the stones of the building will not be left attached to one another hearkens back to the rules for house affliction ("leprosy") in Leviticus 14:33-53.[24] If the affliction in the walls of the house proves irremediable, the priest is to "tear down the house, its stones, and its timbers, and all the plaster of the house, and he shall take them outside the city to an unclean place" (Lev. 14:45).

From the verse just cited, it is clear that house affliction applies only to a house inside a walled city. An examination of the history of the application of the laws of house affliction sheds considerable light on certain events in the Gospels, for the primary house to come under these rules is the temple.

In Ezekiel 8:7-13, Ezekiel is told to dig into the wall around the temple. In his vision the wall is hollow and has a chamber inside of it. All over the inner walls of this chamber are carved various idols, and the leaders of Israel are worshiping them secretly.[25] This is a graphic picture of house affliction, the "greenish or reddish" marks under (within) the walls of a house.

Of more immediate relevance is Zechariah's fifth Night Vision (Zech. 5:1-4). The prophet sees a huge flying scroll, having the dimensions of the Holy Place of the tabernacle. The Holy Place was a symbol of the firmament heavens, and this scroll appears in the firmament. It goes forth from God, as the "eyes" of Yahweh have gone forth in the previous vision (3:10 & 1:10-11; 6:1-8). From Genesis 1, we know that God's eyes evaluate what He sees. In Zechariah 5, then, his eyes are also an evaluating scroll, the law of God in its judging function. The scroll

---

24. On the translation of "leprosy" with "affliction," see my monograph, *The Touch of Affliction: The "Plague" of "Leprosy" in Leviticus 13,* Biblical Horizons Occasional Paper 31 (Niceville, FL: Biblical Horizons, 2002).

25. These people were not actually worshiping idols or engaging in idolatry. We know from Jeremiah that they had turned the temple itself into an idol and regarded Yahweh as their own national god who would always protect them. What Ezekiel sees in his vision is their true hearts, not their outward beliefs.

measures every house in Israel to see if it conforms to the holy dimensions of the Holy Place. Two specific sins are judged: false swearing (worship) and theft. We have noted this pair already in our study. The houses of those who swear falsely and/or who steal will be consumed with house affliction, according to Zechariah 5:4, "[The curse] will dwell within that house and consume it with its timber and stones."

When we come to Jesus' "cleansing" of the temple, we find that He condemns the people for these two sins: "My house should be a house of prayer [true swearing], but you have made it a den of thieves" (Matt. 21:13). Later on, in Revelation 13:14-16, the "Beast Image," which is the idolatrous worship house of the apostates, also requires false worship and a mark that governs buying and selling.

We know from a full reading of the Gospels, Matthew through John, that Jesus "cleansed" the temple twice. As the living Scroll or Word of God, He arrived at the house two times. This is in accordance with the laws of house affliction in Leviticus 14. Making allowances for a general application of the principles in Leviticus 14, we can see Jesus fulfilling them as follows:

First, if greenish or reddish marks appear inside the walls of a house, the priest is to quarantine it for seven days. This corresponds to Jesus' first inspection of the temple, recorded in John 2:14-22. From that time, Jesus did not go again to the temple, as far as we are told, until His final arrival in Jerusalem.

Second, if after a week of quarantine the reddish and/or greenish marks have spread, the priest is to tear out the stones and plaster that have the marks in them and repair the place in the wall. This corresponds to Jesus' second temple inspection, as recorded in Matthew 21:12-14. Jesus drove out the bad stones, for the temple is made of human stones, and then restored the blind and lame, restoring the human temple. This dual action of tearing down the bad and restoring the crippled as a true human temple is a microcosm of Jesus' entire earthly ministry of restoring Israel—which then falls anew by rejecting Him.

Third, if the affliction reappears in the house, the house is to be torn down completely. Jesus as priest, as Zechariah's Flying Scroll, comes in the late AD 60s, finds that the temple has not been repaired—i.e., the people are still apostate—and destroys it.

D. On the Mount of Olives

Speaking of the Church, Romans 11:16-17 says, "And if the root be holy, the branches are also. But if some of the branches were broken off and you, being a wild olive, were grafted in among them and became partaker with them of the root of the fatness of the olive tree…" (cf. also vv. 18-24).

The Olive Tree is taken as a symbol of Israel, but it is quite a bit more specific than that. The Olive Tree is a symbol of the Temple of God, created by the Holy Spirit, and it is especially a symbol of the Holy of Holies. Let us consider the Olive in its revelation in the Bible.

First, on the third day we find fruit trees and grain plants created, and only these plants. At least some other plants were not made before Adam was created (Gen. 2:5). Thus, the olive was one of the semi-sacramental plants, like wine (fruit) and bread (grain). Oil and grain, the components of sacramental bread, were made on the third day. We don't know when grape vines were created. Wine, associated with kings and thus with Noah's new rule over the earth, is not mentioned until after the Flood. Accordingly, the Israelite is always said to have a vineyard, a field, and an oliveyard (e.g., Exod. 23:11; Deut. 6:11; Josh. 24:13). These are to lie fallow in the sabbath year (Exod. 23:11). Gleaning laws are phrased in terms of these three (Deut. 23:19-22). The curse is phrased in terms of these three (Deut. 28:38-40).

Second, bread is associated with priesthood and the Word (the Son), wine with kingship and rule (the Father), and olive oil with anointing and presence (the Spirit). It is with the last that we are concerned. All the articles of the tabernacle and courtyard, as well as the priests, were anointed with olive oil (Exod. 30:22-33), signifying the impregnation of these items with the Spirit of God. Symbolically, the tabernacle was an olive grove.

Third, the Holy of Holies in the temple was guarded by the olive. Two large cherubim of olive wood stood next to the Ark in the temple, and

81

the doors leading into the Holy of Holies were of olive wood. The doorposts of both the Holy of Holies and the Holy Place were of olive wood (1 Kgs. 6:23-34). Thus, the olive has a particular association with guarding God's holiness, and with the Holy of Holies. Along these lines, notice Psalm 52:8, "But as for me, I am a green olive tree in the house of God."

Fourth, the olive was the first tree to grow after the Flood, signifying obviously the re-creation of the Kingdom of God as the first order of events after the Flood (Gen. 8:11). Note that it was a dove, later associated with the Spirit, who delivered the olive branch to Noah.

Fifth, very significant is the vision in Zechariah 4, where the prophet sees the two olive cherubim as two olive trees, feeding the oil of the Spirit into the lampstand of Israel's witness. See also Revelation 11:4 for a further exposition of this imagery.

With this background, we can see that when Jesus moves to the Mount of Olives at the end of His ministry, He is moving into the garden-form of the Holy of Holies to complete His work. Let us now turn to the passages that mention this.

In Matthew 21, Jesus is specifically said to move in His triumphal entry from the Mount of Olives to the temple, where He judges the temple. Part of what is being "fulfilled" here is God's fiery judgment of Nadab and Abihu from His throne in the Holy of Holies (Lev. 10:1-2).

Luke 21:37 says that Jesus spent each night on the Mount of Olives (cf. John 8:1). He went to the temple each day from this Holy of Holies and returned to it each night.

In Matthew 23–24, Jesus departs from the temple for the last time and moves to the Mount of Olives to pronounce judgment upon the temple and Jerusalem. Again the Holy of Holies judges the temple. Moving to the Mount of Olives replicates Jesus' earlier action when, as Yahweh, He left Jerusalem and moved to the Mount of Olives to destroy the city (Ezek. 10:18-19; 11:22-23).

In Matthew 26:30, we find that after celebrating the Passover and instituting the Lord's Supper, Jesus and His disciples went to the Mount of Olives. Then Jesus went to Gethsemane, which means Olive Press, to pray to God. Here we see the high priest in the Holy of Holies. Here in the Mount of Olives, in the very Holy of Holies, Jesus was captured and arrested.

Now, this is not all. A careful reading of the text will reveal that Jesus was crucified on the Mount of Olives. Matthew 27:33 says that Jesus was crucified at "a place called Golgotha, which means Place of a Skull." While some have tried to find a hill around Jerusalem that looks like a skull, this is clearly wrong. Golgotha comes from the Hebrew *gulgoleth*, meaning "head" or "skull," but the Greek interpretation of Golgotha is not "skull" but "place of a skull." Is there someone whose famous skull was placed near Jerusalem? We get a clue from the fact that Golgotha may also be, by way of a pregnant pun, a contraction of Goliath of Gath (Hebrew: Goliath-Gath = Gol-Gotha). 1 Samuel 17:54 says that David took the head of Goliath to Jerusalem, but since Jerusalem was to be a holy city, this dead corpse would not have been set up inside the city, but someplace outside. The Mount of Olives was right in front of the city (1 Kgs. 11:7; 2 Kgs. 23:13) and a place of ready access. We can surmise that Jesus was crucified at the place where Goliath's head had been exhibited. Even as His foot was bruised, He was crushing the giant's head! This was at a place right outside Jerusalem, and likely on the Mount of Olives. But there is more certain evidence.

While Jesus was being crucified, the veil of the temple was ripped in half from the top to the bottom. For this event to have been seen, or its effects perceived, those viewing it would have to be due east of Jerusalem, on a line with the temple's doorways. Luke 23:44-47 indicates that the centurion did perceive this event. It cannot have been the darkening of the sun that shocked the centurion, for that had been going on for three hours. And it could not have been Jesus' death, because that was an expected event, hardly unusual in the case of crucifixion. Thus, the centurion must have been standing up the slope of Olivet and been able to see westward into the temple area. This puts the crucifixion on the Mount of Olives.

Another rather clear indication comes from John 19:20, which reads (literally), "Therefore this inscription many of the Jews read, for near was the Place of the city, where Jesus was crucified." What is the Place of the city? Routinely, the Place is the temple (John 11:48; Acts 6:14; 21:28). Thus, the statement seems to mean that Jesus was crucified near to the temple, in some relation to it, and not in some random spot around Jerusalem somewhere.

Indeed, several passages in the Bible indicate that Jesus was crucified on a living tree, which in this case would be an olive tree (Acts 5:30; 10:39; 13:29; Gal. 3:13; 1 Pet. 2:24). The *stauros* or pole that Jesus carried was the crosspiece, which was affixed to the tree. After all, why would the Roman soldiers want to go to the trouble of cutting down a tree, planing it down into a stake, digging a hole, and then planting the stake when there were lots of trees around that would do just as well? We surely cannot be as certain of this suggestion as we are that Jesus died on the Mount of Olives, but it makes a great deal of sense.

Thus, the site of Goliath's head and the site of the crucifixion were on the Mount of Olives. Here, in the garden-form of the Holy of Holies, Jesus presented His blood to the Father (see Leviticus 16 for background).

According to John 19:41, the garden-tomb was also located on the Mount of Olives. When Mary Magdalene thought Jesus was the gardener of this olive orchard, she was certainly right, for He is the New Adam of the New Garden, which both is and houses the Bride (John 20:15). Even more to the point, when Mary looked into the tomb, she saw the slab where Jesus had lain, with an angel at either end of it (John 20:12), clearly an image of the Cover on the Ark of the Covenant, the meeting place of God and humanity in the Holy of Holies.

Naturally, Jesus also ascended into the heavenly temple from the Mount of Olives (Acts 1:12).

Jesus' crucifixion on the Mount of Olives and the rending of the veil in the Temple of Olives can now be seen as the fulfillment of the prophecy in Zechariah 14:4, "And in that day His feet will stand on the Mount of Olives, which is in front of Jerusalem on the east, and the Mount of Olives will be split in its middle from east to west..." The Mount of Olives before Jerusalem corresponds symbolically to the olive-wood doors before the temple and the Holy of Holies. Their opening from east and west—from the Holy of Holies to the doors of the temple to the doors of the courtyard—released God's energy into the world. Similarly, the mountain-olive-veil before the city would be split, so to speak, so that God's energy could flow out into the whole world.

In conclusion, the reference to the Church as an Olive Tree, rather than as some other kind of tree, tells us that the Church is positioned in the temple of God, in the Holy of Holies, and is impregnated with the oil of the Spirit. Like the olive cherubim, we now guard God's throne and praise Him day and night. This is made possible because Jesus shed His blood before the Father in the Holy of Holies of the Mount of Olives.

For our purposes in this study, we note that Jesus sat down (enthroned) Himself in this arboreal Holy of Holies and from that position passed judgment on apostate Jerusalem, as He had done once before in the days of Ezekiel. Counterfeiting Jesus, the Man of Lawlessness in 2 Thessalonians 2 would "take his seat in the temple."

We should also note that Jesus' enthronement on the Mount of Olives is symbolically far greater than the seat of Moses occupied by the scribes and Pharisees.

E. The Sign of His Parousia: The Sign of Jonah

The Greek word *parousia* is often translated "coming" in the New Testament, but that is not its actual meaning. I have rendered it "manifestation." As the distinguished New Testament scholar N. T. Wright has put it,

> The Greek word *parousia* does occur, in Matthew (24:3, 27, 37, 39; these are, surprisingly enough in view of its popularity among scholars, its only occurrences in the Gospels). But why should we think—except for reasons of ecclesiastical and scholarly tradition—that *parousia* means "the second coming," and/or the downward travel on a cloud of Jesus and/or the "son of man"? *Parousia* means "presence" as opposed to *apousia*, "absence"; hence it denotes the "arrival" of someone not at the moment present; and it is especially used in relation to the visit "of a

85

royal or official personage." Until evidence for a different meaning is produced, this should be our starting-point.[26]

Wright adds in a footnote: "From this, the most natural meaning for the word as applied to Jesus would be something like 'arrival on the scene,' in the sense of 'enthronement.'"

Wright continues by explaining what the disciples were actually asking in their question.

> They had come to Jerusalem expecting Jesus to be enthroned as the rightful king. This would necessarily involve Jesus taking over the authority that the temple symbolized. They were now confronted with the startling news that this taking over of authority would mean the demolition, literal and metaphorical, of the temple.... The disciples now "heard" his prophetic announcement of the destruction of the temple as the announcement, also, of his own vindication; in other words, of his own "coming" ... to Jerusalem as the vindicated, rightful king. What the disciples had naturally wanted to know was, when would Jesus actually be installed as king?[27]

The temple's destruction would constitute Jesus' vindication and be the sign of His assumption of full kingship.

The disciples recognized that they were living in "the present evil age." They had just heard Jesus denounce the "best" leaders of that age. They saw Him, in Matthew, as a new Moses come to deal with Egypt; in Mark as a new David come to deal with Philistines and Edomites. So, when would He "appear" again, as He had on Palm Sunday, and *really* take over as King of kings? When would the people again acclaim Him, saying "Blessed is the One coming in the Lord's Name"? When would be the consummation of the Old Age and the enthronement of Jesus?

They now knew that the old temple had to be torn down, but that was not really surprising to them. They knew that the tabernacle had

---

26. N. T. Wright, *Jesus and the Victory of God,* Christian Origins and the Question of God 2 (Minneapolis: Fortress, 1996), 341.

27. Wright, *Jesus and the Victory of God,* 342.

been wrecked in the days of Samuel and the earlier temple torn down in the days of Ezekiel, Daniel, and Jeremiah. Thus, it was not really a surprise that a temple built by Herod and ruled by the Sadducees would be torn down. Jesus would then build another temple. But when, and how?

Jesus' answer was that there would be a short period of time leading down to the destruction of Jerusalem, itself the core/center of the Old Creation. That event would be His vindication and the sign of His enthronement. Certain events preceding that event would signal to the disciples that Jesus' vindication was shortly to occur.

It is sometimes argued—I have argued this in the past—that the disciples ask two different questions: one about Jesus' near appearing and the other about the consummation of the age. Following this line of thinking, the earlier part of Matthew 24 discusses the "end" of the age, while the later part of Matthew 24 and all of Matthew 25 discuss the "consummation" of the (new) age. These two events are the destruction of Jerusalem and the end of the world.

We cannot press such a distinction out of the disciples' question, however. The distinction between "consummation" and "end" is not one of time but of meaning. The vindication and enthronement of the Messiah was what the entire history of the Old Creation had led to, and thus would be its consummation. As part of that consummation, the Old Creation would come to an end.

The disciples asked for a sign. Jesus had already told them that the only sign that would be given was the sign of Jonah (Matt. 16:4; 12:39-41). Were the disciples asking for something else? Not necessarily. The "sign of Jonah" is a complex of signs that embraces the events about which the disciples asked.

Recall the full history of Jonah. The Kingdom of Israel had sinned to the point where God turned away from them and sent His prophet to the Gentiles. Jonah underwent a symbolic death and resurrection and then took the gospel to the Gentiles, who gladly heard it. The Gentile Assyrians began to be built up as a significant power in the world; meanwhile, Israel declined further into apostasy. After a while, God brought the Assyrians to destroy Israel and take them into exile. Yet, among these Assyrians were remnants of faithful Gentiles, and so the exiled Israelites could find a pillow upon which to land as they fell. The Assyrian Empire passed to the Babylonian, and the same history was repeated with respect to the Kingdom of Judah. In this second history, the temple's destruction was the final sign that the old (kingdom era) order had ended and a new (oikumene era) order had come.

This history is now replicated. Since the Jews have rejected Jesus, He will go (in the Spirit) to the Gentiles, after His own death and resurrection. A new Church will be built up, and then judgment will be brought by a Gentile army.

That, however, is only part of the sign of Jonah. The name "Jonah" means "dove." It is the word used for the dove Noah sent out from the Ark, which would not light her foot on anything unclean. This is somewhat parallel to Jonah's initial refusal to go to pagan Nineveh. Jonah's work there, however, was to build a new Ark. We notice that in Jonah 3 the animals are also put into mourning. The last statement in Jonah 4 shows that God intended to save the animals as well as the people. Assyria becomes an ark that will carry the Israelites through the Gentile sea, as the Great Fish carried Jonah, until the coming of the New Age. The Assyrian Ark becomes Babylonian, then Persian, then Greek, and then Roman. Then, in Acts 27, the political Ark sinks. This is because Jesus is now the new Ark.

Jesus as New Jonah makes the Ark and is the Ark. The dove that came upon Jesus at His baptism was not merely some sign of "peace," but was the sign of Jonah. It made Jesus the New Jonah. Hence, He and His people replay the story of Jonah. Simon Peter's father's name is given both as John (Johanan) and as Jonah (Matt. 16:17). Peter was called while at Joppa to go and visit the Gentile Cornelius (Acts 10). Joppa is where Jonah set out from (Jonah 1:3). Like Noah's dove and the prophet Jonah, Peter did not want to go to the house of a Gentile (Acts 10:28). As with Jonah, God persuaded Peter otherwise. In union with Jesus, Peter was another Jonah, as Paul was after him, and as are we all.

Jesus as New Ark is revealed in Matthew 14:24-33. The disciples were in a boat in a stormy sea (compare Jonah 1). Jesus appears walking on the water, as a New Boat, a New Ark. Peter steps off the old boat (compare Jonah going into the sea) but walks on the water with Jesus as long as he fixes his eyes on Jesus. The minute Jesus steps into the old boat, the storm ceases. The meaning is clear: Jesus is the New Ark.

This is the full "sign of Jonah," and the "sign" that Jesus gives in Matthew 24–25 is part of it.

F.   Of Stones and Sight

There are a couple of other themes in Matthew 23:37–24:3 that we should notice. The first is the theme of stones.

Jesus accuses Jerusalem, the holy, priestly city, of stoning those sent to her (23:37). He then states that not one stone will be left upon another in Herod's temple (24:2). In between, He quotes from Psalm 118:26, which is in the midst of a section dealing with the building of a true temple of God, a house of His people:

> ²²A stone the builders rejected
> Became the chief cornerstone.
> ²³Yahweh accomplished this.
> It is marvelous in our eyes.
> ²⁴This is the day Yahweh has made;
> Let us rejoice and let us be glad in Him.
> ²⁵We beg, Yahweh, save, please!
> We beg, Yahweh, prosper, please!
> ²⁶Blessed is the one coming in Yahweh's name,
> We bless you from Yahweh's house.
> ²⁷Yahweh is the Mighty One,
> And He has shined light on us.
> Join the feast with boughs,
> Up to the horns of the altar.
> ²⁸You are my Mighty One, and I will give You thanks.
> You are my Fearful One, and I will exalt You.
> ²⁹Give thanks to Yahweh, for He is good,
> For His lovingkindness is everlasting.

Jesus is the rejected stone, which appears to be wrong for building walls but which is the right shape for the cornerstone of the building. The rejected stone becomes the first stone of the new building, the stone that (a) by its location establishes where the temple will be built, (b) by its placement establishes the lines of the building with respect to east and north, and (c) by its size perhaps indicates the size of the building.

If we meditate on this picture, we see the following: The Jews have used some stones to build their anti-temple and others to kill God's true temple people. God's people are buried under piles of raw rocks. Both of these groups of stone are "anti-rocks." Now this will be reversed. Their precious temple will be reduced to a pile of rocks, and God's people will be built up as a temple with a rejected rock, Jesus (God) as cornerstone. A full study of this theme would lead us further into the Psalter, where God is the Rock and His people are stones.[28]

There is a similar play on sight in this passage. In the section of Psalm 118 to which Jesus alludes, the new temple is "marvelous in our eyes," because Yahweh from His temple has "shined light on us." Jesus picks this up when He says that in no way will they see Him again until they recognize and affirm the meaning of Psalm 118 (Matt. 23:39). That is, they will have to recognize that He is the true Cornerstone of the temple and that those with Him are the true temple.

With this in mind, the meaning of what follows take on a deeper aspect. The disciples point to the buildings of the temple, asking Jesus to look at them. Jesus asks them, "Do you see all these things?" (24:2). Sitting in the context of the True Temple, the disciples and Jesus contemplate the false one. On the true Holy of Holies of the Mount of Olives, which is holy because Jesus is there, they consider the fate of the false Holy of Holies opposite them.

Thus, there are two different things to see. One is the outward glory of a false temple, doomed to destruction though temporarily powerful

---

28. See James B. Jordan, *Through New Eyes: Developing a Biblical View of the World* (Brentwood, TN: Wolgemuth & Hyatt, 1988; reprint, Eugene, OR: Wipf & Stock, 1999), chapter 6.

and influential. The other is the hidden temple formed by Jesus' words and people, to which the future belongs. Which is marvelous in our eyes? Christians who have left behind large Church buildings because they have been taken over by apostates and who have had to meet in basements and school cafeterias have answered this question many times.

We can note that Jesus begins His next section of warnings with the command "See to it" (v. 4). Verses 2 and 4 contain the only uses of *blepo* in the passage. The other word used for seeing in Matthew 23–25 is *horao*. These are close synonyms, and both have to do with intellectual perception as well as with physical sight. *Blepo* has a slight tilt toward the idea of watching and penetrating discernment, rather than mere recognition. Thus, the three phrases in our immediate section might be rendered thus:

23:39 "In no way will you recognize [*horao*] Me again until you say, 'Blessed is the one coming in the Lord's name.'"

24:2 And Jesus said to them, "Do you not discern [*blepo*; really understand] all these things?"

24:4 And Jesus answered and said to them, "Discern [*blepo*], lest anyone mislead you."

From this we see that Jesus is not merely pointing to the temple and saying, "Do you see this? It will be torn down." Rather, He is asking the disciples if they really and truly understand what the temple is all about. Do they see why it must be destroyed? Do they understand (a) that it has outlived its usefulness now that Jesus has come and (b) that in its present manifestation it is a false temple?

A true discernment of the temple is parallel to a true discernment of the times to come. If they discern the falseness of the Jewish temple and of the Jewish religion, they will not be misled by false Jewish teachings and rumors of prophets and Messiahs. Such discernment will require the kind of penetrating insight that the Apostle Paul will provide them in his discussions of Judaism and of the Judaizers.

5
FALSE PROPHETS AND MESSIAHS
(24:4-5, 11, 24-26)

B ack in the Introduction we saw the overall chiastic structure of
this discourse, and we saw that the theme of false prophets lies at
the very heart of it, in 24:11. We also saw that warnings against
false prophets are situated chiastically around this central part of
Matthew 23–25. Let us therefore consider these three sections together.

⁴And (*kai*) answering, Jesus said to them,
a. "Discern, lest anyone mislead you.
   b. ⁵For many will come in My name,
   b' saying, 'I myself am the Messiah,'
a' and (*kai*) many they will mislead.

¹¹And (*kai*) many false prophets will arise, and will mislead many.

a. ²⁴For there will arise false *Messiahs* and
   b. false prophets,
      c. and (*kai*) will give great *signs and wonders*,
         d. so as to mislead, if possible, even the elect.
      c' ²⁵Behold, I have *foretold* you.
   b' ²⁶If therefore they say to you, 'Behold, in the *wilderness* he is,'
   go not forth;
a' 'Behold, in the *inner chambers*,' believe it not."

In all three of these sections, the notion of false prophecy is linked with the notion of misleading, of tricking. Climactically, the third section adds that if it were possible, even God's elect would be misled.

The first statement says that many false Messiahs will arise. The second statement says that many false prophets will arise. The third statement joins the two.

The first statement, verses 4-5, says that the false Messiahs will come in "My" name. This does not mean that they come claiming to be Jesus' followers or disciples. Rather, each himself claims to be the Messiah (the Anointed One) or a delegate of the Messiah. They come in Messiah's "name" in the sense that they claim His office or anointing. Perhaps they claim to be the Messiah apart from Jesus, or perhaps they claim to be a new manifestation of Jesus Himself.

The third and climactic statement, in verses 24-25, is arranged chiastically. The false Messiahs will be reported as being in the "inner chambers," while the false prophets will be reported as being in the wilderness. The chiasm indicates that the false prophets are like John, associated with the wilderness, while the false Messiahs are like Jesus, associated with the temple. Since the prophet John was Jesus' forerunner, we can link the false prophets in the wilderness with Jesus also.

As related to the rest of the center of the discourse, these three statements govern the content. The opening warning is against the false Messiahs. The central warning is against the false prophets. The final warning is against both. All the other evils Jesus mentions—war, famine, persecution, tribulation—pale when considered next to the threat posed by these false Messiahs and prophets. And though this warning is particularly directed for the apostolic age, it speaks to the Church of all ages also. The greatest enemy is always the false church.

Jesus had made it plain to the disciples that He was going to take His throne and rule. They had asked when He was going to do so. Soon, He replied. In one sense, He assumed His rule in AD 30, when He ascended to the Father. But the sign of His rule, and the great manifestation thereof, would come in AD 70. At that time, as the book of Revelation shows, the saints would join Him in His heavenly rule (Rev. 20), or as

Daniel 7 puts it, the body of people called "one like a son of man" would inherit the kingdom. (Like the four beasts, the "one like a son of man" in Daniel 7 is a corporate figure; Daniel 7:18, 22, 27.)[29]

So, since Jesus was shortly going to manifest His power and rule and was going to "come" in that sense, there would be those who would say that He had already come and was on the scene. Jesus wanted them to know that His coming was not going to take the form of His physical appearance among men. They would not see Him walking around in the land of promise. He would not show up in the temple, nor would there be another prophetic forerunner in the wilderness. No, His next coming would be a manifestation of His heavenly rule, like lightning when it strikes from east to west from the sky.

There is surely nothing new about this kind of appearance or coming. Throughout the history of Israel, the prophets had repeatedly said that Yahweh was going to come and judge His people, but never did that mean Yahweh was going to appear visibly to the people. Rather, the appearance or coming of Yahweh meant earthquake, famine, invasion, captivity, and the like.

The false prophets should be likened to false John the Forerunners. They would herald this supposed second coming of Jesus, but it would be a false heralding. Like John, they would be in the wilderness and perhaps would say that Jesus had returned "in the wilderness," like a prophet of old, like Moses, to lead the Jewish people to a political deliverance from Rome.

The false Messiahs should be likened to false Jesuses. They would claim to be coming in the power of Jesus, to be Jesus Himself in some new form. The rumor would be that Jesus had returned and was in the "inner rooms." Commentators seem to miss the point here, for the overall context of this passage is the temple, and the reference to "inner rooms" is not to some vague hidden appearance, but to His supposed

---

29. See my *The Handwriting on the Wall: A Commentary on the Book of Daniel* (Atlanta, GA: American Vision, 2007), 679.

coming to the inner chambers of the temple. That is why Jesus does not warn, "Do not seek Him out," but "Do not believe it." After all, the disciples would not have been allowed to go into the temple (not being priests), so they would not have been able to check out the story literally. Jesus just says, "Don't believe it. You don't need to go into the temple to see whether I'm there or not. I'm not going to be there."

The chiastic structure of these verses points to the opposition of miracles and words. The false prophets and Messiahs would do miracles and signs, but the disciples are to rely upon Jesus' words: "Behold, I have told you in advance."

Those expositors who choose to ignore Jesus' statement that this prophecy concerns the generation to which He ministered are free to imagine whatever kinds of false prophets and messiahs they can dream up for their projected future catastrophes. Sober expositors, however, must consider that Jesus' prediction was fulfilled in a large and definitive way in the apostolic era, though of course it continues to be relevant to all times in the New Creation era.

Generally speaking, commentators call attention to a few contemporary figures mentioned in the Bible. Simon the Sorcerer of Acts 8 is said to have become a false prophet/messiah. We must say, however, that while this may be true historically, the Bible gives no hint of it. The last thing we see Simon doing is asking the apostles to pray for him. At the very least, this is an ambiguous ending. The Scriptures do not hint that Simon became a false prophet.

Revolutionary leaders like Judas and Theudas (Acts 8:36-37) are mentioned, but they pre-dated Jesus and certainly did not claim to come in His name. Nor is there any hint that the Egyptian mentioned in Acts 21:38 has any relation to the apostolic church and the name of Jesus. There is no reason to think that ordinary Christians would be drawn off, seduced, misled by such men.

There is plenty of evidence in the Scriptures, however, that there was a group of Christian leaders who claimed to have the anointing (*messiah*) of apostles, who claimed to be prophets and teachers, and who did indeed mislead many believers. They were a constant danger in the apostolic era, and a great deal of Paul's writings in particular deal with their deceptions. We are thinking, of course, of the Judaizers.

The Judaizers were the heirs of the tradition-serving Jewish teachers who were Jesus' worst enemy. The Judaizers are the constant enemy in Acts and the Epistles. They are the anti-christs of the Johannine letters, who claimed to have been sent out by the apostles but who were not "of us" (1 John 2:18-19; 4:1).[30] They are the main enemy in the book of Revelation.

The Judaizers fit perfectly Jesus' predictions. They claimed to come in His name. They misled many. They claimed an anointing, but it was false. They were false prophets.

---

30. John is not writing about people who professed faith for a while and then departed from the church. That is a misuse of these passages.

6

WARS, FAMINES, EARTHQUAKES
(24:6-8)

Jesus continues with other characteristics of the end of the Old
Creation, things that will happen during the Apostolic Age but which
are not to disturb the believers.

> [6]And/but (*de*) you will be hearing of wars and rumors of wars.
> Watch carefully so that you are not startled,
> for it is necessary for this to happen;
> but (*alla*) not yet is the *end*.
>
> [7]For nation will rise up against nation,
> and (*kai*) kingdom against kingdom.
> And (*kai*) there will be famines and earthquakes in various places.
> [8]And/but (*de*) all these are a *beginning* of birthpangs.

Chiastically, the mention of wars is matched by verses 15-23, dealing with
the great persecution of believers that is coming. The "end" in verse 6b
is matched by the "end" in verse 14b. The mention of nations and their
conflicts in verse 7 is matched by the witness in the nations in verse 14.
The birthpangs of verse 8 are matched with enduring to the end in verse 13.

The phrase "But not yet is the end" is the important statement. The
conjunction *alla* implies a stronger contrast than it is possible for the
mere particle *de* to imply. Wars, famine, and earthquakes are not signs
of the end of the world in any sense. As we shall see, they are indications
that the kingdom is coming into history, and as such they are necessary
to the growth and development of the New Creation.[31]

---

31. The text behind the King James Version adds "and pestilences" in verse 7. Because
there is virtually no manuscript evidence for this phrase, I have chosen to omit it.

The believers should not be startled to hear about these things. It is a naive and childish faith that thinks that the gospel of peace produces instant peace. Rather, it produces instant conflict, setting father against son, brother against sister, and so on. It is only over the course of time that peace between men grows out of the peace of God.

Commentators mentions various commotions and uprisings around the Roman Empire during the Apostolic Era (AD 30–70). We don't need to list these, because there has never been a time when there weren't wars. Moreover, it is known to everyone that various Jewish groups continually provoked the Romans in Palestine, so that various conflicts arose near to the early Christians during this time. Acts 11:28 mentions a famine in the days of Claudius, which set in motion the events of Acts 12. Secular sources tell us of earthquakes during this period of history.

Wars, famines, and earthquakes are God's tools to tear down the Old Creation. He pits one nation against another. He starves the wicked and drives them to seek Him. He shakes down their empires and cultures. These events, we are told in verse 8, are the beginnings of birthpangs. They are not signs of the end of anything, but they do manifest the death throes of the old order. The new kingdom is being born, and these are the tribulations through which it comes into the world. If anything, these events are positive signs, signs of a new birth for this old world. Similarly, in verse 32, Jesus will say that these events indicate the coming of summer, a time of warmth and productivity, not the end of the world!

I believe Jesus is speaking of wars, famines, and earthquakes in the physical realm. Revelation 6, however, speaks of these same three phenomena in the realm of human life. After the white horse of the gospel comes the red horse that takes peace from the land; that is, the gospel has the effect of pitting people against each other. Following this comes the black horse of a spiritual famine, starving the old order (bread), while protecting the new order (oil and wine, the Church). Then comes a land-quake, which shakes down the old order entirely. Thus, the wise eye will see that national wars, economic famines, and geological earthquakes do not indicate the near coming of the kingdom, but that their spiritual equivalents do indeed indicate the coming of the kingdom into history, into a particular culture.

Finally, the reference to birthpangs should indicate to us that Jesus is not speaking of the end of history, but only the end of the Old Creation and the beginning of the new history of the New Creation.

A. WARS

There have always been wars, and there always will be until the time comes when the knowledge of God covers the earth as the waters cover the seas. At one level, Jesus' statement about wars continues to be true. Specifically, though, He spoke of wars during the forty-year period between His ascension and the destruction of Jerusalem and of the Old Creation.

While there were wars on the borders of the Roman Empire that might partially fulfill this prophecy, the primary wars and rumors of wars took place among the Jews, as they repeatedly rebelled against their God-appointed Roman overseers. When wars are rumored, and even more when they actually come, people become excited and anticipate changes. Jesus warned the people not to fall in with the multitude in this matter.

The Jewish believers in Palestine during the Apostolic Age repeatedly faced the temptation to become excited and enthusiastic about reported attempts to overthrow the Roman yoke. All their unconverted friends were excited, and it was natural to feel a desire to go along with them. Jesus warned them that when the Jewish nation rose up against the Romans and the Jewish kingdom against the Roman kingdom, they were not to count it as anything important. They were to stay out of it, because it meant nothing as far as the coming of the Kingdom of God was concerned.

Some wars are necessary, of course; but Christians must keep their heads and not run after a mob in wartime. Wars let loose psychological forces in society that must be resisted by believers.

B. FAMINES

Jesus' allusion to famines did not come in a Biblical vacuum. More than once famine had been the cause of God's people journeying to a better place, from which they returned with great spoils. Abram went to Egypt to avoid a famine and returned a much wealthier man (Gen. 12). Isaac had the same experience in Gerar (Gen. 26). Jacob went to Egypt to avoid a famine, and later his descendants emerged very wealthy. Elijah won a great victory for God after three years of drought and famine (1 Kgs. 18). God delivered His people dramatically during a famine in the days of Elisha (2 Kgs. 6–7).

Thus, the presence of a famine might well cause the believers to think that their deliverance was very close at hand. Jesus warned them not to think in such a short-term way. Yes, the famine was a sign of the beginning of birth-pangs, but not a sign of immediate rescue.

Jesus would shortly give them a sign to look for, a sign that they should pack up and make an exodus out of the land of Palestine. He tells them that any famine that might come would not be that sign.

C. EARTHQUAKES

Earthquakes were also signs of the coming of God's judgment in the Biblical history. The believers would remember the prophecy of Zechariah 14:5: "And you will flee by the valley of My mountains, for the valley of the mountains will reach to Azel; yes, you will flee just as you fled before the earthquake in the days of Uzziah king of Judah. Then Yahweh, O my God, will come, all His holy ones with Him!" They would remember that Amos prophesied two years before this great earthquake (which, thus, came in the third year). They would associate Jesus with Amos, and an earthquake with the prophecy of Zechariah.

As in the case of famine, the believers might interpret rumors and experiences of earthquakes as a sign that the end was near at hand. They were not to do so. Earthquake would not be the sign for them.

D. BIRTHPANGS

Because of Original Sin, women experience travail in birth, and before the modern era, many died (Gen. 3:16). Jacob's wife Rachel died giving birth to the Son of the Right Hand (Gen. 35:16-20). The history of God's people from the promise of the Seed of the Woman forward was one long labor, one long birthpang, to give birth to the Son and His people (Rev. 12:2). Jesus' suffering on the cross was His travail or birthpangs, issuing in His resurrection and the coming of the Kingdom (Acts 2:24). The whole creation groaned and travailed (same word) with the Church, until the formation of the Church was completed at the end of the Apostolic Age (Rom. 8:22).

In the same way, the Church suffers in union with Christ (Col. 1:24). The suffering of the Apostolic Church led to the victory over the Old Creation in AD 70 and the raising of the saints to sit on the angelic thrones in heaven (Rev. 20). The suffering of the present Church leads forward to the redemption of our bodies at the Last Day. All such suffering, then, is but birthpangs.

Some women die giving birth; others live. The Woman of the Old Creation would live in Christ, even if many of her last members would die in the Great Tribulation. Those members of the Woman who rejected Christ and who persecuted His bride would die in the birthpangs of the New Creation (1 Thess. 5:3).

Jesus said that the wars, famines, and earthquakes that His people would endure along with the rest of the people (Acts 11:27-30) would only be the initial stages of labor for the Church. The Church would move into transition, heavy labor, when she began to be persecuted in earnest, as Jesus mentions in His next breath. The climax of the birthpangs would come with the martyrdom of the Apostolic Church in the Great Tribulation and with the destruction of Jerusalem immediately thereafter.

7
TRIBULATION
(24:9-10)

Jesus now moves to the tribulation that His followers will experience as the time draws to an end. This is the beginning of the Great Tribulation, which He will mention again in a few sentences.

9At that time they will deliver you up to tribulation,
and (*kai*) will kill you,
 and (*kai*) you will be hated by all nations on account of My name.
10And (*kai*) at that time many will be scandalized,
and (*kai*) they will betray one another,
 and (*kai*) hate one another.

These two statements are parallel to one another. In each case the third statement says that the believers will be hated.

The "they" of verse 9 is unclear, but in context Jesus has been speaking of nations and kingdoms, both Jewish and Gentile. It seems that the enemy in verse 9, then, is those outside the Church. Horribly, there will be enemies within the Church as well, as verse 10 states and as its matching verse 12 amplifies: The love of many within the Kingdom will grow cold and they will turn on their former brethren.

A. THE ENEMY WITHOUT

Throughout the book of Acts we see the unbelieving Jews trying to deliver up the believers for persecution at the hands of Roman authorities. Occasionally we also see those who practiced pagan religions trying the same thing. Usually the Romans stand firm in defending the believers, thus fulfilling their role as God-appointed Guardian Beast.[32]

The book of Revelation carries forward the history left incomplete at the end of Acts. There we are told that in a short time after the Revelation was given to John, the Roman Beast would turn against the Church he was supposed to protect. His Palestinian agents, the two-horned Land Beast (Herods and high priests) would put to death any who did not delight in the temple completed in AD 64 (the Image of the Beast) (Rev. 13).[33] The saints would be slaughtered in Jerusalem (Rev. 11) and everywhere (Rev. 14).

B. THE ENEMY WITHIN

Painful as persecution is, more painful is betrayal at the hands of friends and colleagues. Jesus predicts this as well, and we see it all over the Epistles as the Judaizers trouble the Church from within. In the book of Revelation, the enemy of the "land" is both unconverted Jew and apostatized Judaizer.

"Judaizers" is what we call those within the Church who insisted on imposing the peculiarly Jewish ordinances of the Old Covenant upon all believers. The Bible is very clear that God-fearing Gentiles did not need to be circumcised to be saved. True, they were not to attend Passover (Exod. 12:43-49), but they were to be welcomed at all other Feasts (Deut. 16:11, 14). They were to be allowed and encouraged to offer

---

32. For the first (Petrine) phase of tribulation at the hands of the Jerusalem officials, see Acts 4:1-21; 5:17-40; 7:54-60; 8:3; 12:1-17. For the second (Pauline) phase, when the Romans usually protected the church, see Acts 13:44-48, 50; 14:1-6, 19; 16:19-40; 17:5-9, 13; 18:12-17; 19:23-41; 21:27-35.

33. See Peter J. Leithart, *Revelation 12-22* (London: T&T Clark, 2018), 71-72.

sacrifice at the sanctuary, on a par with Jewish believers (Num. 15:14-15). They did not have to keep the dietary laws and the other laws of uncleanness, for these applied only to circumcised people and their families, members of the peculiar priestly nation.

I suspect that all Jews recognized these facts, but we can readily believe that some of them encouraged Gentile converts to become "first class" Yahwists and be circumcised. With the coming of the gospel, things changed. Jesus after all had said that He had not come to destroy the Law but to fulfill it. He had said that all nations were to be discipled along the lines of everything He had taught. Well, then surely that meant that now all believers were to be circumcised and come under the Law.

It was this false gospel of the Judaizers that Paul had to deal with. Paul had to argue that Abraham was saved by faith before he was circumcised and that the whole business of dividing the human race in half by circumcision had now expired in Christ. Rather than everyone needing to be circumcised, now nobody needed to be.

Clearly, the true gospel would not sit well with proud Jews; and even more fanatical, we may well imagine, were those Gentiles who went along with this error and had themselves painfully circumcised. Such people were strongly motivated to insist that others do the same. The book of Revelation refers to the Judaizers as Balaamites ("People Eaters") and Nicolaitans ("People Conquerors") (Rev. 2:6, 14, 15).

When Jesus says that many will be "scandalized," He refers to such people. They were scandalized by the liberties enjoyed by the Gentile converts and by those Jewish converts who understood rightly that they were no longer obligated to the laws of circumcision and uncleanness.

In an interesting study, René Girard has argued that "scandal" is a kind of offense that provokes people to join together to find a scapegoat and punish or even murder him. The Greek word for "scandal" has its root in the idea of a trap set in the ground that trips a person up; hence the Bible associates scandal with a stone of stumbling (e.g., Rom. 9:33, 11:9). A person who is tripped up, even by an inanimate object, immediately seeks to strike back, even striking at the stone that tripped him. At a social level, the presence of such an offensive person or group of people brings about the presence of a mob to rid the community of him or them. Such happened to Jesus, and such will happen to His people, for He was a scandal, and so will they be.[34]

People who are scandalized by proper Christian liberties have a choice. They can either repent of their false belief or they will in time begin to persecute those who have liberty. We see exactly the same thing today in many Christian communities. Those who falsely believe, for whatever reason, personal or traditional, that drinking alcohol is always wrong, become scandalized by believers who enjoy a can of beer, a glass of wine, or a shot of Scotch. Such scandalized persons will be motivated to gossip about the "loose behavior" of their brethren, giving out bad reports concerning their lives. Plug in whatever artificial "sin" you wish, whether it be using birth control or going to movies, and you have the root of scandal. The root of scandal is false doctrine.

Jesus went to saloons and presented Himself to drunkards and prostitutes (Matt. 11:19; Luke 7:34). For His pains, He was rewarded by being called a drunkard. The Judaizers and those like them have given the same kind of reward to faithful believers throughout the centuries.

Jesus' statement to His disciples reveals the progression. First, the "legalistic" churchmember is scandalized. After a while, he acts to betray his fellow churchmember through gossip and slander. Finally he comes to hate his fellow churchmember.

C. The Coming Outbreak of Persecution

Anticipating what we shall come to shortly, we should note that the beginning point of the Great Tribulation was the completion of the temple of Herod in AD 64, the same year Old Rome burned and Nero accused the Christians of burning it. The completion of the temple was

---

34. See Girard, *I See Satan Fall Like Lightning,* trans. James G. Williams (Maryknoll, NY: Orbis Books, [1999] 2001). This book, and all of Girard's later writings, also explain the Judaizers. When a scapegoat dies, his death is in order to set everything back in order as it was before. That is how the Judaizers understood Jesus' death: it was an even more powerful reset of the Torah system. Jesus, however, was far more than a scapegoat, and His death reset the entire universe.

naturally greeted with great exultation by the Jews and Judaizers. The result was twofold. One, they felt that God was on their side, and they revolted against Rome as never before, eventually bringing upon themselves their own destruction. Two, full of false confidence, they persecuted Christians as never before. After all, the Christians were saying that this temple was nothing, and that they were the new temple of God. Naturally, this was extremely scandalous to the Jews and Judaizers, and they retaliated. This retaliation is the concern of Revelation 11–14.

8
APOSTASY AND PERSEVERANCE
(24:11-13)

---

[11]And (*kai*) many false prophets
   will arise,
   and (*kai*) will mislead
many.

[12]And (*kai*) because lawlessness has been multiplied,
the love of the many will grow cold.
[13]And/but (*de*) the one enduring to the end,
that one will be saved.

We have commented on verse 11 already. It remains only to take note of its place in this context. To begin with, note that this verse is the chiastic center of Matthew 23–25, and is itself chiastic. The central thought of the entire passage is that false prophets will arise and mislead.

We must also note that the three *kai* statements in this section follow on the six statements we discussed in chapter 7 above and again should be taken as parallel:

⁹At that time they will deliver you up to tribulation,

and (*kai*) will kill you,

and (*kai*) you will be hated by all nations on account of My name.

¹⁰And (*kai*) at that time many will be scandalized,

and (*kai*) they will betray one another,

and (*kai*) hate one another.

¹¹And (*kai*) many false prophets will arise,

and (*kai*) will mislead many.

¹²And (*kai*) because lawlessness has been multiplied,

the love of the many will grow cold.

Note that the third statement in each triad speaks of love and hatred. Accordingly, the following three ideas from the second statements are also parallel: killing, betraying, and misleading. And the ideas from the first statements are also linked: those who deliver the disciples to tribulation, the many who are scandalized, and the false prophets who lead them.

The entire paragraph, which we have broken in half for discussion purposes and in order to do justice to the overall chiasm of the passage, consists of ten statements: nine predictions of tribulation, and a climactic statement of reassurance, that those who endure to the end will be delivered (v. 13). A list of ten is a complete list. Compare the tenfold list in Matthew 23:33-36, discussed in chapter 3 above.

While there have been false Messiahs—and by implication false prophets—right along, at this point *many* such false prophets arise and at this time mislead *many*. This is in the wake of the persecution and scandalization just mentioned in verses 9 and 10. We have seen that these false prophets are the Judaizing preachers and teachers, who primarily opposed Paul. Paul was the man appointed to be tent-maker for the new Church, the new "one body" of Jews and Gentiles without distinction.

Verses 12 and 13 have a parallel and contrasting structure. Lawlessness (falling away) is set against enduring. *Multiplying* lawlessness is set against enduring to the *end*. Falling away into coldness and apostasy is set against salvation.

Verse 12 is chiastically matched with verses 9-10, which speak of persecution and apostasy.

Verse 13 is chiastically matched with verse 8: enduring to the *end* (death) being linked with the *beginning* of birthpangs.

A.   THE GREAT APOSTASY

The misleading of many, or the falling away (apostatization) of many, is noted in 2 Timothy, an epistle that was written after the close of the book of Acts, while Paul was imprisoned in Rome (2 Tim. 1:17). In 2 Timothy 1:15 we read, "You are aware of the fact that all who are in Asia turned away from me, among whom are Phygelus and Hermogenes." Also, 2 Timothy 4:10 states that "Demas, having loved this present age, has deserted me." A few verses later, Paul adds: "At my first defense no one supported me, but all deserted me" (4:16).

Notice that it is to these Asian churches that Jesus directs His threats in Revelation 2 and 3. Revelation was written about the same time as 2 Timothy.

I think we can infer that when Paul was captured in Jerusalem and put on trial, and then sent to Rome under house arrest, his enemies rejoiced greatly. They did not understand, because they did not want to understand, that Paul had gone to Rome in order to conquer it. Rather, they saw it as a judgment on Paul for his "false gospel." They capitalized on this, doubling their efforts with great enthusiasm and persuading many of their Judaizing heresies. Thus began a great apostasy in the Church, which not only carried many away, but also for a time neutralized many of Paul's supporters, who were cowed into temporary silence.

The great apostasy in the Apostolic Church had been predicted by Paul in one his early letters, in 2 Thessalonians 2:3: "Let no one in any way deceive you, for the apostasy comes first and the Man of Lawlessness is revealed, the Son of Destruction." The apostasy and the revelation of the Son of Satan (see below) are very closely linked, but it appears that the apostasy comes first, followed immediately by the appearance of the Son of Apollyon. First a company of Judaizing false prophets arise, and then their captain appears.

Second Peter 2 is entirely concerned with a prediction that false prophets are about to arise in the Church. The epistle of Jude is written after their appearance and repeats much of what Peter had written earlier.

Jesus tells us that the reason for the great apostasy is that lawlessness had increased, so that the love of "the many" (the "many" of verse 11) grows cold. Recall that this is also the condemnation Jesus pronounces on the church at Ephesus in Revelation 2:4-5, that they had left their first love and had fallen away. This warning, coming in the first letter to the seven churches, applies to all of them—all the churches in Asia that had turned away from Paul.

This falling away of so many from Paul and the other apostles simply repeats what happened to Jesus when He was arrested. All forsook Him. The things that happened to Jesus must also happen to His Church, and first of all to the Firstfruits Church of the Apostolic Age. This pattern can be seen in the last part of Acts, when Paul sets his face to go to Jerusalem, arrives in Jerusalem, and, when a riot is provoked, is arrested. He is then put on trial by the same three courts that tried Jesus: the Jews, Herod, and the Roman Governor. Paul is not put to death on this occasion, but the pattern is clear.

The passages about the great apostasy show that in the years just prior to the destruction of Jerusalem, the Bride of Jesus would go through the same things He went through. She would be attacked by all and betrayed by those closest to her. She would be falsely accused. She would be "crucified" and put to death. And then she would rise again after the destruction of Jerusalem, at the beginning of the millennium (Rev. 20:4).

The root of the Judaizing heresy, and of all legalism, is lawlessness. Those who add new laws to the Law of God are invariably guilty of taking away part of the Law He actually commanded. Those who refuse to drink wine are lawlessly refusing to drink the wine Jesus commanded for the Lord's Supper. But more generally, one can lay it down as a rule that churches focusing on obeying human traditions are simultaneously turning a blind eye to such genuine sins as gossip and fornication.

Human beings were created by God to need laws, rules. They cannot live without laws. When they reject God's laws, they invent new ones out of their own sinful consciences. When they decide that they don't need to tithe a full ten percent of their income, they balance this lawlessness by creating some new law, such as that smoking tobacco is always sinful. At the present time in the United States, it is virtually a crime to speak out against homosexuality, and at the same time it is virtually a crime to smoke tobacco. What we see written large in an apostate nation like the United States is written in smaller letters in legalistic churches all over that country.

As the Great Apostasy got underway, the Man of Lawlessness appeared. He is the captain of those who live lawlessly and whose love has grown cold. He is also called the Son of Destruction, and the word "destruction" is the same as the name of Satan, Apollyon, in Revelation 9:11. Revelation 9:1-11 discusses the rise of the army of false prophets, of Judaizers, led by Apollyon from the pit. The human agent of Satan-Apollyon is the Son of Apollyon. He is the chief of the Jews, and thus of the Judaizers, who takes a seat in the temple (2 Thess. 2:4); in short, the high priest. As the chief False Prophet, he is the Land Beast of Revelation 13, the high priest sponsored by the Herods, who built his temple for him.

B. STANDING FIRM

In his justly famous poem "If," Rudyard Kipling wrote (anticipating Girard): "If you can keep your head when all about you are losing theirs and blaming it on you…" Jesus says that while the *many* are apostatizing, the *one* who stands firm will be saved. As we have seen from 2 Timothy, the apostle Paul was such a one, standing firm when deserted by virtually everyone. Jesus Himself had stood firm when deserted by all. Long before Him, so did Job. Jesus thus warns us that in times of distress, when everyone is following a war leader or a false prophet, it can be very lonely to stand firm for the truth, especially since the one who stands firm draws the wrath of the mob to himself.

The man who stands firm and refuses to follow the crowd is implicitly, if not explicitly, condemning the crowd. The crowd is thus motivated to silence him. His friends, family, and neighbors will work hard to convince him to go along with them because he has become a thorn in their flesh. He will have to endure and persevere. Eventually, they may well come to kill him.

During World War I, the great American Reformed preacher Herman Hoeksema was once set upon by armed men. Why? Because he refused to have an American flag in the worship hall of the church he pastored. He maintained, rightly, that the Church is not part of any earthly nation and that no earthly national symbols belong in the meeting place of the Church. Americans were tremendously excited about the war against Germany, and nationalism was the religion of the day. Hoeksema's refusal was so scandalous that it created a great uproar in the minds of certain people, and for a time he was a marked man.

In the book of Revelation, it is those who stand firm who are said to "overcome" and who are eventually martyred for the truth. They are said to be blessed, those massacred in the final years of the Old Creation (Rev. 14:13-20).

Jesus says that the one who endures to the "end" will be saved. The "end" in view in this passage is the end of the Old Creation. Many believers, however, would not live to AD 70. For them, the "end" was their deaths.

9
TO THE OIKUMENE
(24:14)

[14]And (*kai*) this gospel of the kingdom will be proclaimed in the whole Oikumene,
for a witness to all the nations,
and (*kai*) at that time the end will come.

A. THE OIKUMENE

Jesus' statement here is quite specific, and if the translators had rendered it accurately a great deal of confusion might have been avoided. Jesus does *not* say that the gospel will be preached in the whole world, to the entire earth, but to the Oikumene.

The Oikumene is specifically the Guardian Beast Empires that God set up in Daniel 7 to house and protect His people. In the Apostolic Age, the Oikumene that housed the Jews was the Roman Empire. What we see in the New Testament writings, and particularly in Paul, is a movement into this commonwealth, the Hellenistic Oikumene governed by Rome. We do not see the apostles going to the Persian empire to the east, though doubtless they did do so. The covenant-historical movement in the New Testament is from Jerusalem to Rome. The gospel goes to Jew and Greek, with the Greeks (the Hellenistic Oikumene) standing for all the Gentiles of the whole rest of the world.

The events around AD 70 brought to an end both the Jews, as a nation of priests, and also Rome as a Guardian Beast empire. By AD 70, both Israel and the Oikumene had finished their purposes in the plan of God and both were removed.

Jesus' statement is, thus, quite specific and would have been understood quite specifically by His hearers. The end would come after the gospel had gone to the entire Roman empire. The end would come after both the Jews and the Guardian Beast empire had received the witness.

B. THE KINGDOM

Jesus identifies the good news, the gospel, as a message about the coming of the Kingdom. For the most part, we today think of the gospel as the message that God saves sinners on the basis of the substitutionary death of Jesus Christ. In fact, however, this was not really news in the first century. The righteous had always known that God was going to save them on the basis of the substitutionary death of the seed of the woman, the son of Adam, the Messiah. That was the promise in Genesis 3, and it was made explicit in Genesis 22. In that chapter we read that God called upon Abraham to sacrifice his only son, Isaac. Then God substituted an animal for Isaac. This meant two things that were quite clear to God's people. First, it meant that their animal sacrifices, specifically called "sons of the herd" in Leviticus, were substitutes for a human son. (The bullock or "son of the herd" is the first sacrifice and the weightiest. Its sonship-status carries to the other four animals by implication.) Second, it meant that no human being descended from Adam was worthy to be such a sacrifice, since even the son of the greatest man of faith, Abraham, was inadequate. From these two facts they knew that God was going to take away sin on the basis of the substitutionary death of a sinless man, the anointed one, the Messiah. At least the faithful understood this, and the facts were plain to all the rest.

Thus, the good news is not that God saves sinners, but rather is an historical message. It is the message that at last God has actually accomplished what He promised.

But there is more. It was clear from Genesis 1:29 that the prohibition on the Tree of the Knowledge of Good and Evil was only temporary and that if Adam had proven faithful he would eventually have been given to eat of its fruit. It was clear from the use of the phrase "knowledge of good and evil" in the rest of the Bible that it referred to maturity and rulership.[35] This was also clear from God's statement in Genesis 3:22 that man had, in a perverse way, become like God, knowing good and evil. The word "god" in the Bible is used for human rulers (e.g., Ps. 82:1, 6). In short, it was clear that the new Adam, the Messiah, would become king of the world.

And that is the specific content of the gospel in the New Testament. It is the good news that Satan is no longer the ruler of the world, for the new Adam has taken back the world that the old Adam gave away. It is the good news that Jesus has ascended to the throne of glory and that "God has made Him both Lord and Messiah" (Acts 2:26). A study of the gospel message in Acts will show that it is the resurrection, ascension, and enthronement of Jesus that is at the heart of the proclamation.

It is precisely this message that must go to the Jew first and then to the Oikumene and eventually to the entire earth. The message is this: You are no longer in charge. You must submit to King Jesus and rule as His servant.

It is right and proper that this message go to the Jews first and then to the Hellenistic Oikumene. (Remember that Rome was a Greek-type city-state, and that the language of the Roman empire was Greek. It was basically a Greek civilization.) God had established the Jews through Abraham and the Oikumene through Daniel. He had a special relationship to the Jews and their leaders and to the Oikumene and its leaders, starting with Nebuchadnezzar (Dan. 1–4). The Jews were given a chance to accept the new kingdom before they were removed as a priestly nation. The Oikumene was given a chance to accept the new kingdom before it was removed from the plan of God.

Both the Jews and the Oikumene had no place in the new kingdom of God, where all are on an equal footing in the unified body of Christ. The calling of the Jews and of the Oikumene had been temporary all along, and now that calling had been fulfilled in Jesus Christ. As the final

---

35. For a full discussion, see my books *Primeval Saints: Studies in the Patriarchs of Genesis* (Moscow: Canon, 2001) and *Trees and Thorns: Studies in the First Four Chapters of Genesis* (Monroe, LA: Athanasius, 2020).

sacrifice, Jesus had fulfilled the mission of the Jews. As the new ruler of humanity, Jesus had fulfilled the mission of the Oikumene. Thus, both Israel and the Oikumene needed to disappear. Before this happened, however, God fulfilled His promises to them, promises uttered to Israel and implicit in the call of the Oikumene empire. He gave a special witness to them before moving out to the rest of the world.[36]

C. THE WITNESS

The proclamation of Jesus' Kingship to the entire Oikumene is said to be a witness to the nations. In verse 7, nation rose against nation, but now the gospel goes to the nations. This can mean two things, and probably both. First, it means that preaching the kingdom to the Oikumene is the same thing as bearing witness to the nations within the Oikumene. This is probably the first-order meaning of Jesus' statement.

Second, however, it means that preaching the kingdom to the Oikumene, as recorded in Acts and the Epistles, stands as a witness to all the other nations of the earth. The spread of the gospel throughout the Roman empire, and the consternation and conflict that it provoked, would have been noticed by the nations around the Roman empire. Moreover, the inspired record of that proclamation would stand as a witness to all nations of all periods of history.

There is a huge and important contrast between what Jesus says here in Matthew 24:14 and what He says later on in the Great Commission, Matthew 28:19-20. Here the proclamation is only a witness, and then the end comes. In the Great Commission, it is not only proclamation but theocratization that is in view. All the nations are to become Christocracies. They are to submit to the rule of King Jesus and adopt the Bible as their fundamental standard and law in all of life, observing everything Jesus taught. At the time I am writing this essay, this command

---

36. On the final witness to the Jews, see my monograph on Romans 11, *The Future of Israel Reconsidered*, Biblical Horizons Occasional Paper 18 (Niceville, FL: Biblical Horizons, 1994).

has by no means been carried out. Only a few nations have ever become outwardly Christian, and only in rather meager ways has any nation been discipled.

Thus, in Matthew 24:14, Jesus said that the end would come after proclamation and witness had been made to all the nations of the Oikumene. The greater end of all human history will come only after all the nations of the earth have been discipled to obedience to the word of Jesus.

10
THE ABOMINATION OF DESOLATION
(24:15-20)

B riefly let us remind ourselves of the chiastic structure of the central part of Matthew 23–25:

    F. The Temple (23:38-24:2)
        G. Jesus' Arrival (24:3)
           H. False Prophets (24:4-5)
             I. Wars (24:6a)
               J. End (24:6b)
                 K. Nations (24:7)
                   L. Birth (24:8)
                     M. Persecution (24:9-10)
           H' False Prophets (24:11)
                     M' Lawlessness (24:12)
                  L' End (24:13)
                K' Nations (24:14a)
             J' End (24:14b)
           I' War (24:15-21)
           H" False Prophets (24:22-24)
        G' Jesus' Arrival (24:25-27)
      F' Corpse (24:28)

The "wars and rumors of wars" of verse 6 now come into their fullness, as all out war is waged against the believers.

Verses 15-28 are one full paragraph:

¹⁵When, therefore, you see the abomination of desolation, which is spoken of through Daniel the prophet, standing in the holy place (he who reads should understand/interpret),

¹⁶at that time let those who are in Judea flee into the mountains.
¹⁷The one who is on the housetop, let him not go down to take anything out of his house.
¹⁸And (*kai*) the one who is in the field, let him not turn back to get his cloak.
¹⁹And/but (*de*) woe to those who are with child and to those who nurse babes in those days!
²⁰And/but (*de*) pray that your flight may not be in the winter, or on a sabbath.

²¹For at that time there will be a great tribulation, such as has not occurred since the beginning of the world until now, nor ever shall be.
²²And (*kai*) unless those days had been cut short, no flesh would have been saved; but for the sake of the elect those days will be cut short.

²³At that time if anyone says to you, "Behold, here is the Messiah!," or, "Here!," do not believe it.
²⁴For there will arise false messiahs and false prophets,
and (*kai*) will give great signs and wonders,
so as to mislead, if possible, even the elect.
²⁵Behold, I have foretold you.
²⁶If therefore they say to you, "Behold, in the wilderness he is!," go not forth; "Behold, in the inner chambers!," believe it not.
²⁷For just as the lightning comes (*erchomai*) forth from east and appears as far as west,
so will be the manifestation (*parousia*) of the Son of Man.

²⁸For wherever will be the corpse, there will be gathered the eagles.

This passage covers the following themes:

The abomination (v. 15)
At that time, flee (v. 16)
Four warnings to the elect (vv. 17-20)
At that time, the Great Tribulation (v. 21).
Preservation of the elect (v. 22).
At that time, false prophecy (v. 23).
False messiahs (v. 24a).
False prophets (v. 24b).
False manifestations (v. 24c).
Warning to the elect (v. 24d).
True teaching (v. 25).
False prophets (v. 26a).
False Messiahs (v. 26b).
True prophecy of the true Prophet (v. 27).
The judgment on the abomination (v. 28).

Our concern in this chapter will be with verses 15-20.

A. THE ABOMINATION OF DESOLATION

It is only Jews, and particular the priests, and in most particular the high priest, who can commit the sin called "abomination of desolation." Therefore, we can exclude from consideration all those multitudes of commentators who wrongly think that the abomination of desolation is an army of Romans or Edomites surrounding Jerusalem. (On Luke 21:20, see below.)

The word translated "abomination" is from the Hebrew word *sheqets/shiqquts* and never is used for Gentile sins. Rather, it means "sacrilege," and is a sin that can be committed only by members of the priestly nation. In this case, since it relates to the temple, it means sins committed by religious leaders. A different word, *to'evah,* is used for more general "abominations" that are committed by men in general. As regards the temple, it did not defile the temple or its furniture for birds to drop on it, or for dogs to urinate against it, or for Gentiles to defecate inside it or offer pigs on its altar. Only the priests could commit a "desolating sacrilege" against the temple. Clear instances of this sin are seen when Aaron, the high priest, makes the Golden Calf and God desolates the camp of Israel (Exod. 32–33); when the sons of Eli, the high priest, seize God's prerogatives and the Ark deserts Israel (1 Sam. 2–4); when the priests and leaders engage in idolatry and God deserts Jerusalem (Ezek. 8–11).

The chiasm in our passage links the abomination with the full manifestation of false messiahs and false prophets. In a general way, it is the full apostasy of Judaism that is indicated by the abomination of desolation, as the Jews began to follow various wicked leaders with a fullness of heart they had not previously employed.

We have alluded previously to the fact that Herod's temple was completed in AD 64.[37] The writings of Josephus indicate that finishing touches were put on Herod's temple at the time Gessius Florus became procurator, which was in AD 64 (*Antiquities* 20.9.7). As we shall see, the arrival of Gessius Florus entailed the beginning of the end for the Jewish commonwealths.

Luke 21:20 is often taken as a parallel to Matthew 24:15, so that the "abomination of desolation" is the same as "Jerusalem surrounded by armies." While Luke is recounting the same speech of Jesus, he recounts many different parts of it from what Matthew records. Matthew focuses on the tribulation that comes upon the Christians, while Luke focuses on the wrath coming upon the Jews. I don't think Luke 21:20 is speaking of the same event as Matthew 24:15. He might be; that is, armies might have gathered around Jerusalem at about the same time as Herod's temple was finished. Or perhaps Luke means by "armies" the hosts of apostate Jews gathering for some festival at Jerusalem. But there is absolutely no way that the phrase "abomination of desolation" can refer

---

37. Under the entry for AD 64, we read "Jerusalem's Third Temple is completed after 84 years of construction," in James Trager, *The People's Chronology*, 2nd ed. (New York: Henry Holt, 1992).

to a gathering of armies. More likely, Luke's account is speaking of the gathering of Roman armies a few years after the abomination of desolation was set up.

Possibly the completion of the temple, now wholly dedicated to preserving the dead forms of Old Creation religion against Jesus Christ, is the specific event Jesus was prophesying. The abomination of desolation stands in the "holy place." The word "place" here is not the word used for the Holy Place of the tabernacle and temple, the outer room of God's Palace, the word *hagios*. Rather, the word for "place" here, *topos,* indicates a general area, in this case a holy area. What is in view is the temple mount, and the abomination is the temple.

Jesus had claimed that He was the true Temple. By continuing to build Herod's temple, the Jews were explicitly rejecting Jesus' claim. The completion of that false temple brought to a fulness that sacrilegious rejection, and at that point God completely abandoned the Jews.

The completion of that temple naturally caused great rejoicing among the Jews. Now they were sure that God was on their side. Their leaders, the false messiahs and false prophets, encouraged them to revolt against Rome and to wipe out the obnoxious Christians. The restraint that God had exercised over the Jews had been removed and they attacked in full fury, doubtless also encouraged by Nero's imperial persecution of the Christians, which began at this same time.

The other alternative is that the sin called "abomination of desolation" is the attack upon the Christians by the Jews. We shall explore this possibility further as we proceed.

B. DANIEL'S PROPHECY[38]

Daniel did not write his prophecies; he only wrote them down. Thus, the oracles, which came from God, were spoken *through* him.

---

38. For a fuller discussion of everything in this book about Daniel, see my *The Handwriting on the Wall: A Commentary on the Book of Daniel* (Powder Springs, GA: American Vision, 2007).

Daniel 11:31 speaks of an earlier abomination committed by the high priests Jason and Menelaus, which God punished by bringing Antiochus Epiphanes against the Jews. The specific sin of these two men was their removal of the true high priest, Onias III, and their takeover of the priesthood. They could not have succeeded in this without the connivance of most of the priests and of the leading Jews of Jerusalem. Daniel 11:22 speaks of the shattering of the "chief" or "prince," a term that refers to the son of the high priest (1 Chr. 9:11, 20; 12:27; 2 Chr. 31:10, 13; Neh. 11:11; Jer. 20:1). The shattering of the son of the high priest means that the *line* of high priests has been shattered by the removal of the true line of such priests. Daniel 12:7 says that beginning with this shattering until the shattering of the saints has been completed will be a set-time, set-times, and a half; and this is explained in Daniel 12:11 as starting with the abomination of desolation and lasting three times 430 "Egyptian captivity" days (1290 days). Accordingly, the sacrilege that causes God to desolate His temple was the shattering of the high priestly line, the attack upon God's messianic agent.

The shattering of the high priestly line, the abomination of desolation, begins a time of tribulation for the saints (Dan. 11:33-35). This time of tribulation reaches a climax after the coming of Jesus (Michael), and this time of tribulation is said to be "such as never occurred" (Dan. 12:1). Jesus refers to this statement when He characterizes the Great Tribulation upon the Church as the greatest since the beginning of the world (Matt. 24:21).

We now have a beginning of the time of tribulation, marked by the commission of the desolating sacrilege, and a climax of that time in the Great Tribulation, again marked by the commission of the desolating sacrilege. Daniel 9:27 had prophesied this second abomination of desolation, and Jesus refers to it here in Matthew 24:15. Since the first abomination of desolation consisted of deposing and then murdering the high priest, and since Jesus has already linked the desolation of the temple to the murder of the prophets in Matthew 23:34-38, it seems likely that the outbreak of persecution against the Church, the sons or line of high priests following Jesus, is the prophesied "abomination of desolation."

The abominable sin consists of defiling the temple of God. Recall the series of such abominations: Aaron defiled the holy camp, and God forsook them. The sons of Eli defiled the tabernacle, and God forsook them. The priests of Ezekiel 8 and 11 defiled the temple, and God forsook them. In the late AD 60s, the priests and Jews defile the temple, which is the Church, by persecuting and murdering Christians, and God forsook them.

Thus, the completion of the temple is not the main sin. It is only a sign to the believers that the Great Tribulation is about to start. That great persecution of believers is the actual abomination that brings about the destruction of Jerusalem, as the blood of the martyrs of Revelation 14 calls down God's wrath in Revelation 16–17.

As we have seen from Matthew 23:37-38, Jesus states that the temple will be left desolate because Jerusalem had murdered the faithful. Thus, in context, Jesus has already identified the outbreak of persecution as the abominable act that results in desolation.

The tabernacle and temple were symbols of the Israelite society organized for worship and service around God. The Church of the New Creation is the new temple. The completion of Herod's temple was a symbol of the completion of a body of evil men, an anti-Church worshiping an anti-Christ, identified in Revelation 8:10-11 as Satan-Wormwood, now enthroned in the temple and sending out his own poisonous laver-of-uncleanness waters (cf. Rev. 12:15).

The history of the Apostolic Church is a history of the formation of the new body of the Church, weaving Jew and Gentile into one New Man in Christ. That work was completed by, let us say, AD 64. Then that new body was slain and resurrected to become the new permanent Church. Simultaneously a false body was being woven together, of Jews and Gentiles opposed to the Christians, an alliance of Sea Beast and Land Beast. That false body was also completed in AD 64, and the symbol of its completion was the completion of the physical temple. That false body, the anti-Church, then murdered the true body, the true Church, thereby committing the abomination of desolation.

If the outbreak of persecution rather than the completion of the temple *per se* is the sacrilege that causes God to desolate the Jews, then what does "standing in the holy environment" mean? The "holy location" is the Church. The desolating sacrilege stands up within the Church herself. We have already seen the prophesied apostasy of many within the Church. Now the apostates within the Church, or formerly with her and still claiming to be the true Church, begin to join with the Jews in persecuting the Church. Apostates within the "holy place" (Church) act to shatter and bring tribulation upon the true saints.

In a way, there is nothing new about this. The good prophets of old had been attacked primarily by false prophets within Israel. And while the unconverted Jews will attack the Christians, it will once again be primarily the false Christians who will attack the true saints. Initially, of course, as we read in the book of Acts, it was Jews who attacked the fledgling Church. But after a course of time, the Church developed false members of her own. It is these, who "stand in the holy place," who will attack the saints.

C. THE INTERPRETER

Matthew adds in parenthesis, "he who reads should understand." Many commentators, noting the reference to Daniel, hold that this means that the reader of Matthew should meditate on what Daniel has written so as to understand its relevance—as we have sought to do above.

I don't think this is correct, for two reasons. First, if the reference is to Daniel, the parenthetical statement should follow "which is spoken of through Daniel the prophet," instead of "standing in the holy place." Matthew is not calling on the reader to understand Daniel *per se*, but to understand what Jesus Himself is saying

Second, when Mark writes up this same sermon, he omits any reference to Daniel, but retains "he who reads should understand" (Mark 13:14). While Mark has a different perspective from Matthew—which is why there is more than one Gospel—and thus might be saying something slightly different from Matthew, it is more likely that he is saying the same thing here. The reader is called upon to understand what Jesus is saying.

Some commentators assume that Matthew is addressing Bible students. Those reading his text should endeavor to understand this cryptic saying of Jesus. This is most unlikely. Since many if not most people did not know how to read and had no reason to learn, they heard the Bible as read by a scribe, someone who could read and write. Revelation 1:3 speaks very clearly to this situation: "Blessed is the one who reads and those who hear the words of the prophecy."

Thus, it should be clear that the reader in Matthew 24:15 is the person reading this text out loud to the congregation of hearers. Matthew is addressing him. And Matthew is not saying that he should seek to understand the matter for himself alone. Rather, Matthew is calling on the reader to interpret and explain Jesus' remarks to the congregation.

Matthew is saying, "Jesus spoke in symbols here, and I have written down what He said. But you need to interpret this symbol and explain it to the congregation, so that they will be able to understand it and will know what to watch for in the near future."

D. The Mountains

Jesus says that when the abomination takes place, those in Judea are to flee to the mountains. From this we see that the abomination is a very public event. A celebration connected with the completion of the final touches on the anti-temple would be such an event, a celebration accompanied by an outbreak of violence against the Church.

Jesus uses the plural, "mountains," because no particular mountain is in view. All the same, the alert first century Jewish Christian would rather quickly make some important connections. He would recall the times when God's people had fled to a particular mountain to escape wrath coming upon the wicked.

To start with, we recall from Revelation 11 that Jerusalem is called Sodom and Egypt. When the angels delivered Lot, they told him to flee to the mountain (19:17), which in context is the mountain where Abraham was (18:16, 21, 22). Lot was to flee to Abraham, but he did not want to and went to Zoar instead. As regards Egypt, we instantly remember that when the Hebrews fled after the first Passover, they went to the Mountain of God.

While these two exoduses are perhaps primary, since Revelation calls attention to Sodom and Egypt, others should be mentioned as well. Noah's exodus from the old evil world to a new world landed his ark on mountains (Gen. 8:4). When Jacob fled from Laban, he went to the mountains of Gilead (Gen. 31:21-54). When the spies fled from cursed Jericho, they went to the mountains (Josh. 2:16, 22). Elijah fled from Jezebel to the Mountain of God (1 Kgs. 19:8; recall that Jezebel in Revelation 2:20 links with Harlot Babylon).

Thus, Jesus' admonition to flee to the mountains stands right in line with the typological pattern of going to a mountain after making an exodus. Moreover, since mountains and high places are where God meets with man in the Old Creation—recalling that every altar is a miniature holy mountain[39]—fleeing to the mountains is also a way of saying "Flee to God." The Church is the holy mountain of the New Creation, as the pyramid-shaped New Jerusalem of Revelation 21–22 shows us, and all men are called to flee to her.

E. THE HOUSETOP

Jesus now expands on fleeing to the mountains with four examples. First, He says that the person on the housetop should not go down to get anything out of his house. This seems to imply the situation in a city, where a person might run across the rooftops and get out of town. Some have taken this command literally and assumed that it refers to a point in time during the investiture of Jerusalem. The abomination of desolation is not, however, the investiture of Jerusalem, so I think we are constrained to see Jesus using a figure of speech, along the lines of His telling us to cut off our hands and rip out our eyes (Matt. 5:29-30).

The meaning of the hyperbole is clear: Don't try to take anything of the old world with you when you flee to the new. Don't be like Lot's wife,

---

39. See Jordan, *Through New Eyes*, 158-159.

who kept thinking about the things she left behind. Don't be like those who murmured against Moses and wanted to go back to the leeks and onions and melons of Egypt. Don't be like Ananias and Sapphira.

I think there is another dimension as well. The housetop was a place for prayer because it was a high place. We see this in Acts 10:9, when Peter went to a rooftop to pray.[40] In the city, booths for the Feast of Booths were erected on the rooftops (Neh. 8:16). Thus, Jesus was saying that they should continue in prayer, trusting God to take care of them.

F. THE CLOAK

In Exodus 22:26-27, the pre-incarnate Jesus said, "If you ever take your neighbor's cloak as a pledge, you are to return it to him before the sun sets, for that it is his only covering; it is his cloak for his skin. What else will he sleep in? And it will come about that when he cries out to Me, I will hear, for I am gracious."

This law, with which every first-century Jewish Christian was familiar, lies behind what Jesus says about the cloak. The man working in the field is not to bother going back for anything, not even his cloak. The cloak is the one thing that is so precious and needful that it cannot be taken as a pledge during the nighttime hours but has to be returned each night to its owner. Leaving the cloak behind, then, means leaving everything behind.

Jesus had already made this point in the Sermon on the Mount, where He told His followers to be ready to give up their cloaks if that was demanded of them (Matt. 5:40).

Did Jesus mean that the believers should literally leave their cloaks behind, even in winter, when they would need them on the road? I don't think so. Again I think we have to take Jesus' command as an epigram. First it means to be ready to leave everything behind, just as Jesus left His tunic at the foot of the cross and soldiers gambled for it. But it probably has a deeper meaning also.

---

40. Compare Jeremiah 19:13; 32:29; Zephaniah 1:5.

In Matthew, Jesus has said that no one sews a patch of new cloth on an old cloak, but instead turns the old one into a rag and makes a new cloak of new cloth (Matt. 9:16). The new cloak is the white cloak of the saints in Revelation 3:4, 5, 18; and 16:15.

Leave behind the cloak of the Old Covenant. You won't need it any longer.

G. THE MOTHERS

Jesus expresses emotional sorrow for those who are pregnant or nursing in the days of the Great Tribulation. Naturally, it will be particularly hard for them to travel.

We could stop with that observation, as most of the commentators do. But since Jesus has already compared the Great Tribulation to the labor pains of childbirth, I think we are encouraged to meditate on deeper aspects of what He says here. These women exemplify in their own personal lives the situation of the Apostolic Church as a body, as the Woman, the Mother of the Seed, and ultimately the Bride of Christ. The Apostolic Church is laboring to give birth to the Worldwide Church. At the same time, the Apostolic Church is the guardian of infants within her bosom, who will inherit from her.

If we take this larger picture, we can imagine the situation of some of the strong believers at this time. They know that it is time to flee, but they have friends who are weak believers, who are being caught up in the great events around them, who don't want to flee. Should the strong believer abandon these babies or stay behind and try to persuade them? Should the pastor abandon his weak flock? The choice would be hard, because the believer who decides not to flee knows that he may well be martyred. The picture of the 144,000 Jewish martyrs in Revelation 14 indicates to me that many Christians elected not to flee but to stay and minister.

Does that make them superior to those who fled? Not at all. Each person acted as the Spirit moved him. It was necessary that some flee, so that the Church would have some continuity into the future.

H. WINTER AND SABBATH

Winter would make the flight more difficult, not only because of the cold, but also because it is a time of much rain. The word translated "winter" can also mean "storm, tempest," as in Matthew 16:3. "Winter" is literally "the season of stormy weather." The wet and freezing cold would be a major danger, especially for people without cloaks!

The sabbath would be a problem, not because the Christians would have any scruples about fleeing on the sabbath but because the wicked Jews had invented rules about how far one might travel on the sabbath. Christians fleeing on the sabbath would be highly visible, and those seeking to put them to death would be able to identify them.

The dangers of flight in stormy weather or on the sabbath would cause some Christians to waver in their determination to flee. This provides yet another reason to pray that the flight not be necessary at such a time.

There is an implied contrast between storm and sabbath, for the sabbath is the day of peace and rest. They are two extremes. The feasts God appointed for Israel all took place in spring and summer, not in the time of storm and tempest and cold.

Both winter and sabbath are to be left behind. Shortly Jesus will say that the events He is predicting are a sign that summer is near (Matt. 24:32). These events are, thus, springtime events, constituting a new and greater Passover, when the angel of death will destroy the enemies of the believers and they will pass into a new world. The sabbath is to be left behind, because the sabbath day has been fulfilled in Jesus and has been replaced by the new Lord's Day, the first day of the week.

Being caught in winter or sabbath, then, is being caught in the coils of the Old Creation. They must pray that this not happen, in any way, spiritual or literal, so that their flight to the mountains of God may be rapid and easy.

11
DANGERS OF THE LAST HOUR
(24:21-24)

---

²¹For at that time there will be a great tribulation,

such as has not occurred since the beginning of the world until now,

nor ever shall be;

²²And (*kai*) unless those days had been cut short,

no flesh would have been saved.

And/but (*de*) for the sake of the elect those days will be cut short.

²³At that time if anyone says to you,

"Behold, here is the Messiah!",

or, "Here!",

do not believe it.

²⁴For there will arise false messiahs and false prophets,

And (*kai*) will give great signs and wonders,

so as to mislead, if possible, even the elect.

A.   THE GREAT TRIBULATION

It is often assumed that the Great Tribulation refers to the horrors experienced by the Jews during the Jewish War, as recorded in awful detail by Josephus. This is not the case. The Great Tribulation is experienced by the believers.

Without exception, every time the verb *thlibo* and the noun *thlipsis* are used, they refer to the sufferings of believers. Matthew 24:9 has already made it clear that it is the believers who are delivered up for tribulation. Daniel 12:1 had predicted it.

From Josephus's *The Jewish War* 2:14:1-3 we learn that in AD 64 the former Roman procurator Albinus was replaced with one Gessius

Florus. Unlike all the previous Roman rulers, Florus made no attempt to get along with any of the Jewish leaders at all, but began to impose a total and cruel tyranny. Like all Romans, Florus would have made no distinction between traditional Jews and Christian Jews. Josephus states that he intended to provoke the Jews to rebel against Rome, in order to justify his actions. The war against Rome began in the summer of 66. The Jews were initially successful, but the resulting conflicts led to many serious massacres of Jews, and doubtless Christian Jews also, throughout Palestine. Nero sent General Vespasian in the Spring of 67 to quell the rebellion. The war was conducted all over Judea and Galilee, and the Romans had pacified the whole area by around the end of November of 67 and began to prepare to take Jerusalem.

Now, while all of this is approximate, I believe we can fill in the details from the data of Scripture. Following the establishment of the abomination of desolation, a persecution of Christians arose along with the revolt against Rome. The Romans who entered Palestine were also motivated against the Christians, since they believed the Christians had burned Rome in 64 and since they made no distinction between Christian and non-Christian Jews. According to Revelation 14, the blood of massacred Christians filled the land. Thus, it was important for Christians to flee the lowlands and to take refuge in the mountains right at the beginning of this period.

By the end of November of 67, the battles in the lowlands were over and the Romans were again in power. The reimposition of law would bring to an end the persecution of the Christians, which we can put in the Spring of 68. But the blood of the slain believers had called up the Divine Avenger of Blood, and immediately God's agent, Vespasian, laid siege to Jerusalem.

Thus, Jesus lays out two phases of the end of the age:

1) Fall of 64 to Spring of 68: the Great Tribulation.
2) Spring of 68 to Fall of 70: the Days of Vengeance (Luke 21:22, Destruction of Babylon-Jerusalem).

The book of Revelation hints that the Great Tribulation was to last 3½ years (Rev. 11:3; 13:5). Our reconstruction provides such a period of time. Notice, though, that this period is only six, not seven years in length. The Days of Vengeance only lasted 2½ years. The seventh year was, thus, a sabbath, the first year of the fullness of the New Creation.

Jesus states that the tribulation through which the Apostolic or Firstfruits Church will pass is to be the greatest period of Christian suffering that will ever happen. Believers had never suffered as much before, and they never will again.

Jesus experienced the greatest tribulation of all on the cross, where He suffered directly under the wrath of the Father and the Spirit. All Christian suffering is counted in union with Christ, so that we fill out His suffering on behalf of the world, so that the blood of martyrs is the seed of the Church (Col. 1:24). In a very particular way, however, the suffering of the Apostolic Church during the Great Tribulation filled out the suffering of Jesus. Jesus' suffering and death gave birth to the Apostolic Church, and the suffering and death of the Apostolic Church gave birth to the Worldwide Church. It is in large measure the purpose of the book of Revelation to unfold the meaning of this suffering and victory. Jesus' suffering and death made the Groom ready, while the suffering and death of the Apostolic Church made the Wife ready (Rev. 19:7).[41]

We should also point out that the Great Tribulation of the Apostolic Church was not only the greatest time of suffering for believers of all time, but as Jesus says, it was the greatest time of suffering for humanity. When we consider the horror experienced by Jews and others under Nazism, the horrors of the GULAG prison system in the Soviet Union, the horrors experienced by the Chinese in the Great Cultural Revolution, the horrors experienced by the Cambodians under the Pathet Lao, and the horrors of the endless war of the Hutus and Tutsis in West Africa,

---

41. By the way, the death of the Apostolic Church in the Great Tribulation explains why the post-Apostolic Church displays such great ignorance of the Bible. The continuity of knowledge was broken, and the Church had to start anew. The so-called Church Fathers are really the Church Babies.

we stand in amazement. But Jesus tells us that His people underwent worse in the years between AD 64 and 68.

In this, His first eschatological discourse, Jesus focuses on the tribulation of Christians in Palestine. In His second eschatological discourse, the book of Revelation, He includes the suffering of Christians in the Roman Empire as well.

B.   FOR THE SAKE OF THE ELECT

Commentators debate over why the days are cut short. It is in order to save the lives of the elect or to save their souls? Is it because of physical danger that they are cut short or because of spiritual danger?

I believe we can answer firmly in favor of the second view. Jesus follows His statement about the days being cut short by warning about false prophets and messiahs, who might mislead the elect.

As we have seen, the tribulation through which the Church was called to go at this time was the worst she will ever have to endure. Physical persecution was only a small part of that tribulation. The greater suffering was the temptation to give in. This is parallel to what Jesus underwent in His suffering and death. The physical suffering was only a small part of His tribulation. The far greater suffering was His sense that the Father and the Spirit had cut Him off: "My God, My God, why have You forsaken Me?" This is why He asked that this cup of suffering, if at all possible, pass from Him (Matt. 26:39).

I believe that God's desolation of Israel left the true believers in a dark night of the soul. They also experienced a sense of desolation. They experienced what Job experienced, what Heman experienced in Psalm 88, what Jesus experienced on the cross (though Jesus experienced it to the ultimate degree). Friends and family were against them. Former associates in the Church had apostatized into the Judaizing counterfeit; former close friends were leading the attack. The whole society was full of enthusiasm about fighting the Romans and about the completed temple. Meanwhile, the believers did not feel the comforting presence of Jesus. They experienced what the Puritans called an "abandonment," what other Christians have called "the dark night of the soul." In short, they experienced death and hell. Paul had predicted in his letter to the Hebrews, "You have not *yet* resisted as far as blood in your striving against sin" (Heb. 12:4). In union with Jesus, who *did* resist temptation to the point of shedding blood in His garden agony, they would be privileged to come to that point (Luke 22:44).

Of course, they had not really been abandoned. Rather, they had been given the privilege of participating in the same cross-bearing as their Savior. The same is true of believers today who pass through that valley of the shadow of death, as most of us do at some time in our lives. None of us will ever suffer as much as Jesus did, however, and none of us will ever suffer as did the Apostolic Church in the Great Tribulation. And that can be a comfort to us. Agony of desolation

The agony of desolation is the great trial in the life of a believer. It is then that he or she is tempted to look for a quick fix. Perhaps Jesus has returned! Perhaps He is in the inner chambers, or in the wilderness with a new John-like prophet! Perhaps the Jewish prophets are really harbingers of Jesus, because they are doing signs and wonders just as He did.

This is the heart of tribulation. Jesus promises, however, that He will not let the agony go on for too long. He will cut short the time of tribulation, so that the elect are saved. The tribulation is designed to winnow the flock, to shake them so that only those who cannot be shaken remain (Heb. 12:25-27). That promise is still for us today, as 1 Corinthians 10:13 assures us.

C. THE DAYS CUT SHORT

The fact that the days are cut short implies that the days should properly have lasted longer. We can only guess at how much longer they would have lasted if they had not been cut short, but I think we can make a good guess.

We have seen that the tribulation lasted about 3½ years. That is half of a week. The time of the Old Creation, when humanity was cut off from the kingdom of God, was symbolically one week. The New Creation began with Jesus' resurrection on the eighth day, the beginning of a new week for a new humanity.

Jesus' tribulation lasted a week. He arrived in Jerusalem on the first day of the week, which we call Palm Sunday. Initially everything was light and joy, but then immediately He began to be challenged and rejected by those He came to save. This time of conflict lasted until Thursday evening, when Jesus celebrated a Passover meal with His men—3½ days. Then Jesus was arrested, beaten, crucified, slain, and buried—another 2½ days.[42]

If the believers are, as a body, to go through an equivalent tribulation, then they will have to endure a period of six-almost-seven also. As a community, they will endure six-almost-seven years (the period of a sabbath for the land) instead of six-almost-seven days (the period of a sabbath for a man).

The time is cut short, however. First, the Great Tribulation itself only lasts for half the week of years. Second, the entire period (Great Tribulation + Days of Vengeance) only lasts for six rather than seven years.

It is the first foreshortening that is in view. Had the Great Tribulation lasted longer, even the elect might have been seduced by the false prophets and false messiahs. But God acted to shame and destroy these evil people after 3½ years, by bringing the Romans against them in force, thus invalidating their false prophecies and showing their powerlessness as messiahs.

Is it really possible for the elect of God to fall away? Well, if it were up to the elect, yes. The tribulation would be so great that even the elect would indeed fall away. But the elect are not sustained by their faith alone. They are sustained by the grace of God. And God promises to intervene in time, so that the elect will not be lost. Therefore, it is not possible for the elect of God to fall away.

---

42. Matthew 12:40 says that as Jonah was three days and nights in the belly of the great fish, so Jesus would be three days and nights in the heart of the earth. "Heart of the earth" is clearly a figure of speech and does not refer simply to His burial in the tomb. If we start counting the three days with His arrest on Thursday night and continue through Friday and Saturday night until Sunday morning, we find that Jesus' prediction was most accurate. Notice that God calls Jerusalem the "navel of the earth" in Ezekiel 38:12.

It is the "flesh" that is the problem. Note the chiastic structure of verse 22:

And unless those days had been cut short,
  No flesh would have been saved;
  But for the sake of the elect,
Those days will be cut short.

Jesus was shortly to say, "The spirit is willing, but the flesh is weak" (Matt. 26:41). The "flesh" does not mean the physical body, but the connection of human beings to the first Adam. The drag of the Old Creation continues to afflict us as long as we are in our bodies of soil, because that soil is Adamic, the soil of the First Creation. Only when we receive new bodies of purified soil at the final resurrection will we be free of this drag. Until then, we have to fight it.

12

THE MANIFESTATION OF THE SON OF MAN
(24:25-28)

²⁵Behold, I have foretold you.

²⁶If therefore they say to you, "Behold, in the wilderness he is!"
go not forth;
"Behold, in the inner chambers!"
believe it not.

²⁷For just as the lightning comes forth from east
and appears as far as west,
so will be the manifestation (*parousia*) of the Son of Man.

²⁸For wherever will be the corpse,
there will be gathered the eagles.

A.   THE SON OF MAN

We come now to the subject of the "son of man." There is considerable debate and not a little confusion about this title, and we must take some time to unpack its meaning, for it does not always mean the same thing. The primary root of this title is in the book of Ezekiel, and secondarily in the book of Daniel; but because most expositors completely overlook Ezekiel, we shall start with Daniel.[43]

In Daniel 7:13-14, Daniel sees "one like a son of man" approach the Ancient of Days and receive a kingdom. This "one like a son of man" is a corporate symbol. Earlier in Daniel 7, the prophet was shown four

---

43. Psalm 8 is also relevant. See Barach, "The Glory of the Son of Man."

beast-empires that would be brought forth by the activity of the saints (the four winds of heaven; Zech. 2:6). These world empires would be guardians of God's people, who would bare their fangs against their enemies. Like Ezekiel 1, Daniel 7 is a scene set in the heavenly throneroom, and as in Ezekiel 1, the four beasts are guardians. Ezekiel's four beasts are the cherubim, archetypes and overlords of the creation, especially of the animal creation, which comes before the human creation in Genesis 1 and which characterizes the Old Creation before the ascendancy of humanity over the angels and their animal agents. Daniel's four beasts are historical human empires, but they function on earth as the cherubim function in heaven. Whenever one of the human beast-empires falls into sin and turns against the saints, it is replaced by a new one.

Now, the "one like a son of man" should also be regarded as an empire, but a human one. Daniel is shown that the age of animals, of animal tutelage (as in Proverbs) and of animal sacrifices (as in Leviticus), is going to be replaced by an age of true humanity come of age. As Paul writes, humanity will no longer be children under (angelic) tutors, but adults in union with Jesus the Messiah (Gal. 3–4). Just as the four beasts are not individuals, neither are the "little horn" and the "one like a son of man." Rather, the son of man's receiving of dominion, glory, and a kingdom is explained as the saints of the Most High receiving the kingdom and possessing it forever, and as the sovereignty, dominion, and greatness of the kingdoms under the whole of heaven being given to the people of the saints of the Most High (Dan. 7:14, 18, 27). The "little horn" represents the company of those opposed to the saints.

The Ancient of Days is not God the Father, but Jesus Christ. That is, this Person is He who anciently became Israel's king at Mount Sinai and will be incarnated as Jesus Christ. The description of the Ancient of Days in Daniel 7:9 correlates with the description of the glorified Jesus in Revelation 1:14. The chariot throne of Daniel 7:9-10 is the chariot throne of Ezekiel 1, and the person enthroned on both is the Angel of Yahweh, ruler of Israel, the second person of God, eventually Jesus Christ. The opening of the books in Daniel 7:10 is seen in Revelation 4–6, as Jesus comes to the throne in heaven, receives the book, and opens it. It is after a brief period of time, during which the Little Horn is destroyed and the beasts are judged, that the "one like a son of man" comes to Jesus Christ and the saints are given the kingdom (Dan. 7:11-14, 18, 22, 27).

Mark this well. The Ancient of Days who takes His seat and opens the book is Israel's ruler, and that Ruler is not the Father but the Son. Daniel 7 does *not* picture Jesus coming to the Father to receive His kingdom but the saints coming to Jesus to receive theirs (cf. Ezek. 2:8–3:3).

We are so familiar with Jesus' calling Himself "the Son of Man" that this may be surprising, but a simple reading of the chapter will make it obvious. In Daniel 7, the "one like a son of man" is identified as the "saints of the Most High" no less than six times in the passage (Dan. 7:18, 21, 22, 22, 25, 27).

In view of this, it is remarkable that so many scholars persist in thinking that when Jesus called Himself "the son of man," He was referring to Daniel 7. In fact, He was referring to Ezekiel, as we shall see, and Daniel 7 also alludes to Ezekiel. What, then, does "son of man" mean?

THE MEANING OF "SON OF MAN"

First, it should be obvious that the "son of man" is the son of Adam. Accordingly, the term can be used to mean "human being" (e.g., Num. 23:19; Ps. 146:3). In view of this, some older expositors took "son of man" to refer to Jesus' humanity, considered apart from His divinity, and "Son of God" to refer to His divinity, considered apart from His humanity. But while keeping these two aspects of Jesus distinct is essential to Christian theology, the difference is not signaled by the terms "son of man" and "son of God." Others have said that when Jesus calls Himself "son of man," He means nothing more than "I" and "me," but this is absurd. Jesus routinely referred to Himself with the first person pronouns and clearly used "son of man" as a title to allude to Himself in some particular fashion that could be recognized by His audience.

Thus, second, if the "son of man" is the son of Adam, he is the promised "seed of the woman." The two phrases are parallel, referring to the same person, though not in precisely the same sense. The son of Adam is the one who will do what Adam did not do: He will obey God and bring humanity to mature, adult, regal status. The parallel phrasing in Psalm 8 implies this quite pregnantly:

> What is man, that You remember him;
> And the son of man, that You care for him?
> You made him a little lower than God (angels),
> And crown him with glory and majesty (vv. 4-5).

That is, Adam in the beginning was made lower than the angels, but was destined to be crowned over them. Since Adam fell, it remained for his son to fulfill his original destiny. From Psalm 8, then, to call someone "son of man" is to identify him as the one who will be crowned with glory and honor, and exalted over the angels.[44]

Similarly, Psalm 144 implies the same distinction:

> Yahweh, what is man, that You take knowledge of him;
> Or the son of man, that You think of him?
> Man is like a mere breath.
> His days are like a passing shadow (vv. 3-4).

Here it looks as if "man" and "son of man" are synonyms and that both are a mere breath whose lives are like a passing shadow. But the psalm continues in the next stanza (vv. 5-11) by calling on Yahweh to bring down His throne-judgments, put down the wicked, and exalt the righteous. Then the psalm concludes (vv. 12-15) with praise to God for having done just this and recounts many rich blessings that stand in stark contrast to "mere breath" and "passing shadow." It would seem that the transition from death to abundant life is parallel to a transition from Adam to the son of Adam.

Third, the implication that the "son of man" is the exalted man, the faithful man, the new man, brings us to Ezekiel. With one exception, Ezekiel is the only person in the Bible except Jesus who is called "son of

---

44. Once again, see Barach, "The Glory of the Son of Man."

man" by God, and not just once: ninety-two times by my count. (Dan. is called this once, but by Gabriel; Dan. 8:17.) Since Ezekiel was an exact contemporary of Daniel,[45] it is likely that "one like a son of man" would have been taken as an allusion to Ezekiel; and the more so since the vision of Daniel 7 was given many years after Ezekiel had completed his ministry. Daniel and all of his contemporaries knew who the "son of man" was and thus knew that "one like a son of man" was "one like Ezekiel." So, who was Ezekiel, and why would this phrase be used uniquely of him?

Ezekiel was a priest in exile in the Chebar settlement in Babylon. At the age of thirty, he was anointed by God Himself to serve as an interim high priest among the exiles. His high priestly status is seen in two ways. First, he is given a vision of the four cherubim around the throne of God, which was architecturally represented by the Ark-Cover in the Holy of Holies, a place into which only the high priest might go. Second, when Ezekiel's wife died, he was forbidden to engage in public mourning, a stricture imposed only on a high priest (Lev. 21:1-15; Ezek. 24:16-18). The death of Ezekiel's wife was a sign of the death of Yahweh's wife, Israel (Ezek. 24:19-27), which again puts Ezekiel in close proximity to the symbolic role of the high priest.[46]

Jesus' frequent reference to Himself as the Son of Man would have been understood by His contemporaries as an allusion to Ezekiel far more readily than as an allusion to Daniel 7. Ezekiel, in fact, preaches a message very similar to that of Jesus. Both men predicted the destruction of Jerusalem, and the fulfillment of that prophecy was the proof of the validity of their ministries. Jesus gave no sign except the "sign of Jonah," which linked Nineveh to Jerusalem. Besides His own death and resurrection, the destruction of the temple and Jerusalem was the one thing He repeatedly prophesied in parable and sermon. The fulfillment

---

45. Ezekiel refers to Daniel in Ezekiel 14:14.

46. For more on the ordination of Ezekiel, his assumption into the heavenly court, and his symbolic character, see my paper, *Chariots of Fire: The Ordination of Ezekiel*, Biblical Horizons Occasional Paper 13 (Niceville, FL: Biblical Horizons, 1991).

of that prophecy in the immediate future would be the confirmation of Jesus' own ministry and its public vindication. (Jesus' resurrection was His first, but more private, vindication.) Similarly, Jerusalem's destruction in Ezekiel's day confirmed his words.

More, both Jesus and Ezekiel formed new communities and created new temples and cities. Ezekiel's community formed around him before Jerusalem was destroyed, and his temple and city were presented in a vision, a symbol of the glories of the Oikumenical Era. Jesus' community formed around Him, and the Church was and is His new temple and city, pictured as the New Jerusalem.

We have considered the "exodus from Egypt" theme in Matthew. We must now take into consideration that the book of Ezekiel is a recasting of the book of Exodus. Jeremiah 34 had identified Jerusalem as Egypt, where the faithful were held as slaves. Thus, moving into Babylon was moving into the wilderness, before moving to a new "holy land" eventually under Cyrus. Ezekiel goes into the wilderness before the destruction of Jerusalem-Egypt and prophesies its destruction. Indeed, like Moses, Ezekiel actually brought destruction upon Egypt-Jerusalem. In an all-important statement that is so startling that most translations don't render it properly, Ezekiel writes that when he saw the Glory return to the visionary temple, it was "like the appearance of the vision that I saw, like the vision that I saw when I came to destroy the city" (Ezek. 43:3). Ezekiel states that he destroyed the city!

Ezekiel saw the Glory depart the city in the vision of Ezekiel 8–11. In the course of that vision, he also saw "a certain man" go through the city and put a Passover-mark on the foreheads of the righteous so that they would be spared the judgment. Six other "men," the servants of the "certain man," then went through the city and killed all the rest. The "certain man" was clothed in linen, like the high priest on the Day of Coverings. Wearing a writing case at his side, he is like Ezekiel, a writing prophet. It seems clear that the "certain man" is Ezekiel himself (though symbolically also a foreshadowing of Jesus). This is all in Ezekiel 9.

Then in Ezekiel 10, the prophet has a second vision of the destruction of Jerusalem. This time, the "certain man" is commanded to take altar-fire from among the cherubim and scatter it over the city.

Finally, in Ezekiel 11, the prophet is shown a third parallel vision of the destruction of Jerusalem. He himself (not "a certain man") is told to prophesy against the wicked in the city, and as he does so, they fall and die.

These three pictures of the destruction of Jerusalem (via personal judgment, sacramental fire-judgment, and preaching) each require a man to approach the throne of God and then execute His judgments. Ezekiel 43:3 states that Ezekiel was that man ("I came to destroy the city"). It is without question that Ezekiel was the "son of man" who approached the throne and then passed judgment in the third vision, and because of this we are not likely to be wrong in saying that the "certain man" is also at least partially a picture of Ezekiel. Ezekiel's ministry, like that of Jesus, would have the effect of marking out the elect before the coming judgment, and then, like Jesus, Ezekiel would (though only in a vision) destroy the apostate city.

Following out the Exodus pattern, Ezekiel then predicts the restoration of the people to the land and ends with nine chapters of architectural description, parallel to Exodus 25–40.

Thus, it is no surprise at all that Jesus identifies Himself as the Greater Ezekiel by calling Himself the Son of Man. This is how alert Jews of Jesus' own day would have understood His self-designation.

Returning to Daniel 7, though, we can see that vision building upon Ezekiel's earlier visions. This statement corresponds exactly with Ezekiel's visions of judgment in Ezekiel 9–11:

> And behold, with the clouds of heaven
> One like a son of man was coming,
> And he came up to the Ancient of Days,
> And was presented before Him (Dan. 7:13).

Remember that Ezekiel came to the Ancient of Days as He was enthroned in the "cloud" of angels and cherubim and fire and smoke. Thus, the "one like a son of man" is "one like Ezekiel." Unlike Ezekiel, who only predicted the coming of the reign of the saints, this "one like a son of man" (the saints) will actually receive the kingdom.

It remains to be noted that one other prophet is called "son of man," and that is Daniel in Daniel 8:17. This statement is important because it elucidates some aspects of Daniel 7. Daniel is given a vision in the first part of Daniel 8, and then he seeks to understand it. Daniel says "standing before me was one with the appearance of a man. And I heard the voice of a man between the (banks of the) Ulai (canal), and he called out and said, 'Gabriel, give this one an understanding of the vision.' So he came near to where I was standing…, and he said to me, 'Son of man, understand that the vision pertains to the time of the end.'"

We see "one like a man" standing above waters, a new-creation image drawn from Genesis 1:2. He tells a spirit angel to speak to Daniel, and Daniel is called "son of man." The "one like a man" is the Ruler of Israel, the pre-incarnate Jesus Christ. Daniel is "son of man." What this implies is that Daniel is a member of the community of the saints of the Most High, the community that is "one like a son of man" in Daniel 7.

Calling Daniel "son of man" also implies that from this point on, at least, Daniel's life and work will be a foretaste of the life and work done by the Greater Son of Man. A few aspects of this should be noted before we move to Jesus Himself. On more than one occasion, Daniel undergoes a symbolic death and resurrection experience (Dan. 8:17, 27; 9:3, 20-21; 10:2-3, 8-10). Each time, after his "resurrection" Daniel is given a message concerning the future that is a message of "death and resurrection" for the people of God (the saints of the Most High, the "one like a son of man.") Thus, the exalted Daniel (son of man) proclaims the coming victory of the Kingdom through persecution, exactly as the exalted Son of Man does in the book of Revelation.

JESUS, THE SON OF MAN

When Jesus uses the phrase "Son of Man" to describe Himself, He thus means, first, that He is a true man; second, that He is the new man, the promised Messianic son of Adam; and third, that He is the Greater Ezekiel.

In Matthew 8:20, for instance, Jesus says that the foxes have holes and the birds have nests, but the Son of Man has no place to lay His head. This is not something that is true of humanity as a whole, but it is a good way to express the condition of exile. Ezekiel did have a house, but being in exile from the "hole," the "nest" of the land of promise, did not really have a place to lay his head. The Chebar settlement was not permanent. Like Ezekiel, Jesus was in exile and was taking upon Himself the exile that we sinners deserve.

In Matthew 9:6, the Son of Man has power on earth to forgive sins. Here again, this is what Ezekiel (the "certain man") did when he put the passover-mark on the foreheads of those who mourned for their sins and the sins of Jerusalem.

Matthew 11:19 has a different nuance. Here Jesus says that the Son of Man came eating and drinking, but was charged with being a drunkard and a glutton. This charge comes from Deuteronomy 21:20, where the stubborn and rebellious son is charged precisely with being a drunkard and a glutton and is put to death for it. Ezekiel is not in view here, but sonship certainly is, and so is the cross.

Jesus' statement in Matthew 12:8 that the Son of Man is lord of the sabbath does not obviously allude to Ezekiel. Rather, it means that Jesus is the New Adam, the Mature Adam, the Adam who has come into his own sabbath, the replica of God's, because He has finished His work. Just as God worked for six days and then sat down, enthroned, to rest on His sabbath, so Adam was to work for a time and then be elevated to rule. In Jesus this came to pass. Here in Matthew 12, Jesus is by anticipation already lord of the sabbath.

Other passages that use the phrase "Son of Man" as New Adam and that speak of the work of the New Adam without referring to Ezekiel, include Matthew 12:32, 40; 16:13ff.; 20:2. A note on Matthew 12:32 is worth making at this point, because the influential Geerhardus Vos badly misinterprets this saying. "And whoever shall speak a word against the son of man, it will be forgiven him; but whoever shall speak against the Holy Spirit, it will not be forgiven him, either in this age or in that to come." Vos points out that Jesus is closely tied to the Spirit, so that to speak against the Spirit is to speak against Jesus; therefore, the "son of man" must refer to human beings other than Jesus. Words spoken against ordinary people will be forgiven, but words spoken against the Spirit-filled Jesus will not be.[47]

What Vos misses is the redemptive-historical framework in which this saying must be fit. God gives a testimony of two witnesses: Jesus and the Spirit. The Spirit comes into the world at Pentecost, after Jesus has departed. The Jews, who rejected Jesus, will be forgiven, but if they reject the additional testimony of the Holy Spirit after Pentecost, they will not be forgiven.

This, by the way, is why Jerusalem was not destroyed right after Jesus' ascension and enthronement. The Jews were given a second chance, as it were, by being sent a second witness. When they rejected the second witness, the Holy Spirit working through the Apostolic Church, they were destroyed. Their rejection of the Spirit is seen in their persecution of the Church, which in the book of Revelation and in Matthew 25 is stated as the reason why they were destroyed. Thus, contrary to Vos, the term "Son of Man" in Matthew 12:32 definitely refers to Jesus.

The Parable of the Sower in Matthew 13 alludes to Ezekiel. Like Ezekiel and all the prophets, Jesus sows the seed of God's Word. Like Ezekiel specifically, He sends fire to destroy the wicked who do not receive it (Matt. 13:37-43).

I believe Ezekiel's story also forms a background to the statement in Matthew 17:9, where Jesus tells the disciples not to tell about the transfiguration until the Son of Man is risen from the dead. In Ezekiel 14:15-27, Ezekiel is told that Jerusalem is about to be destroyed. His wife

---

47. Geerhardus Vos, *The Self-Disclosure of Jesus*, 2nd ed. (Nutley, NJ: Presbyterian & Reformed, 1953), 50.

is slain. He is told to be dumb and to withdraw from the community of the exiles until the news of Jerusalem's destruction reaches the community. Then, in chapters 33 and following, he can proclaim the good news of a coming restoration from exile. Now, it should be obvious from the Gospels that Jesus identifies Himself as the true Temple and City, and that His death fulfills the destructions of the temple and city at one level. (Thus, the Church has always applied the Lamentations of Jeremiah to the crucifixion, for instance.) Like Ezekiel's wife, Jesus becomes the bride and dies. Like Ezekiel himself, Jesus is absent and silent for a time. Thus, I suggest that it is entirely appropriate for Jesus to refer to Himself as the "Son of Man" when speaking of His coming death (cf. also Matt. 17:12, 22).

Matthew 18:11, "For the Son of Man has come to save that which was lost," is a sentence that does not appear in all manuscripts. Taking it as authentic for the moment, we notice that immediately Jesus compares His work to that of a shepherd who leaves the ninety-nine sheep and looks for the one lost. By using the phrase "son of man," Jesus recalls Ezekiel 34, a long oracle about good and bad shepherds.

Mark 9:12 states that it is written of the Son of Man that he should suffer many things and be treated with contempt. Nowhere in the foundational Scriptures ("Old Testament") do we find such a statement. Rather, it is the Suffering Servant of Isaiah 53 of whom this is predicted. Why does Jesus' use "son of man" here and in Mark 9:31 and 10:33? There are two possible answers that I see. One is that Jesus is Himself for the first time linking the Son of Man to the Suffering Servant. The other is that there is such a link in the Scriptures and that Jesus alludes to it. We should explore this second possibility before deciding the question.

I suggest that Jeremiah is the "near fulfillment" of the prophecies Yahweh made through Isaiah about the Suffering Servant. A reading of the book of Jeremiah certainly shows that he was despised and rejected of men; indeed, that is his complaint for the first twenty chapters of his book, and it is shown in the events in the rest of the book, which include more than one "death" event (such as his being cast into a pit). The

"Weeping Prophet" is certainly a suffering servant! Now, Ezekiel is Jeremiah's near contemporary. Indeed, as I have shown elsewhere, he is Jeremiah's successor.[48] Thus, if Ezekiel is a "son of man," then so is Jeremiah.

In John 1:51, Jesus tells Nathanael that he will "see the heavens opened and the angels of God ascending and descending upon the Son of Man." There is an obvious allusion here to Jacob's ladder, and back to the Tower of Babel, that false ladder to heaven. Jesus is the True Ladder that connects heaven and earth. But by using the term "son of man," Jesus also alludes to the opening of heaven and the descent of angels upon Ezekiel in Ezekiel 1.

I shall break off this survey here. We have seen that very often when Jesus calls Himself the "Son of Man," the book of Ezekiel is in the background. We must now turn our attention to apparent citations of Daniel 7 in the Gospels and the rest of the New Testament.

THE COMING OF THE SON OF MAN

As we have seen, in its original statement Daniel 7 speaks of God's corporate people as coming to the Ancient of Days to receive the kingdom, and does so with the symbol of "one like a son of man." It is those who are faithful, like Ezekiel (and Daniel), who will receive the kingdom.

It is important to see that the "coming of the son of man" is not a coming to the earth but a coming to the heavens to receive the kingdom. The Greek word *erchomai*, translated "coming" in the English versions of the Gospels, is very general and can just as easily mean "going." It all depends on one's perspective. From the standpoint of those on the earth, the son of man is "going" to the Ancient of Days.

But beyond this, we need to understand that some passages speak of Jesus as "son of man" coming to Jerusalem to judge it and others speak

---

48. See James B. Jordan, *Countdown to Exile: The End of the Kingdom of Judah,* Biblical Horizons Occasional Paper 26 (Niceville, FL: Biblical Horizons, 1997).

of the Church as "son of man" ascending to heaven to receive the kingdom. As we saw, in Ezekiel 8–11, Ezekiel (the son of man) came in a vision to Jerusalem and destroyed it. This is how Jesus "comes" as Son of Man. But in Daniel 7, the saints (ones like a son of man) come to the Ancient of Days and join with Him in receiving the kingdom. Other passages, those that particularly cite Daniel 7, refer to this event.

Now let us look at the specific passages. As before, we shall begin with Matthew, which is the first Gospel.

In Matthew 10:23, Jesus tells the disciples that they will not finish preaching the kingdom in the cities of Israel before the Son of Man comes. Since the particular phasing of Daniel 7 is not used here, we can assume this refers to Jesus' coming as the Greater Ezekiel to inspect and then destroy Jerusalem. In context, it has nothing to do with the coming of Jesus back to the earth at the end of history (Acts 1:11).

In Matthew 16:27-28, Jesus says, "For the Son of Man is going to come in the glory of His Father with His angels, and will then recompense every man according to his doing. Truly I say to you, there are some of those who are standing here who will not taste death until they see the Son of Man coming in His kingdom." Several comments are needed on this saying.

First, "seeing" the Son of Man coming does not refer to physical sight, but to perception.

Second, the second part of this prediction obviously does not refer to the Final Coming of Jesus at the end of history, for it is a near event: Some disciples will still be alive.

Third, some have said that the Transfiguration, which follows immediately, is what is in view (Matt. 17:1-8). But there is no time for anyone to die between Jesus' prediction and the Transfiguration, which happened only six days later.

When we remember Ezekiel 8–11, we can understand what Jesus means here. Ezekiel was picked up by the Glory of God and taken to Jerusalem in a vision. There, with God's holy angels, Ezekiel destroyed the city. Matthew 16:27 alludes back to that event. Jesus will come in His Father's glory, with the angels, and will pass judgment on men. Since this judgment is but a foretaste of the Final Judgment at the end of history, we can certainly apply Jesus' words to that great event also. But since Jesus goes right on to say that some of those hearing Him will live to see the Son of Man coming in His kingdom, we should limit the primary meaning of His prophecy to the time of that generation.

But did any of the disciples live that long? Tradition says that John outlived the destruction of Jerusalem, but a careful reading of Revelation 10:9-11 with 11:3-12 indicates that John died before Jerusalem was destroyed. The harvest of the Apostolic Church, pictured as a harvest of bread and wine in Revelation 14, hints that all the disciples were martyred before vengeance was poured out on those who killed them.[49] Perhaps, then, Jesus was predicting that John, and some others, would "see" the Son of Man coming in His kingdom in the sense that John was given a vision of it in the book of Revelation. Or, perhaps a few of the disciples listening to Jesus did live past AD 70.

In Matthew 19:28, Jesus says, "Truly I say to you, that you who have followed Me, in the regeneration when the Son of Man will sit on the throne of His glory, you also shall sit upon twelve thrones, judging the twelve tribes of Israel." Here Ezekiel and Daniel come together. Jesus as Ezekiel Son of Man sits on the throne of His glory (as Ancient of Days), and the saints (the "one like a son of man") will also receive the kingdom. Here again, the book of Revelation fills out this statement. The martyrs under the altar, who expected to ascend to the twenty-four thrones when Jesus ascended, are told to wait until the AD 70 vindication. One by one the twenty-four archangels leave their thrones until heaven is empty of them. Then the saints ascend and sit on thrones, ruling with Jesus for the millennium (Rev. 6:9-11; 15:5-8; 20:4.) This statement is discussed more fully in chapter 16.B. below.

We shall skip the references to the son of man in Matthew 23–25 for now and take them up as they come. Matthew 24:27 is discussed in the next section of this chapter: "The Manifestation."

---

49. See my *The Vindication of Jesus Christ: A Brief Reader's Guide to Revelation* (Monroe, LA: Athanasius Press, 2009).

In Matthew 26:63, Jesus tells Caiaphas that from now on he will see (perceive) the Son of Man sitting at the right hand of the Mighty One, coming on the clouds of heaven. The false high priest will see the true high priestly people ascend to God. This is a direct allusion to Daniel 7, and "Son of Man" here is not Jesus but the saints.[50] Jesus is not saying that Caiaphas will see some particular event, but that he will know in his heart that this is true. For the rest of his life, he will know that Jesus is the Messiah and the Son of God. He will know that the kingdom of the saints, prophesied in Daniel, has arrived. For one fulfillment of this prophecy, see Acts 4:6ff., where Caiaphas perceives the power of that kingdom as it is already becoming manifest.

In Mark 8:38, Jesus says, "Whoever is ashamed of Me and of My words in this adulterous and sinful generation, the Son of Man will also be ashamed of him when He comes in the glory of His Father with the holy angels." This statement applies specifically to the then-present generation, which was going to be judged by angels as their last act as the wardens of the Old Creation. Once again, it is Ezekiel's coming with angels to judge Jerusalem that is in the background.

In Luke 18:8, Jesus asks, "When the Son of Man comes, will He find this faith on the earth [land]?" The faith spoken of is the kind of faith that perseveres, as the widow of verses 1-7 persevered in demanding

---

50. Editor's note: For a different perspective, R. T. France points out that "*Coming on the clouds of heaven* (together with the phrase 'the Son of man') is a clear allusion to Daniel 7:13, already similarly alluded to in 24:30.... We have seen that its natural application in terms of its Old Testament source is to the vindication and enthronement of the Son of man in heaven, not to a descent to earth. It is therefore in this verse a parallel expression to 'seated at the right hand of Power'; the two phrases refer to the same exalted state, not to two successive situations or events. In this verse the appropriateness of this interpretation is underlined by the fact that this is to be true 'from now on' (*hereafter* is a quite misleading rendering of the more specific phrase *ap' arti*, which, as in 23:39 and 26:29, denotes a new period beginning *from now*). Indeed it is something which Jesus' inquisitors themselves *will see* (an echo of Zc. 12:10, as in 24:30?), for it will quickly become apparent in the events of even the next few weeks (not to mention the subsequent growth of the church) that the 'blasphemer' they thought they had disposed of is in fact now in the position of supreme authority." *Matthew: Tyndale New Testament Commentaries* (Grand Rapids, MI: Eerdmans, 1985), 381.

justice. Although the fulfillment of this saying is popularly pushed off to the Final Coming, it has no such meaning. Again, it is the coming of Ezekiel to judge that is in view.

THE SON OF MAN IN REVELATION

With all this in mind, we can turn to the two references to Jesus as Son of Man in Revelation.

First, in Revelation 1 we have a sustained allusion to Daniel 7, beginning in verse 6. There we are told that the saints, the "one like a son of man," are "a kingdom, priests to His God and Father; to Him the glory and the dominion forever and ever." These phrases hint at Daniel 7, and the next sentence directly quotes from it: "'Behold, He is coming with the clouds,' and every eye shall see [perceive] Him…" This does not refer to the Final Coming or to a coming to destroy Jerusalem. Rather, it is a way of saying that He is enthroned in heaven. He is enthroned as Ancient of Days. Every eye will perceive it; that is, that the time for the public vindication of Jesus' ministry has come. The events He predicted concerning Jerusalem and the Oikumene will now take place, with the result that everyone will know that He is who He said He was.

Now that we have Daniel 7 in mind, we are not surprised that when Jesus actually appears, He appears as "one like a son of man" (Rev. 1:13). He walks among the church-lampstands and evaluates each in turn, thus passing the kinds of judgments He predicted in Matthew 25.

In Revelation 1 we find, for the first time I believe, a use of the "one like a son of man" of Daniel 7 to refer to Jesus Himself rather than to the saints. This usage is not odd, of course, because "one like Ezekiel" in Daniel 7 can easily include "Ezekiel" himself. Jesus is the Head of the "one like a son of man" community, and thus the language of Daniel 7 can be applied to Him, even if in its first meaning it did not refer to Him. The "one like a son of man" in Revelation 1:13 includes the saints, for Jesus holds the seven stars, who are the pastors and thus also the communities, in His right hand.

Moreover, since "coming with the clouds" in Revelation 1:7 seems to come from Daniel 7, it can include the saints as well, for the judgments that befall Babylon in Revelation come about not only because Jesus Himself was pierced, but also because His fledgling Church has been pierced in the Great Tribulation.

Also, Ezekiel is never absent from Revelation, and so he is here as well. Jesus' judgments on the seven churches correspond to Passover in the festival calendar of Revelation. In one way, Jesus is searching out the old leaven in the churches. In another way, He is, like Ezekiel, going through the churches and marking out the faithful in preparation for the tribulation to come. (Compare Rev. 7:3.)

There is only one other place in Revelation where Jesus is called "one like a son of man," and that is 14:14. The seven actions of this chapter are arranged chiastically, with the Son of Man at the center:

Angel of Yahweh (v. 6)

Spirit Angel (v. 8)

Spirit Angel (v. 9)

Son of Man (v. 14)

Spirit Angel (v. 15)

Spirit Angel (v. 17)

Angel of Yahweh (v. 18)

An interesting arrangement. As this is the judgment of the Old Creation, spirit angels are very much involved, and so is their Captain, the Angel of Yahweh (who is also Jesus). At the center, however, is the "One Like a Son of Man," the new ruler of the cosmos. On His cloud, He initiates the actual series of judgments, judgments that begin with the martyr-harvest of the wheat and grapes, the sacramental host. Spirit angels then judge Babylon and the Beasts, the apostate remnants of the Adamic Order. The Son of Man, however, harvests the Apostolic Church. The Great Tribulation and its martyrdoms are under His oversight all along, and the blood of the martyrs, spread over the land, calls forth the Avenger of Blood against Jerusalem.

Note that Jesus is sitting on the cloud to perform these acts. He is not pictured as returning to the earth to harvest the saints or to judge Jerusalem.

But notice also that the phrase "one like a son of man" rather than merely "son of man" has to include the saints as in Daniel 7. Jesus acts here in Revelation 14 as the Head and Representative of the whole community, and as their Harvester and then their Avenger. As Jesus reaps the wheat (14:16), He acts not apart from the saints, but in union with them. As He had been harvested, so now they are also.

A final fulfillment of Daniel 7 is found in Revelation 11:12, where the "two witnesses" (who correspond to the 144,000) are called up to heaven in the cloud. This is the ascension of the "one like a son of man" spoken of directly in Daniel 7, the ascension of the saints of the Most High to rule. The second picture of this event, or sequence of events, is given, as we have seen, in Revelation 14. In Revelation 15, we see the saints standing on the sea of glass before the throne of God.

B. THE MANIFESTATION

Following on what He has just said, Jesus tells the disciples that He has told them in advance (Matt 24:25). In other words, they know in advance that the words of the false prophets and messiahs will be false. Anyone who believes that Jesus has returned bodily and secretly is simply wrong, because that is not how He will return, and it is not how He will manifest His rule in the events He is predicting.

In the first place, He won't be manifesting Himself secretly to a few disciples, as He did after His resurrection. No, this time He will be manifest as openly and publicly as a lightning flash that brightens the entire firmament.

In the second place, He won't be manifesting Himself in His personal body. Rather, He will be manifesting His enthronement in the form of an inescapable display of power: the power of lightning falling from heaven. In case the disciples don't understand this and still think of some visible return of Jesus to the earth in the near future, He adds that the sign of His manifestation will be the gathering of vultures around the corpse of Jerusalem (v. 28).

(Acts 1:11 tells us that Jesus will return to the earth bodily at the end of history, and it won't be secretly either. But that event is not in view in our passage.)

A different word for "coming" (*parousia*) is used in Matthew 24:27, 37, and 39. This word means "presence" rather than "coming/going," and here means "manifestation." In verse 27, Jesus says that the manifestation of the Son of Man will be like the lightning's coming from the east and flashing to the west. The lightning "comes" from the east, but its effect is noted in the west. In other words, the source is the east, but there is a manifestation in the west. In the same way, Jesus remains on His throne in heaven (the "east"), but His rule is manifested in an earthly event (the "west"); to wit, the destruction of Jerusalem will be a dramatic and visible manifestation of the heavenly rule of the Son of Man.

Originating in the east but manifesting in the west with the destruction of Jerusalem is exactly what happened in Ezekiel 8–11. Ezekiel remained in the east, in Babylon; but his spirit moved to the west, to Jerusalem, and destroyed it. Thus, Jesus's analogy is precise, and alludes to the original son of man's destruction of Jerusalem.

In verses 37 and 39, that manifestation is said to be as sudden and unexpected as the coming of the Flood in the days of Noah. The fact that "manifestation" rather than "coming" is in view here is strengthened by the parallels in Luke 17. There the equivalent terms are the "day" or "days" of the Son of Man, and the "revelation" of the Son of Man (Luke 17:22, 24, 26, 30). "Day" means "light-time" in the Bible (Gen. 1:5). Thus, "day" correlates with "lightning flash."

We need to note that Jesus sets Himself directly against the false prophets and false Messiahs. All four claims begin the same way in Greek:

Behold, here is the Messiah (v. 23).
Behold, I have foretold you (v. 25).
Behold, in the wilderness he is (v. 26a).
Behold, in the inner chambers (v. 26b).

We have discussed the wilderness and inner chambers (temple) in chapter 5 of these studies. At this point, I only wish to make the point that the wilderness sets up verse 27, where Jesus manifests Himself like lightning, while the temple sets up verse 28, where eagles gather at the corpse.

C. LIGHTNING

For Jesus to associate His manifestation with lightning would call two matters to the minds of His Jewish hearers.

First, they would remember that when God's cloud of glory appeared, one of its manifestations was lightning (Exod. 19:16; Ps. 77:18; 97:4; Ezek. 1:13; Dan. 10:6; Matt. 28:3; Rev. 4:5). Lightning flashes are just a more particularized form of the light that streams from God's glory whenever it appears, for God's glory is the Day of the Lord, and wherever He is, it is perpetual day (Gen. 1:5; Rev. 22:5).

Second, they would remember that God's lightning is His heavenly sword and His heavenly arrows, with which He destroys the wicked (Deut. 32:41; 2 Sam. 22:15; Job 20:25; Ps. 144:6; Ezek. 21:10, 15, 28; Nah. 3:3; Hab. 3:11; Zech. 9:14).

Thus, for Jesus to liken His manifestation to lightning was to say that in the coming Day of the Lord, He would be sending forth His spear, His arrows, to destroy the wicked. That is why the next verse mentions a corpse.

D. FROM THE EAST

We have noted above the link to the manifestation of Ezekiel (the son of man) in the west, at Jerusalem, while he was still located in the east. But there are some further allusions here also.

The throne of God in the tabernacle and temple was positioned in the west, with the altar in the east. It would seem, then, that lightning should flash from God's throne down to the miniature holy mountain of the altar, from west to east.

By reversing the expected direction, Jesus associates Himself with another pregnant image from the Bible, that of the rising sun. Already in Malachi, Jesus had been called the "sun of righteousness who rises with healing in His wings" (Mal. 4:2). Earlier, in Psalm 19, the firmament was said to be a sanctuary for the sun, which travels from east to west through it, a picture of the priest ministering in the earthly sanctuary moving from altar to temple.

Additionally, that sun in Psalm 19 is said to be a bridegroom. The allusion is to Samson, whose name means "Sun," and who started out as a frustrated bridegroom, and whose whole life is encapsulated with three stories of his relationships with women. Samson himself was a fulfillment of Deborah's prayer that the righteous be like the sun's rising in their strength (Judg. 5:31), a prophecy already fulfilled once in the history of Gideon (Judg. 8:13, "ascent of Heres" means "rising of the sun"). Deborah's prayer, in turn, was based on the fact that the victorious Jacob crossed into God's land while the sun was coming up over the river (Gen. 32:31). The name of Deborah's associate, Barak, means "Lightning Bolt."[51]

In the book of Revelation, Jesus is pictured as the *Other Angel*, as the *Sunrise Angel*, in 7:2, and as such is the *Captain of the Host from the Sunrise* in 16:12.[52]

Thus, by saying that the lightning flashes from the sunrising to the west, Jesus is saying that His manifestation will be a Day of the Lord and a new dawn after a night of tribulation.

The sunrise imagery also correlates with the fact that the wilderness was east of the promised land. This is in line with what Jesus has said. Don't look for some secret visit by Jesus in the wilderness, because when Jesus' manifestation appears, in the wilderness to the east, so to speak, it will be clearly visible from within the promised land to the west.

Moreover, when Israel came out of Egypt and crossed the sea, travelling eastward, Yahweh came from the east and met them at Mount Sinai. He came from the east in cloud and lightning and thunder. Deborah calls attention to this in Judges 5:4-5, and she is alluding to part of the blessing of Moses: "Yahweh came from Sinai, and rose on them from Seir. He shone forth from Mount Paran [perhaps Bright Beauty], and He came from the myriads of His holy ones. At His right hand there was fire become law for them" (Deut. 33:2; my translation; cf. Hab. 3:3).

---

51. See my *Judges: God's War Against Humanism* (Eugene, OR: Wipf & Stock, 1999).

52. For more on this, see my "The Day of the Lord and Its 24 Hours," *Special Studies in the Book of Revelation*, Biblical Horizons Occasional Paper 40 (Niceville, FL: Biblical Horizons, 2011).

Thus, the idea of a bright light flashing in the wilderness is a sign of God's sunrise coming to rescue His people.

E. THE CORPSE

The Greek manuscripts vary as to whether verse 28 should begin with "for." If it should, then it stands in close parallel with verse 27. If not, then it still may be parallel in a broader sense. I take it that Jesus' statement about coming like lightning correlates in a general way with the false claim that He is in the wilderness, and that the statement about the corpse correlates in a general way with the false claim that He is in the temple.

Some translations render "carcass," which might imply dead animals; but the Greek clearly means "corpse," referring to human beings. The two phrases in verse 28 are exactly parallel:

wherever	will be	the corpse,
there	will be gathered	the eagles.

The statement is a virtual proverb, from Job 39:30, which, speaking of the eagle, says, "Where are the slain, there is he."

There are those who interpret verse 28 as a prediction of the eagle banners of the Romans surrounding Jerusalem, but while this might be an extra layer of meaning over the statement, it is not its basic meaning. Every Jewish hearer of Matthew would immediately remember that God had repeatedly pronounced judgment upon Israel in terms of eagles descending upon their corpses (Deut. 28:49; Jer. 4:13; Lam. 4:19; Hos. 8:1; Hab. 1:8). More than that, a basic part of the covenantal curse is to be devoured by birds of the air (Gen. 15:9-12; Deut. 28:26; Prov. 30:17; Jer. 7:33; 15:3; 16:3-4; 19:7; 34:18-20; Ezek. 39:17-20; Rev. 19:17-18). Specifically, the curse was to be hanged up after death on a tree or stake for the birds to eat (Deut. 21:23; 2 Sam. 21:9-10).

When God made the covenant with Abram, He caused the patriarch to divide a set of animals. These animals, made of soil, represented both Abram and the land, which were estranged from one another because of the death-curse of Adam's sin. God's living Shekinah Spirit passed between the dead parts, sealing them back together with His transfiguring fire, uniting Abram to the land in terms of the promise of the covenant (Gen. 15:7-21). Now, in this visionary ritual, the birds tried to devour the divided animal carcasses before God could reunite them, but Abram drove them away (15:11).

The meaning is that it is one thing to die, but another to die and be eaten by birds and wild animals. To die and not be eaten by the world is to have the prospect of being raised again, but if one is eaten by the world after death, then there will be no resurrection to newness of life, only a resurrection to eternal fire. For that reason, the person put to death and hanged up for all to see was not to be left to the wild animals, but to be buried. This rule was fulfilled when Jesus was taken down from the cross and buried, not left for the birds to eat.

The birds seeking to devour the divided animals before Yahweh could reunite and resurrect them represent a prophecy of the Egyptian attack upon Israel in the years preceding the exodus. In Genesis 15, God said that after four hundred years He would bring about this resurrection, this binding of Abraham's people with the land. The Egyptian birds tried to prevent this by keeping the people in Egypt. As Abram drove away the birds, so God drove away the Egyptians. With this in mind, that the birds can represent enemy nations, we can see that the suggestion of the Romans as devouring birds is not without basis.

Jesus' choice of "eagles" rather than the more general "birds" may be significant here. We ought not to think of Roman eagle insignia, but of the fact that the Oikumene empire set up by God is linked to the eagle in Ezekiel 17. The Romans, as Oikumene, would fulfill the prophecy, both in a literal way and in the deeper sense we have been exploring, as God's eagles to bring the curse of the covenant upon the corpse of the temple and Jerusalem.

Yahweh threatened in Deuteronomy 28:26 that if His people provoked Him too far, they would be slain and left for the birds, "and there will be no one to frighten them away." In other words, they would be abandoned by Abraham. They would not be taken to Abraham's Bosom in death, but would be carried by the birds to Torments in Hades (Luke 16:22-23).

In such a way did Jezebel die (1 Kgs. 21:23-24; 2 Kgs. 9:33-37). In Revelation, the harlot city that rules over the kings of the land is not only mystical Babylon but also spiritual Jezebel (Rev. 2:20). Thus, for the harlot city to become a corpse devoured by the birds is right in line with Biblical prophecy and the imagery of Revelation.

Now to the temple. God is Life, and His Spirit is the Spirit of Life. From His temple flow rivers of living water from the Laver and Sea of cleansing (Ezek. 47; Rev. 22). But if the temple becomes a corpse, then all it can produce is uncleanness, symbolic death. This is what God told the people through Haggai the prophet, in Haggai 2:10-19. Yahweh reminded the people that the holiness of sacrificial meat offered to Him did not pass holiness through the wings of the garments of the priests who carried it. On the other hand, if the people's hands were unclean, their defilement passed to the sacrificial meat and defiled it. Then Yahweh explained that the people were unclean (dead), and that their sacrificial offerings were dead, and for that reason the temple (which symbolized them) was a corpse in their midst. But since they had resolved to rebuild the temple, they had stopped being a corpse, the temple had come to life again, and their sacrifices were no longer unclean (dead) but once again holy and acceptable.

This passage stands in the immediate background of Jesus' proverb. The temple was a symbol of God's people gathered around Him, and Jerusalem, as "Holy City," was part of the wider temple complex. Because the people were dead in trespasses and sins, however, both they and their temple and city were corpses. God, the animating Spirit of Life, had abandoned the temple, and thus the temple had died and become a corpse. Now, zombie-like, the temple had a new resident, Wormwood (Satan; Rev. 9:10-11). From his death-dealing person flowed rivers of death-dealing waters (Rev. 12:15-16). Wormwood-Satan had brought Adam into the estate of death in the beginning, and now he was doing the same from his seat in the corpse of the temple.

Thus, Jerusalem and the temple are the corpse. The eagles were coming to devour it. Jesus, the Greater Abraham, would not drive them away; in fact, He had invited them (Rev. 18:2; 19:17-18).

161

F.   A SIGN AND A WONDER

With all this background information in mind, we can return to the context of Matthew 24. The false prophets and messiahs were going to claim that Jesus was in the wilderness. Not so, said Jesus, for when He manifested Himself it would be like lightning in the eastern wilderness, visible to all observers to the west. The false prophets and messiahs were also going to claim that Jesus was in the temple. Not so, said Jesus, for the temple is a corpse, and when He comes to the temple, He will come with an army of eagles to devour it. And this destruction of the temple and city would be a very public act, not a secret one.

The false prophets and messiahs offered false signs and wonders. Jesus offers a sign and a wonder. The sign is the lightning flash. The wonder is the birds devouring the corpse of Jerusalem. The destruction of God's city is spoken of as a wonder in the Hebrew Scriptures. Repeatedly it is said that the nations will look upon the desolation of the city and will suck in their breath ("hiss") in horror, and that the city will become a proverb and a curse ("May you become like Jerusalem!"). In short, the nations will observe and marvel and wonder at this great proof that Yahweh is God and that He means business. Here are just some of the passages that make this point: Leviticus 26:32; Deuteronomy 28:37, 45-46; 1 Kings 9:7-9; Jeremiah 19:8; 22:8-9; 25:18; 29:18; 42:18.

It is interesting to consider some of the deeper foundations that are implied in these few compact sentences. The movement from the wilderness and Sinai to Jerusalem and Zion is a movement that embraces the whole of Israel's national history, from alpha to omega as it were. Jesus promises to manifest His victory at both poles of the history.

Also, a movement from the wilderness westward into the land is a new conquest. Jerusalem becomes Jericho, a city completely destroyed because of its wickedness, the firstfruits of the conquest of the world. The early chapters in the book of Acts parallel the events in the first half of Joshua, and Jerusalem is definitely associated with Jericho in Acts. Jesus' lightning-fast arrival as the Greater Barak reduces Jerusalem-Jericho to a corpse for birds to feed on and dwell in.

13
THE GATHERING
(24:29-31)

²⁹And/but (*de*) immediately after the tribulation of those days the sun will be darkened,

and (*kai*) the moon will not give her light,

and (*kai*) the stars will fall from the heaven,

and (*kai*) the powers of the heavens will be shaken.

³⁰And (*kai*) at that time will appear the sign of the Son of Man in heaven;

and (*kai*) at that time will mourn all the tribes of the land,

and (*kai*) they will see the son of man coming (*erchomai*) on the clouds of the heaven with power and great glory.

³¹And (*kai*) He will send His messengers (angels) with a great trumpet sound,

and (*kai*) they will gather together His elect from the four winds,

from [one] ends of heavens to [other] ends of them.

In Matthew 23–24, this section on the gathering of the elect matches chiastically Jesus' wish in Matthew 23:37 that He might have gathered Jerusalem together as a hen gathers her chicks.

Structurally, this section begins with a temporal "and" followed by a series of explicative "ands." That is, all the events described here are part of one complex event that happens immediately after the Great Tribulation. The tribulation spoken of is that which came upon the saints, not the destruction of Jewry. It is the tribulation of "those days," spoken of earlier in verse 22, the tribulation that threatened the faith even of the elect. Now the elect are gathered.

Specifically, the structure is as follows:

A. Immediately after: heavenly removals (v. 29)
B. At that time: heavenly appearance (v. 30a)
C. At that time:
   1. earthly mourning (v. 30b)
   2. heavenly ascension (v. 30c)
D. He will send:
   1. heavenly messengers (v. 31a)
   2. heavenly removals (v. 31b):
      a. from four heavenly winds (v. 31c)
      b. from two heavenly extremities (v. 31d)

Although some Bibles have parts of these verses in quotation marks, nothing in these verses actually quotes from the Hebrew Scriptures. Rather Jesus, as the Author of those earlier Scriptures, states in a new way things that He has said before. Earlier Scriptures are alluded to but not quoted with any degree of precision.

A. ASTRAL IMAGERY

Anyone familiar with the Hebrew Scriptures would recognize immediately that what Jesus says about the sun, moon, and stars is not to be taken to refer to the physical cosmos but to the political cosmos. I suppose it is not surprising that many twentieth-century expositors either don't know this or choose to ignore it in favor of their own apocalyptic predilections. Before we consider what Jesus says, however, we should understand the language He uses.

The Bible speaks of the purpose of the heavenly lights in Genesis 1:

Then God said, "Let there be lights in the firmament of the heavens to separate the day from the night, and let them be for signs, and for seasons [festival times], and for days and years; and let them be for lights in the firmament of the heavens to give light on the earth"; and it was so.

And God made the two great lights; the greater light to govern the day, and the lesser light to govern the night; He made the stars also. And God placed them in the firmament of the heavens to give light on the earth, and

164

to govern the day and the night, and to separate the light from the darkness; and God saw that it was good. (Gen. 1:14-18)

The first thing said about the astral bodies is that they are lights. Light is an aspect of God's glory cloud, and it is as a reflection of God's glory that these heavenly bodies are made as lights. They represent glory, and so the Bible can say of the glorified saints that "the righteous will shine forth like the sun in the kingdom of their Father" (Matt. 13:43). Similarly, Solomon wrote, "Who is this that grows like the dawn, as beautiful as the full moon, as pure as the sun?" (Song 6:10). Or as Paul wrote, "There is one glory of the sun, and another glory of the moon, and another glory of the stars; for star differs from star in glory" (1 Cor. 15:41).

As lights, the astral bodies are glorious. But, second, they were given for signs, or symbols. All created things point back to God, but all things also relate to other creatures, and in this case, the astral bodies symbolize rulers and governors. The lights are positioned in the firmament, which is called heaven (Gen. 1:8). Heaven rules the earth. Thus, those things positioned in the firmament symbolize rulers of the earth.

Third, they are said to be for seasons, or more literally for festival times. This applied to the Old Creation, which was regulated by these creational clocks. It was particularly the moon, regulator of months, that governed the Israelite calendar. The moon established which day was the first of the month and which was the fifteenth. Such festivals as Passover, Pentecost, and Booths were set on particular days of the month (Lev. 23:5-6; 34; Num. 28:11-14; 2 Chr. 8:13; Ps. 81:3). The moon, of course, governs the night (Ps. 136:9; Jer. 31:35), and in a sense the entire Old Creation took place at night. With the rising of the Sun of Righteousness (Mal. 4:2), the "day" of the Lord is at hand (Mal. 4:1), and in a sense the New Creation takes place in the daytime.[53] As Genesis 1 says over and over: first evening and then morning. In the New Creation we are no longer under lunar regulation for festival times (Col. 2:16-17).

---

53. See Judges 5:31; 1 Thessalonians 5:1-11; Genesis 15:12; 32:33-30; Exodus 12:29; 2 Samuel 23:4; Isaiah 60:1-3; Zechariah 1-6; Mal. 4:1-2; Luke 1:78; John 3:2. If you have time, it would be good to consider these passages in order.

In that regard, Christ is our light (Matt. 24:29-30; Rev. 21:23-25; 22:5).

Fourth, they are said to be clocks, for days and years. Long before our mechanical clocks and watches were invented, people told time by the position of the sun, the occurrence of solar equinoxes and solstices, and the precession of the equinoxes. Particularly mentioned are days and years, which are regulated not by the moon but by the sun.

Fifth, they are said to rule over day and night, to govern time. Here again the emphasis is on rule. The astral bodies signified those who are glorified and exalted. While this is true of all the saints, it is also true of all human rulers as well. Revelation 1:20 says that the rulers of the church are like stars, and Jude 13 says that apostate teachers are "wandering stars." Long before this, in Genesis 37:9-10, Joseph had seen the rulers of his clan as sun, moon, and stars. We see this even today. The flag of the United States of America has fifty stars, for the fifty states of that nation. The flags of oriental nations include the rising sun. The flags of near eastern countries feature a crescent moon. Sun, moon, and stars are symbols of world powers.

Sixth, they are associated with the heavenly host, the angelic and human array around the throne of God. This also follows from the fact that they are positioned in heaven. They represent the angelic host in Judges 5:21, Job 38:7, and Isaiah 14:13. They represent the human host of the Lord as well, as we see from the promise to Abraham in Genesis 15:5, reiterated in Genesis 22:17, 26:4, and Deuteronomy 1:10. Christians "appear as luminaries in the world in the midst of a crooked and perverse generation" (Phil. 2:15). The fact that Abraham's descendants were to be like stars implies not only that they would be positioned in the heavenlies (Eph. 2:6), but also that they would be rulers over the Gentiles.

Now, it is neither possible nor desirable to separate these aspects of astral symbolism. The sun, moon, and stars mark time as clocks. Since they mark time, they govern time. Positioned in the heavenlies, they signify governments, ruling day and night. Since they mark time, they can be seen to signify the duration of earthly governments, so that, as we shall see, the fall of sun, moon, and stars is a symbol for the fall of earthly governments.

1. THE SUN

The sun, ruler of the sky and of the day, is used to symbolize the Lord in Psalm 84:11, "Yahweh God is a sun and shield." Similarly, a familiar passage in Isaiah says, "Arise, shine, for your light has come, and the glory of Yahweh has risen upon you. For behold, darkness will cover the earth, and deep darkness the peoples; but Yahweh will rise upon you, and His glory will appear upon you. And nations will come to your light, and kings to the brightness of your rising" (Isa. 60:1-3).

God is like the sun, and when He comes, He glorifies His people so that they also shine. So Deborah could pray, "Let those who love God be like the rising of the sun in its might" (Judg. 5:31), a prayer answered a few years later in Gideon (Judg. 8:13, *heres* is a word for sun), and then again in Samson, whose name means "Sun." Psalm 19 reflects on this: The sun is like a bridegroom, like a strong man. The reference here, first of all, is to Samson, the bridegroom of Judges 14–15. But beyond this we see the Messianic Judge of all the earth, who is to come and bring His Word (vv. 7-11). When John saw that One, "His face was like the sun shining in its strength" (Rev. 1:16).

Night gives way to day, and this is an image of the coming of the Kingdom. If Nicodemus met with Jesus by night, this was in part a reflection of the condition of history at that point, for the whole Old Creation is seen as nighttime. Malachi 4:1 says that a "day is coming," and goes on in verse 2 to predict that "the Sun of Righteousness will rise with healing in its wings." In this way, moon and sun are governors of time, of the Old Creation and New Creation respectively, but they also symbolize the First and Last Adams, who are the real governors of these two eras.

Finally, we should note that in the Bible the sun can also symbolize counterfeit gods, those who falsely pretend to be the true Sun of Righteousness. The Pharaoh of Egypt claimed to be an incarnation of the sun, and thus it was appropriate that in the judgment of Egypt, God put out the sun for three days (Exod. 10:21-23).

2. Starfall

The prophets often see the "sun, moon, and stars" falling to the earth. One of the most frequently encountered mistakes in the interpretation of Biblical prophecy today is the notion that this always refers to the end of the world at the second coming of Jesus Christ. Actually, though, this expression always refers to the collapse of some particular nation.

Suppose we wrote a prophetic poem about the destruction of America, and included in the poem these lines:

> The sun was darkened, the moon eclipsed;
> The stars fell, they fell to the ground;
> Fifty in ranks, trampled under foot;
> Her rulers imprisoned, caged in darkness.

Let's analyze this section of our "poem." It has an ABBA structure. The first line, about the darkening of sun and moon, is explained by the last line about the imprisonment of our rulers. The second and third lines clearly refer to the defeat of the fifty states. This would be obvious to us, would it not? Anyone who has had a high school class in literature could figure it out.

With this in mind, let us briefly survey the Biblical passages that use sun, moon, and stars as symbols of rulers and times.

3. Israel

In Genesis 15, when God cut the covenant with Abraham, He took him outside and told him to "tell" the stars, "if you are able to tell them; thus shall your seed be" (v. 5). Bible exegetes differ on exactly what Abraham was being asked to do. Generally it is assumed that he was being asked to count up the number of the stars and that his descendants would be like the stars of the heavens for multitude, even as they would be like the sand of the sea. Some have pointed out, however, that the Hebrew verb translated "count" can also be translated "tell" in the sense of evaluating (Hebrew *saphar*, as in Ps. 56:8). This is not clearly the case, however, since the verb often just means "count up."

All the same, two alternative interpretations have been suggested. The first is that of M. Barnouin. Barnouin points out that the patriarchs in Genesis 5 and 11 lived lives of curious numerical lengths. Enoch, for instance, lived 365 years, the length of a solar year, making him the original Sun of Righteousness (Mal. 4:2).[54] Kenan lived 910 years, ten times a standard quarter year of 91 days. Lamech lived 777 years, which is the total of the synodical periods of Jupiter (399 days) and Saturn (378 days) (Gen. 5:23, 14, 31). Is it possible that God was saying to Abraham that his seed would be like the great patriarchs of old, the faithful Godly men who were blessed and preserved before the Flood, and in the years after the Flood?[55]

Barnouin suggests that when Abraham looked at the stars, he was considering the planets and how they govern time (Gen. 1:14), and making an evaluation based on this. The years of the patriarchs corresponded to the time-governing periods of the planets and other heavenly bodies. Abraham's seed would be like this. They would be a heavenly people, gathered around God's heavenly throne. Their history would mark time.

Barnouin sees this fulfilled in the censuses of the book of Numbers, in which these same astral periods recur. In Numbers 1, all the men aged twenty and up are enrolled in the Israelite militia, God's army. As God's army, Israel was in one sense a "heavenly host," captained by the Lord of heaven. In this respect, they are spoken of as stars in Deuteronomy 1:10, and as a heavenly host they are commanded by an angel, the Angel of the Lord (Josh. 5:13–6:2; Exod. 23:20-21). Thus, it would not be surprising if the numbering of that heavenly host had some association with astral numbers. At any rate, Barnouin's thesis is a complex one, but certainly also a challenging one.[56]

---

54. Thanks to my student Yevgeni Kruzhkov of Karaganda, Kazakhstan, for calling my attention to this connection.

55. For a full analysis of Genesis 5, see my monograph, *A Chronological and Calendrical Commentary on the Pentateuch*, Studies in Biblical Chronology 3 (Niceville, FL: Biblical Horizons, 2001).

56. M. Barnouin, "Remarques sur les tableaux numériques du libre des Nombres,"

The second alternative view of Genesis 15:5 relates to the constellations of the zodiac. When Joseph saw twelve stars bowing down before him, could this have been the constellations of the ecliptic, and not individual stars?[57]

To conclude our look at Abraham, let me point out that when God made the covenant with Abraham in Genesis 15, He did so by burying the sun and making it "very dark" (Gen. 15:17). This implies to me that if the "seed" is to be like the stars of heaven and dust of earth, it will have to be a new heavens and a new earth.

B. COSMIC COLLAPSE

Let us now briefly survey the passages where sun, moon, and stars are used in a prophetic-symbolic sense. A failure to understand the symbolic nature of these passages has led many popular writers (and, surprisingly, not a few scholarly ones) to assume that such expressions as "the sun turned to sackcloth and the moon to blood" can only be understood as referring to the collapse of the physical cosmos. Nobody takes these verses literally, of course, so the question is: What kind of event does this symbolic language refer to? For modern man, it seems that it can only be speaking of the end of the natural world. For ancient man, it was indeed the end of the "world" that such language indicated, but not the "world" in our modern scientific sense. Rather, it was the end of the "world" in a socio-political sense.

Revue Biblique 76 (1969):351-364; Barnouin, "Recherches numériques sur la généalogie de Gen. V," *Revue Biblique* 77 (1970):347-365; Barnouin, "Les Recensements du Livre des nombres et l'Astronomie Babylonienne," *Vetus Testamentum* 27 (1977), 280-303; English translation, "The Censuses of the Book of Numbers and Babylonian Astronomy"; cf. also Gordon Wenham, *Numbers: An Introduction and Commentary* (Downers Grove, IL: InterVarsity Press, 1981), 64-66; and Wenham, *Genesis 1–15* (Waco, TX: Word Books, 1987), 133-134.

57. I regard this as very likely. For a discussion of the zodiac in the Bible, I must refer the reader to my book, *Through New Eyes*, 59-62, and to my monograph, *Behind the Scenes: Orientation in the Book of Revelation*, Biblical Horizons Occasional Paper 19 (Niceville, FL: Biblical Horizons, 1999).

For instance, Isaiah 13:9-10 says that "the day of Yahweh is coming," and when it comes, "the stars of heaven and their constellations will not flash forth their light; the sun will be dark when it rises, and the moon will not shed its light." It goes on to say in verse 13, "I shall make the heavens tremble, and the earth will be shaken from its place at the fury of Yahweh of hosts in the day of His burning anger."

Well, this certainly does sound like the end of the world! *But*, if we read these verses in context, we have to change our initial impression. Verse 1 says, "The oracle concerning Babylon which Isaiah the son of Amoz saw," and if we read on, we find nothing to indicate any change in subject. It is the end of Babylon, not the end of the world, that is spoken of. In fact, in verse 17, God says that He will "stir up the Medes against them," so that the entire chapter is clearly concerned only with Babylon's destruction.

If we read Biblically, this won't seem so strange. What verse 10 is saying is that Babylon's lights are going to go out. Their clocks are going to stop. Their day is over, and it is the Day of Doom for them. Their time has run out, and the cosmic clocks are going to be turned off as far as they are concerned. And, since these astral bodies symbolize governors and rulers, their rulers are going to have their lights put out as well. All of this imagery arises directly from what is said about the astral lights in Genesis 1:14-16.

The "heavens and earth" in verse 13 refer to the socio-political organization of Babylon. The "heavens" are the aristocracy, roughly speaking, and the "earth" is the commoners.

We find the same kind of thing in Ezekiel 32. In verses 7-8 God declares, "And when I extinguish you, I shall cover the heavens, and darken their stars; I shall cover the sun with a cloud, and the moon will not give its light. All the shining lights in the heavens I shall darken over you and shall set darkness on your land." The end of the world? Yes indeed, but not for everybody. If you don't remember this passage, don't look it right up, but think about it. What ancient people might God be speaking of in using this language? The idea in the Babylon oracle was that the astral bodies would not shine forth any light. Here the idea is that they will be covered over. God's glory cloud will interpose itself between this nation and the heavenly lights. While God's glory cloud shines brightly for His people Israel, it is dark and foreboding to His enemies, with the result that they are in darkness when He appears to them.

These people experienced this once before. Their whole land was darkened, and when they pursued the Israelites, God's cloud came between them and Israel and put them in darkness (Ezek. 32:2; cf. Exod. 10:21-23; 14:19-20).

Similar language is used prophetically concerning Israel, but with a twist. It is in the prophecy of Joel that we find this most clearly set out. Joel begins by reminding Israel of a recent plague of locusts. In his first chapter, he describes the horrors of the locust invasion. Then, in chapter 2, he threatens the people with another locust plague, this time an invasion by human locusts. Such an invasion will be a manifestation of "the day of Yahweh," that is, the day of judgment (2:1).

The expression "day" of Yahweh refers to the rising of the sun—the sun of God's searching light that shows up sin and brings judgment, the sun of God's blazing heat that destroys sin. Yet for Israel, this "day" will be a "day of darkness and gloom, a day of clouds and thick darkness" (2:2). The metaphor is mixed, but apropos: When God brings His day and evaluates their sin, He will cast them into *darkness*.

Accordingly, when God's locust army comes to judge Israel, "before them the earth quakes, the heavens tremble, the sun and the moon grow dark, and the stars lose their brightness" (2:10). This is a reference to the collapse of Israel as a body politic. After all, Abraham had been told that his seed would be like the stars of the heavens. It is possible that the quaking of the earth refers to the Israelite citizenry, the trembling of the heavens to the Levites and priests (since the temple was a symbol of heaven), and the darkening of the astral bodies to the royal court and other rulers in Israel.

If the people repent, however, God will return to them and restore them (2:12ff.). God promises them a great future. He promises them the coming of the Holy Spirit. "And it will come about after this that I will pour out My Spirit on all mankind, and your sons and daughters will prophesy [fulfilling Num. 11:19], your old men will dream dreams, your young men will see visions. And even on the male and female servants I will pour out My Spirit in those days" (2:28-29). We know from Acts 2:16-18 that this was fulfilled at Pentecost.

"And I will display wonders in the sky and on the earth" (Joel 2:30) This is connected with Pentecost and was therefore a warning to the Jews of Peter's day. Wonders in the sky and on the earth is what is foretold. In reverse order, first we read of the earth: "Blood, fire, and columns of smoke." These are the phenomena of war. There will be war. There will be yet another invasion. This was fulfilled when the Romans invaded Palestine and destroyed Jerusalem, AD 66-70.

Wonders in the sky are also foretold: "The sun will be turned into darkness, and the moon into blood, before the great and awesome day of Yahweh comes" (2:31). What is of interest here is the expression "moon into blood." In a solar eclipse the sun turns black, and in a lunar eclipse the moon turns red. Thus, not merely a general darkening but an *eclipse* of powers is spoken of here. But more than that, the turning of the moon to "blood" points, I believe, to something particularly Jewish: the sacrificial system. If they will not accept the blood of Jesus Christ, the final Sacrifice, then they themselves will be turned into blood. They will become the sacrifices. That is what the prophesied war is all about. That is what the destruction of Jerusalem in AD 70 was all about.

But Joel is issuing a warning. Those who listen can escape. "And it will come about that whoever calls on the name of Yahweh will be delivered; for 'on Mount Zion and in Jerusalem there will be those who escape,' as Yahweh has said, even among the survivors whom Yahweh calls" (2:32). Just as Isaac escaped death on Mount Zion because of the substitute ram that God provided (Gen. 22:14), so those who trust in the Lamb of God will escape the destruction of Jerusalem in AD 70. Such is Joel's warning, reiterated by Peter on the day of Pentecost.

And also reiterated by John. Prophesying this same event, the destruction of Jerusalem, John writes, "And I looked when He broke the sixth seal, and there was a great earthquake; and the sun became black as sackcloth made of hair, and the whole moon became like blood; and the stars of the sky fell to the earth, as a fig tree casts its unripe figs when shaken by a great wind" (Rev. 6:12-13). The fig tree is a standard symbol for Israel, especially in this context (Matt. 21:19; 24:32-34; Luke 21:29-32). Both sackcloth and blood remind us of the Levitical system, the blood for sacrifices, and the sackcloth for the mourning associated with affliction ("leprosy") and uncleanness.

In this way, the astral symbols are given peculiar coloring depending on context. The Babylonians worshiped the stars, and so they are extinguished. The Egyptians worshiped the sun, so God darkens it. The Jews continued to maintain the sacrifices, so the moon is turned to blood.

To round out this discussion, we need look at only one more passage. After promising the coming of the Spirit and the judgment upon apostate Israel in Joel 2, God goes on to say in chapter 3 that He will shake down all the nations of the world and bring them to their knees. Speaking of the nations, He says that "the sun and moon grow dark, and the stars lose their brightness" (Joel 3:15).

In conclusion, the symbolism of universal collapse—the extinction of sun, moon, and stars—has reference to the fall of nations and empires. In the Hebrew Scriptures it was used for Babylon, for Egypt, for Israel, and for the nations in general. At the destruction of Jerusalem, the Jewish sun went into black eclipse, mourning in sackcloth, and the Jewish moon went into red eclipse, the blood-red of sacrifice.

C. NEW HEAVENS

We now turn to Matthew 24:29. In the past I have assumed that the Tribulation was the destruction of Jerusalem and have interpreted the shakedown of the heavens as a reference to the evangelization of the world following that event. I now see that this is no longer an interpretive possibility.

The "official" overlap of the Old and New Creations lasted from AD 30–70. This is the overlap of the focused Abrahamic Covenant and the New Covenant. The overlap of the larger Noahic Covenant and the New

Covenant takes place whenever the gospel comes to a new, as-yet-unevangelized location. The overlap of the Adamic world of sin and death with the New Creation continues until the Last Judgment.

The book of Revelation concerns the end of the Abrahamic Covenant in its final focused manifestation: the Oikumenical Covenant. In that Covenant, the Jews were positioned as world evangelists within a larger Gentile Oikumene that was to act as a Guardian Beast of God's people: first Babylon, then Persia, then four successive Hellenistic empires (the last being Republican Rome), and finally Imperial Rome. The sun, moon, and stars of that Oikumenical Covenant were the Jewish and Gentile rulers, signified in Revelation as the Land and Sea Beasts respectively.

According to Revelation 16–19, the fall of Jerusalem was simultaneously the elimination of the Sea Beast of Imperial Rome. Rome continued to exist, of course, but not as God-appointed guardian of the Abrahamic Covenant. Not coincidentally, the Julio-Claudian line of emperors, which had governed the Roman empire since its beginning, came to an end in the late 60s and, after a short time of chaos, was succeeded by a new line. During the same period, old Rome burned to the ground and a new Rome had to be built.

While prophecy in general, and the book of Revelation in particular, are concerned primarily (focally) with Israel, the nations around Israel are always included, and especially in this last period, the Beast Empires are included. For this reason, I am not satisfied to identify the sun, moon, and stars of Matthew 24:29 with the Jews only. Also, the judgment scene at the end of Matthew 25 includes all the nations, and while this judgment points to the Last Judgment, it has a first fulfillment in conjunction with the end of the Old Creation events around AD 70. Nonetheless, Israel is central since Israel was Eden and the center of the Old World, and judgments on Israel were judgments on the entire Old World.

Little noticed but all-important for the passage before us is a prophecy given by Yahweh to Jeremiah:

Thus says Yahweh,
Who gives the sun for light by day,
And the statutes of the moon and the stars for light by night,
Who stirs up the sea so that its waves roar;
Yahweh of Armies is His name:
"If these statutes depart from before Me," declares Yahweh,
"Then the offspring of Israel also will cease from being a nation
before Me forever." (Jer. 31:35-36)

In other words, the removal of the sun, moon, and stars is a signal that the covenant with Israel has come to an end, its role fulfilled. As the heavenly lights are replaced by the shining of Jesus, so Israel is replaced by the larger Church of the New Creation.

An objection to this interpretation can be raised by pointing out that in the context of Jeremiah 31:35-36, it is the New Covenant that is being spoken of (Jer. 31:31-34). At this point, a general failure of Biblical theologians to understand the course of Biblical history has misled interpreters. To be sure, the book of Hebrews and other New Testament passages speak of the New Covenant as that which Jesus brought. But Jesus' New Covenant, which is the "New Covenant" we generally think of, is a _fulfillment of an earlier "new covenant,"_ which was the Oikumenical Covenant. It is quite clear from the context of Jeremiah 31 that Yahweh is speaking of a new covenant to be made with the people when they return from exile, a covenant we see in the latter part of Ezekiel and in the book of Zechariah. This is the first form of the New Covenant, a new covenant made with the house of Israel and the house of Judah (Jer. 31:31; Ezek. 37; Zech. 1-14). Note in this regard the parallel between "Behold, days are coming" in Jeremiah 31:27, 31, and 38. Clearly these are linked, the first speaking of the return from exile, the second of the new covenant, and the third of rebuilding Jerusalem after the exile. Now of course, as with many prophecies, the prophecy of the new covenant points beyond its immediate fulfillment to a larger fulfillment in the future, a Messianic fulfillment. This, however, must not blind us to the first fulfillment and the immediate import of the prophecy.

Thus, Yahweh made a new covenant with His people after the exile, and that covenant was to last as long as the sun and moon and stars stood in their fixed patterns. When Jesus says that the sun, moon, and stars will disappear right after the Great Tribulation, He is saying that this preliminary new covenant has been succeeded by the permanent New Covenant.

Jesus' oracle consists of two pairs of statements. The first pair concerns the sun and the moon, the heavenly father and mother. They will become dark. Their light will no longer be a religious guide to God's people. Festivals will no longer be determined by them. Rather, Jesus' light, His "great glory" (v. 30) will be the religious light of the New Creation people.

To expand just a bit: The times of the daily evening and morning sacrifices were determined by the sun. The times of the annual feasts were determined by the sun and moon together: the sun marking the vernal equinox, and the first new moon thereafter being the first month of the lunar year. The feasts of Unleavened Bread and of Booths began on the fifteenth days of the first and seventh months respectively—in other words, during the full moon, when the moon gives forth her light. Since Jesus calls attention particularly to the moon as a light-giver, I think it is pretty safe to say that it is the moon in her liturgical dimension, not in her physical dimension, that is in view.

So then, the sun and moon will be darkened with respect to their function of determining religious events. Beyond that, as symbols of social leaders, the suns and moons of society will be darkened. In both cases, Jesus and His bride are the replacement Glory Lights. He is the new Sun King, and it is He who determines times of worship (by being available whenever two or three are gathered in His name).

The second pair of statements links the stars of the heaven with the powers of the heavens. They will "fall" or "be shaken." I believe that the book of Revelation informs us of what this means when it shows us the angels vacating their thrones around God (Rev. 4:10), which thrones are then occupied by the saints in Revelation 20. Stars can be symbols of spirit-angels in the Bible (as in Job 38:7), and that is what they seem to symbolize here. The original heavenly court of angels, in place during humanity's childhood, is to be replaced by a court of saints when the

Old Creation is finally removed in AD 70. The first human being to move into a seat of heavenly power will be the Son of Man, as the next phrase in the prophecy tells us. The gathering of the elect from the four winds of heaven in verse 31 speaks of the saints replacing the angels in heaven as the new stars.

D. THE ENTHRONEMENT OF THE SON OF MAN

Verse 30 is mistranslated in some Bibles and misinterpreted by many. It does *not* say, "And at that time the sign of the Son of Man will appear in heaven (in the sky)," as if some sign were supposed to appear in the upper atmosphere. Rather—and the original Greek is quite clear—what will appear will be a sign that shows that the Son of Man is in heaven.

The sign is the destruction of Jerusalem in AD 70, which comes right after the Great Affliction of the saints. This is the sign that Jesus repeatedly said would be His public vindication, the visible proof that He is who He said He is. It is the same as the sign of Jonah, the *only* sign that was to be given to the wayward and perverse generation.

The final destruction of the Old Creation is the public vindication of Jesus Christ. Repeatedly throughout His career, Jesus warned that destruction was going to come soon on the apostate Jews and on the whole old world. Occasionally He also predicted His own resurrection, but not nearly as often. Jesus' resurrection was a more private vindication of who He was and what He did, but few saw it take place, and Jesus appeared to only a few disciples. The destruction of the enemy city, Jerusalem, was His public vindication. Fulfilling Jesus' prophecies, it confirmed Him as a true Prophet, and as the last and greatest Prophet, for virtually all the prophets had predicted the coming destruction of one city or another. It was the proof that He had indeed ascended to heaven and become King of kings and Lord of lords.

Thus, the destruction of the Old Creation is of incalculable importance to Biblical theology. It was not some mere mopping up operation but was the great public historical vindication of Jesus by the Father. Those who fail to see this fact generally discount the importance of the destruction of Jerusalem, and thus fail to see why it occupies so much attention in the Gospels and also fail to see that it is the major concern of the book of Revelation. We might just as well call Revelation "The Vindication of Jesus Christ."[58]

The mourning of all the tribes of the land, which is a consequence of this vindication of Jesus, is often linked to Zechariah 12, though it is not a quotation of any specific phrase in that prophecy. That passage predicts a conversion in the hearts of the people, so that each mourns over his or her sin and what it has cost the Son of God. I do not think that Zechariah 12 is the background to Matthew 24:30b, however. Rather, if we look at Revelation 18, we find a whole series of mourners who weep with frustration and regret over the destruction of Jerusalem. They do not mourn the death of Jesus, but the death of the Whore. They mourn not because they have been converted but because they have been defeated.

Now we must consider the coming of the Son of Man on the clouds of heaven and what this phrase means in this context. The phrase comes from Daniel 7 and must refer to the coming of the saints to Jesus (the Ancient of Days) to receive the kingdom.

The reference is to the enthronement of the saints as seen in Revelation 15–20. Part of the drama of Revelation is this: Initially the saints are under the altar in chapter 6. They are waiting to go into the throne-heavens and are surprised that they did not get to go in with Jesus Himself. They are told to wait a little while. Then 144,000 earthly saints are sealed, bear witness, and are martyred (chs. 7–14). Following this, right after the martyrdom of the Great Tribulation, the saints move up into the heavenly area and stand upon the sea of glass in Revelation 15. At this point, however, the glory of God fills His palace. All the angels have vacated their thrones, but no one has yet entered to replace them. What follows is the destruction of Jerusalem (Rev. 16–17), the mourning of the tribes (Rev. 18), and the enthronement of the saints in heaven (Rev. 20).

The coming of the saints to the throne of the Ancient of Days to receive a kingdom in Daniel 7 corresponds to the ascension of the saints to the sea before God's throne in Revelation 15. The destruction of

---

58. See my *The Vindication of Jesus Christ.*

Jerusalem, which follows right away, is a sign to those on the earth, a sign not only to vindicate Jesus Himself, but also to vindicate His martyred Bride: the two witnesses and 144,000 of Revelation 11 and 14. Those on the earth mourn not only because they perceive the vindication of Jesus, but also because they realize that their massacre of the believers has failed.

Thus, the sign of the Son of Man in heaven in verse 30a refers to the enthronement of Jesus Christ, which is signified in the destruction of Jerusalem. As the passage reads, this Son of Man is already in heaven. Thus, the "son of man" who comes on the clouds in fulfillment of Daniel 7 is just what Daniel 7 predicts: the saints of the Most High receiving the kingdom.

Further confirmation of this interpretation is to be found, I believe, in the phrases that follow in verse 31. There we see messengers gathering the elect not from their graves (which is how the Last Judgment scenes read), nor from all over the earth (which is how an evangelistic passage would read), but from all over the heavens. They are gathered from the four winds, not from the four corners of the earth. They are gathered from the ends of heaven, not from the ends of the earth (cf. Deut. 4:32; Psa. 19:6; Jer. 49:36).

This language might be taken as a general reference to the whole earthly world, except for the fact that it fits so very well with what we find, again, in Revelation. The dead saints "under the altar" are in "paradise" or "Abraham's bosom," a location symbolically equivalent to the firmament heavens that are right below the throne-heavens (Rev. 6:9-11). It is these elect, and their newly-massacred brethren who come out of the Great Tribulation, who are gathered before the Throne in Revelation 15.

Now, to be sure, the four winds are the Jewish saints who minister during the Oikumenical Era. They are spread abroad to carry the gospel and to stir up the nations, who are raised up as Guardian Beasts (Zech. 2:6; 6:5; Dan. 7:2). And since Jesus died to gather together all those, Jew and Gentile, who were scattered abroad (John 11:52), it is possibly the re-formation of the Church after the Great Tribulation that is in view in Matthew 24:30.

Given the parallels with Revelation, however, and remembering that Revelation is the Johannine version of Jesus' eschatological discourse, I am strongly inclined to believe that it is the gathering of the saints in heaven that is here spoken of. The trumpet would be the last or seventh trumpet, which is sounded by one of the twenty-four archangel-elders in Revelation 11:15-18. This event happens right after the Great Tribulation, which in Revelation 11 is pictured as the martyrdom of the two witnesses. Revelation 12–14 recapitulates the trumpets of Revelation 8–11 and ends with the martyrdom of the 144,000, which is followed in chapter 15 by the same kind of praise in heaven as we see in Revelation 11:15-18.

E. SUMMARY

Let us summarize Matthew 24:29-31. Immediately after the great affliction, the great persecution and martyrdom of the apostolic church, the world will be changed from the Old to the New Creation. No longer will sun and moon determine liturgy and worship; the former covenant with its lunar liturgy will be broken forever. No longer will angelic stars and heavenly powers govern humanity, for in Jesus, mankind has at last come of age. No longer will angels rule the world. They will vacate their heavenly thrones.

At that time, the promised sign will be given, a sign that shows that Jesus, a *man,* is truly enthroned in heaven. That sign is the destruction of Jerusalem and the temple. The Jews will mourn over Jerusalem, and they will realize that the Church, which they had hoped to destroy, has now ascended to the Ancient of Days and has been given the Kingdom promised in Daniel 7. Those saints have been gathered by the angels in connection with the seventh and last trumpet described in the book of Revelation, their souls gathered from all the heavenly places in Paradise where they had been waiting for this day. The saints are gathered before the Throne in the highest heavens, and shortly will sit down on thrones with their Lord and Master. They will be the new stars and moon and will sit where the angels formerly sat in heaven.

14
THIS GENERATION
(24:32-35)

---

³²And/but (*de*) from the fig tree learn the *parable*: When already its branch has become tender, and it is putting forth leaves, you know that the summer is near. ³³Thus also you, when you see all these things, know that it is near, at the doors.

> ³⁴Amen I say to you, certainly this *generation* will not have passed away until all these things shall have taken place.

> ³⁵*The heaven and the earth* will pass away,

and (*de*) *My words* certainly will not pass away.
³⁶And/but (*de*) concerning that day and hour:
no one knows,
not even the angels of the heavens,
[nor the Son,]
but My Father only.

The structure of this paragraph is implicitly chiastic. Jesus tells them a parable and ends by saying that His words will not pass away. That is, the parable is certain, though Jesus knows only the approximate time, not the exact time. Sandwiched between these two certainties are two things that will pass away: this generation and the heavens and the earth.

A. THE PARABLE OF THE FIG TREE

We come now to a parable. Contrary to what is often popularly stated
and believed, a parable is not a simple story designed to make some
teaching plain. When Jesus wanted to say something plainly, He did so.
Parables are quite different. They are puzzles that require a good deal of
both insight and Bible knowledge to understand and that provoke deep
thought. Matthew 13:10-17 makes it plain that parables were given to
confuse the ungodly and to teach the righteous. See also John 10:6.

If we are going to understand the Parable of the Fig Tree in any full
and deep way, we must examine what else the Bible has to say about figs.
We begin with Genesis 3:7, where Adam and Eve made aprons to cover
their shame from the leaves of the fig tree. The large leaves of the fig tree
were well suited for this purpose.

Adam and Eve covered their shame with fig leaves and hid among
the trees of the Garden. Since the Garden was the first sanctuary, where
God would meet with humanity, they were hiding in the sanctuary and
clothed in the garments of the sanctuary. This might seem to be very
proper and a sign of faith and trust in God. But it was in fact
presumptuous, because a sinner has no right to seek refuge in God's
sanctuary. In fact, it was very dangerous for them to stay close to God
as sinners. Accordingly, they were cast out.

The later sanctuaries, such as the oak oases of the patriarchs, the
acacia-board tabernacle, and the cedar-olive temple, were extensions of
the Garden. No one was allowed into such places unless his sins had
been forgiven through blood sacrifice. Indeed, only the Aaronic priests,
who had undergone fuller sacrificial rites, were allowed into the
tabernacle and temple. Anyone seeking to enter the tabernacle or temple
apart from such a consecration was to be killed. And, importantly, any
priest who was in rebellion against God had no right to remain in these
new Edenic Gardens. Thus, when the priests rebelled against God, the
tabernacle and temple were torn down and the priests were exiled.[59]

---

59. On the Garden and the later sanctuaries, see James B. Jordan, *Through New Eyes*;
on the duty of the Levites to kill any layman who tried to approach the holy places, see

We return to the fig tree, now aware that it was one of the original sanctuary trees and the one that provided covering for Adam and Eve. We can see that hiding in the trees, covered with fig leaves, is parallel to the situation of the Jews and their priests in Jesus' day. They were in rebellion against God, but they chose to try and hide in God's own house, covered in sanctuary garments—priestly robes parallel the Garden's fig leaves. This sin of presumption only increased their guilt and hastened their doom.

The Bible provides a fuller picture of the fig when it calls attention to people resting under the leafy foliage of its leaves in such passages as 1 Kings 4:25; Isaiah 36:16; Micah 4:4; Zechariah 3:10; and John 1:48. These passages portray the righteous man, who has access to God's garden, as resting under a fig tree enjoying grapes, the wine of the kingdom.

Equally important is what we read in Hosea 9:10, "I found Israel like grapes in the wilderness. I saw your forefathers as the earliest fruit on the fig tree in its first season. They came to Baal-Peor and devoted themselves to shame, and they became as detestable as that which they loved." Israel, God's chosen priestly nation, the first theocracy, was like early figs, but then they turned to shame, like Adam and Eve. They were no longer entitled to be figs and would come into judgment. Note that the word "detestable," in Hebrew *sheqets,* is the term reserved for sanctuary abominations committed by those set aside as priests, or as part of the nation of priests—the "abominations of desolation."

The sprouting of figs is a sign that winter is over and that the kingdom has come, in particular the kingdom of Solomon, prototype of Jesus' Kingdom (Song 2:10-13). This is the background to a strange event recorded in Matthew 21:18-22, which is the immediate backdrop for the Parable of the Fig Tree. We read that Jesus approached a leafy fig tree and sought for fruit in its branches. Finding none, He cursed it and it withered.

Jordan, *The Death Penalty in the Mosaic Law: Five Exploratory Essays,* Biblical Horizons Occasional Paper 3 (Niceville, FL: Biblical Horizons, 1989), ch. 3: "The Death Penalty for Encroachment."

What is strange about this event—and would have been strange to the disciples—is that one would not expect to find figs this early in the year. Jesus' action was parabolic, a riddle, as He explains right away. The fig tree was a symbol for the Jews and the priests. In Jesus, the Kingdom had come. He had just been welcomed as the Davidic King (Matt. 21:1-17). But the Jewish leaders had also just rejected Him. The Kingdom had come, but there were no figs. Jesus explained to the disciples that not only might they also curse such a false fig tree, but that they might also call on God to cast "this mountain" into the sea. The mountain in view was Mount Zion, where Jerusalem and its temple were located. And that mountain was indeed cast into the sea (Rev. 18:21), as the Jews were scattered into the Gentile sea after the destruction of Jerusalem in AD 70.

A similar analogy is found in Revelation 6:13, where God's judgment on Jerusalem is pictured as a stormy wind coming before summer fully arrives, causing the fig tree to drop its first figs to the ground. Such figs are the bad figs spoken of in Jeremiah 24 and 29:17, for they have fallen to the ground, split open, and rotted. Such a bad fig was Judas (Acts 1:18) and all who joined him in betraying Jesus and His Church.

We are now in a position to reconsider the allegorical Parable of the Fig Tree. The Kingdom has come, and the fig tree of the new Garden Sanctuary of the Church has begun to put forth leaves. At the same time, the false fig tree of the rebellious Jews begins to put forth leaves also. Soon will come the Tribulation. Some figs, the bad ones, will fall the ground, split open like Judas, and rot. Others will be harvested as the first-fruits of the Kingdom, as Jesus gathers to Himself the believers massacred in the Great Tribulation.

In terms of the allegory, the period from AD 30 to AD 70 is the springtime, when the fig tree puts forth leaves. As summer approaches the first figs appear, and this time corresponds to the Great Tribulation. Thereafter the fig tree of the Garden-Kingdom will continue to offer shade to God's people, who will bear the fruit of good figs for Jesus.

A couple of other points should be noted. First, Jesus says that the branch of the fig tree "has become tender." Jesus might merely have said that the fig tree begins to put forth leaves, but He adds the notion of tenderness. I don't think it is going too far to say that the true fig tree is tender to the call of the gospel. Good leaves and good figs come from tender branches.

Second, Jesus says that summer is near. Once again we see that this passage is not speaking of the end of the world, but of a new beginning. It is a time of birth-pangs, not of a death rattle (Matt. 24:8). Jesus says to the disciples that when they see all these things (the Great Tribulation and the leafing of the fig tree), they should know that "it" (not "he") is near; that is, summer is near. Allegorically, the full coming of summer is the resurrection of the Church after the Great Tribulation (Rev. 20:4-5).

Third, Jesus mixes His metaphor by saying that summer is "at the doors." Summer is ready to come in. Likely, the doors here would be the doors of the temple, which is in full view during this entire discourse. When the old, fallen temple of the Jews is torn down, the Church will enter fully into the new temple of the Kingdom. This again is quite in keeping with what the book of Revelation teaches, that when old Babylon (fallen Spiritual Jerusalem; Zech. 2) is torn down, the New Jerusalem will appear in its glory, doors wide open for the nations to enter. Of course, in a very real sense the doors of the New Jerusalem were open in the period of the Apostolic Church, but they will be open in a newer and fuller sense when summer fully arrives. Jesus' statement is also in line with what He says later on to the church at Laodicea, that they should open the doors to Him, so that His summer can come in to be with them (Rev. 3:20).

B. THIS GENERATION

Jesus tells them that "this generation will not have passed away until all these things shall have taken place." The word "generation" is sometimes paraphrased to mean "race" and is taken to mean that the Jewish race will not cease to exist until the end of time. That is clearly not the meaning here.

Another suggestion is that "this generation" means "this line of offspring," referring not to the Jews as such, but to the wicked in general. In that case, it would mean that there will be wicked people in the world until the end of time. Again, the context, which is the judgment in the first century, makes this interpretation impossible.

If "all these things" that Jesus has been talking about included events down to the end of history, then we would have to have a reason to take "generation" in such an extended sense. Throughout Matthew, "this generation" always refers to wicked Jews who reject Jesus as Messiah (11:16; 12:39-45; 16:4; 17:17; 23:36).

Thus, the full meaning of Jesus' saying seems to be "this present evil generation will not have died off before all these things take place." Many of Jesus' enemies were about His same age, and would be in their 70s when Jerusalem would be destroyed. *All* the events prophesied in connection with the Cataclysm would be fulfilled before the present evil generation died off.

C. THE HEAVEN AND THE EARTH

Jesus then states that heaven and earth will pass away, but that His Word will remain. It is because "pass away" is used here, as in the preceding sentence, and because many expositors believe the end of the world must be in view, that they try to extend "this generation" down to the end of history. This interpretation fails to understand the meaning of the phrase "heaven and earth" as it is found in the Bible. True, it can mean the physical cosmos, but most often it refers to the social or political cosmos of a given people (e.g., Isa. 14:1-16). In that case, Jesus is saying that the old heaven and earth will pass away, and a new heaven and earth will come, in a societal sense. This use of "heaven" is in line with what we investigated in chapter 13 above concerning the sun, moon, and stars.

The word "heaven" is singular here, while many times it is given in the plural: "heavens and earth." Though scholars have at various times tried to formulate a reason for the difference, either as it is played out in the Bible as a whole or as it occurs in Matthew, that difference has thus far eluded them all—as far as I know; if someone has completely figured it out, I'm not aware of it. It may be that "heavens" is a plural of majesty, speaking of the most glorious heaven that is God Himself, while in the singular a community in heaven is in view; that is, heaven as it relates to angels and/or men. This might explain the change in the Lord's Prayer: "Our Father in the heavens, ... Your will be done, as in heaven, so on earth...." The plural would be a reference to God ("Our Divine Father"), while the singular would be a reference to the place itself considered apart from God and under His rule. In other places, however, the plural seems to imply the multiple heavens (sky, firmament, and highest heaven), while the singular refers specifically to the sky or firmament or throne-heaven. In the passage before us, I suggest that the singular is used because "heaven and earth" are used symbolically for aspects of the covenantal society of man and God.

The Bible repeatedly uses the phrase "heaven/s and earth" to refer to a covenantal arrangement between God and His people, or any people, between the powers of heaven and those of earth. For instance, in Jeremiah 4:23-31, the decreation of heavens and earth means the destruction of the Kingdom of Judah, the dissolution of the covenant between God and His people. The heavens and earth in view was set up at Mount Sinai, according to Isaiah 51:15-16. The destruction of a heavens and earth is also prophesied in Isaiah 34:4, where it refers to the judgment of Edom. The destruction of Babylon's heavens and earth is found in Isaiah 13:13. All of this language is explained by the statement that "the heavens are My throne and the earth is My footstool" (Isa. 66:1). The "new heavens and new earth" of Isaiah 65:17ff. cannot be a new physical cosmos, nor can it be a picture of affairs after the Last Judgment, because people are still giving birth and dying in that new world.

There is nothing new in these observations. The great Puritan expositor and theologian John Owen preached a sermon from 2 Peter 3:11, arguing that the dissolution of the heavens and earth in 2 Peter 3:7 refers to the end of the Old Creation in AD 70.[60] The "elements" that are destroyed in 2 Peter 3:10, he pointed out, are the "elementary principles" of the first covenantal/creational order, as in Galatians 4:3, 9; Colossians 2:8, 20; and Hebrews 5:12.

---

60. Owen, "Sermon on 2 Peter iii," *Works,* 16 vols. (London: Banner of Truth, 1965-68) 9:131-141. More recently, see Peter J. Leithart, *The Promise of His Appearing: An Exposition of Second Peter* (Moscow: Canon, 2004).

Once we become familiar with this way of thinking, we can see that the Bible uses "heaven/s and earth" to refer to a covenantal order in many ways and places. For instance, the tabernacle and temple were, in part, symbolic models of the heavens and the earth. The Holy of Holies symbolized the highest heavens, where God is enthroned among His angels. The Holy Place symbolized the firmament heavens. The courtyard laver symbolized the waters above the firmament, the boundary between heaven and earth. The altar was the holy mountain, raised up in the middle of the earthly courtyard.[61]

Thus, when the tabernacle was taken apart in the days of Eli, and when the temple was destroyed in the days of Jeremiah, an old "heavens and earth" was destroyed, ending the Sinaitic and Kingdom Covenants respectively. Similarly, the destruction of the Oikumenical Covenant temple, built initially by Zerubbabel and enhanced by Herod, in AD 70, was the dissolution of that "heavens and earth."

Using similar language, Jesus said that not one jot or one tittle would pass away from the Sinaitic Law until heaven and earth passed away (Matt. 5:18). Since the Law *did* pass away as regards its jots and tittles in the first century, Jesus was clearly not speaking of the end of history as we think of it. After all, we no longer keep the laws of uncleanness, the sacrificial system, and so on, according to their specific "jots and tittles," but rather we observe them in new, transformed ways (as we avoid sin, worship with sacrifices of praise, and so forth).

We find the same kind of language in Hebrews 12:26-28, where God says that in a very little while He will shake the heavens and the earth so that many things will be shaken down and removed; yet meanwhile the saints will continue to live in a kingdom that cannot be shaken. The horizon of this prophecy is the immediate future, a "little while," the same as in Hebrews 10:25, where the hearers are told to remember to watch for the Day that is drawing near. In Hebrews 8:13, the hearers of

---

61. For a more extended discussion, see James B. Jordan, *Through New Eyes,* and Vern S. Poythress, *The Shadow of Christ in the Law of Moses* (Brentwood, TN: Wolgemuth & Hyatt, 1991).

the letter are told that the Old Creation is just about to be removed because the New Covenant has come.

In a general way, the "heavens" are those powers that are above, while the "earth" is those who dwell beneath. Thus, in one universe of discourse, the heavens are the rulers of a nation and the earth is the people. In another universe of discourse, the heavens is God's heavenly people while the earth is the rest of the world (see our discussion of astral imagery in chapter 13 above). The heavens might also refer to the angelic supervisors of the various nations before the ascension of Jesus. All of these are possibilities inherent in various passages of the Bible, such as those we have mentioned.

We can fill out precisely what a "new heavens and new earth" entail if we look at the New Covenant. For one thing, there is now a human King in heaven, something that never was the case before. As well, angels no longer rule as they did before; man is now over the angels, not "a little while lower than the angels" (Psa. 8:5). And, after AD 70 human souls are admitted to heaven as well (Rev. 6:9-11; 14:1 + 15:2; 20:4). Meanwhile, the Holy Spirit has come down to the earth in a full and final way, at the last Pentecost. Satan has been removed from access to the heavenly court and has been cast down to the earth (Rev. 8:10-11; 12:7-9). Thus, the old heaven and earth passed away in the first century and a new heaven and earth arrived.

It is true, of course, that Jesus' words will *never* pass away, even when the physical heavens and earth are changed at the end of history. But what Jesus means in the context of Matthew 24:35 is that His words will stand after the passing away of the old covenantal/societal heavens and earth in AD 70. They still stand today.

D. The Day and the Hour

Jesus now states that neither He nor the angels knows the exact day and hour of the coming events. Some ancient manuscripts omit "nor the Son" from this verse, but it is definitely found in the parallel passage of Mark 13:32. Whether it belongs here or not, the idea is the same: only the Father knows the day and hour.

190

For a long time I agreed with those expositors who argue that Jesus is changing the venue at this point. "These things" seems to contrast with "that day." Jesus seems to know quite a lot about "these things," and gives many clear predictions concerning them; but concerning "that day" He professes ignorance. Moreover, it is argued, this sentence begins with "but," implying a contrast.

Against this view, which I can no longer hold, are the following considerations. First, the "but" here is just a general connective, and can just as readily be translated "and." It is the Greek connective particle *de*, not the more adversative word *alla*, which means "but" and would imply a strong contrast.

Second, as we shall see, the sentences that follow this statement make much more sense as a description of the coming exile of the Jews, not of the final coming of Jesus at the end of history.

Third, although "that day and hour" may seem to imply more than merely a day and hour, they might mean just that, plainly and simply.

Thus, it seems more likely that Jesus, having given many fairly specific predictions about this coming event, now says that He does not know the precise time they will occur. Accordingly, He tells the disciples to be on their alert and to watch for the signs (vv. 42, 44).

At the same time, I think it would be a mistake to say that Jesus knew the year and month, but not the precise day and hour. Rather, Jesus is saying that these events are going to come fairly soon, before the present generation of Jews has died off, but that no one but the Father knows precisely when.

How can Jesus be ignorant of the precise timing? It is sometimes argued that as a man Jesus was ignorant, while as the Son of God He knew everything. It is theologically very problematic to try to divide the consciousness of Jesus this way, and, in any event, it is not what it in view in this context. Rather, it is Jesus as Revealer of the Word who does not "know." He has just spoken of His "words." Jesus does only what His Father tells Him, and says only what His Father has given Him to say. The Father has not given this to Him to say, and so He does not say it. In that sense, He does not know when the event will take place. As Word-Revealer, both man and God, He does not "know" it.

That this is the correct interpretation is clear from the fact that neither the angels nor the Son is said to know the time. The angels were the revealers of God's Word in the Old Creation, when humanity was in its childhood under angelic supervisors (Heb. 1–2; Acts 7:53; Gal. 3:19; 4:1ff.). The Son is the one who reveals the Word in the last days (Heb. 1:2). In both cases, as perfect servant-priests they reveal only what the Father tells them.

What do "that day and hour" mean? Various very specific events have been suggested, such as the day and hour that the Roman army, or the Edomite army, appeared at the walls of Jerusalem. Or possibly, the day and hour that the completed Herodian temple was dedicated. Such suggestions build on interpreting "let him that is on the housetop not come down to get things out of his house" and the like as warnings of a specific event (Matt. 24:17-18). As we have seen, it is far more likely that these sayings are to be taken as general proverbs that will apply when all these things start to happen. For that reason, I think it unlikely that a specific date and hour are in view.

Rather, it is the Day of the Lord that is in view. The Day of the Lord, as we find it in the Bible, is the time God comes to judge. It may be the Lord's Day, the weekly time of worship, as in Revelation 1:10, or it may be a time of cultural and national judgment, as it is in Zephaniah. Such a "day" extends over a period of time, in this case from the completion of Herod's temple to the full destruction of Jerusalem, about six years.[62]

Similarly, the "hour" is a more pointed temporal event, but still not a precise sixty minute period of time. Jesus spoke of His hour of glorification in John 12:23, but this "hour" extended at least from His being lifted up on the cross to His ascension to God's throne in heaven, and possibly down to His public vindication in the events of the Cataclysm. Similarly, 1 John 2:18 speaks of the "last hour" as a period of time when antichrists are revealed, the last period before the destruction of the Old Creation.

---

62. For an argument that the book of Revelation can be seen from one perspective as occupying one day of twenty-four hours, see my "The Day of the Lord and Its 24 Hours."

Thus, it seems that Jesus is using "that day and hour" as a synonym for the climactic events of the "these things" He has been speaking about, to wit, the last six or so years of the Old Creation. For all the disciples knew, these events could have come in the AD 30s or 40s or 50s or 60s. Jesus does not tell them. Rather, He tells them to be alert and vigilant.

At the same time, it is no contradiction to observe that human beings live in clock time, days and hours. There would come a specific day and hour when the disciples would decide it was time to forsake the housetops of prayer and flee to the mountains of Divine protection. This would be like the specific day and hour when Noah entered the ark (24:38). Yet, it is easy to imagine that various believers would be moved to flee at different times, responding to various events. Jesus' prophetic warnings allow for this, since He predicted a whole complex of events.

15
DAYS OF NOAH; DAYS OF EXILE
(24:37-44)

In verses 37-44, Jesus compares the coming devastation of Israel with the Great Flood, with the arrival of an invading army that takes people into exile, and with a robber who breaks into a house.

37And/but (*de*) just as the days of Noah,
so will be the manifestation (*parousia*) of the Son of Man.
38For just as they were in the days before the Flood, eating and drinking, marrying and giving in marriage, until the day when Noah entered into the ark, 39And (*kai*) they did not know until the Flood came and took away all, so also will be the manifestation (*parousia*) of the Son of Man.

40At that time two will be in the field: One is taken and one is left.
41Two [women] will be grinding in the mill: One is taken and one is left.
42Be watching, therefore, for you do not know what day your Lord comes (*erchomai*).

43And/but (*de*) know this, that if the master of the house had known in what watch the thief comes (*erchomai*), he would have watched and not have allowed his house to be dug through [broken into].
44Therefore also (*kai*) you, be ready, for you do not know what hour the Son of Man comes (*erchomai*).

The first section says that the wicked will not know that the judgment is coming until they experience it. The second section climaxes with the statement that the disciples do not know the *day*. The third section climaxes with the statement that the disciples do not know the *hour*.

The first section portrays the coming Cataclysm as the manifestation or revelation of the reign of the Son of Man, Jesus. The second portrays it as the coming of their Lord, Jesus, who comes to bring this judgment. The third section portrays it as the coming of the Son of Man, which alludes back to Ezekiel's coming to destroy Jerusalem.

A. THE DAYS OF NOAH

While it is tempting to wax expansive on the immoral condition of humanity at the time of the Flood, and while this is indeed in the background (the reference to "this generation"), it is not precisely what Jesus is talking about. He mentions eating and drinking, which are surely not wrong in themselves. And He mentions marrying and giving in marriage, which again are not wrong in themselves, though in the time before the Flood the supposedly Godly Sethites were intermarrying with the wicked Cainites. Jesus mentions these things only to say that the people were going about the ordinary business of their lives, with no perception that disaster was about to come on them. The following two examples have the same meaning: Working in the field and grinding at the mill are not immoral actions, but ordinary daily life.

The sin of the people before the Flood lay primarily in that they did not listen to the warnings of Enoch and Noah. Their other sins were great and important, but secondary. Their primary sin was their failure to repent. They ignored Noah and continued to go about their daily lives, convinced that no judgment was coming.

The situation would be the same before the destruction of Jerusalem. Jesus had, as a Great Noah, provided a whole series of warnings right here in this discourse, and the lesser Noahs, His disciples, the sons of Noah as it were, would preach them to the people. Those who harkened to Jesus would stop living ordinary lives and make preparations. We see this as the Christians sold off all their property in Jerusalem and its environs, transferring their wealth from the old world to the new church, the New Creation (Acts 4:34ff.). Meanwhile, however, those who rejected Jesus' words would go on with their lives and be taken unawares when the disaster came.

Passages like 1 Peter 3:20 and Hebrews 11:7 imply, in the overall context of Biblical theology, that the building of the ark before the Flood corresponds to the gradual building of the Church, the new community of Jew and Gentile, during the period between Jesus' ascension and His parousial manifestation. The completed ark of the Church then was a place of safety during the Cataclysm. As Noah built the ark and then carried his whole family through the judgment to a new world, so Jesus would build His Church and then carry His people through the Cataclysm to the fullness of the New Creation after AD 70.[63]

This paragraph focuses on the parousia or vindication of Jesus. The Cataclysm would manifest the truth of His many words of warning and be the sign of His reign.

We should also note that Daniel 9:26, which predicts this same event, speaks of the destruction of Jewry as a flood.

B. EXILE

One is taken and the other is left behind. This statement has been read as a prophecy of some kind of "rapture" of the saints before some future tribulation. It is assumed that the person who is taken is caught up into the air, a misapplication of 1 Thessalonians 4:17.

Rather, what is in view here is exile. The disciples, knowing the covenant history of the Bible, would not have misunderstood what Jesus was saying. They could tell from the attitudes of their countrymen that the Romans would eventually come and suppress a rebellion, just as Nebuchadnezzar and the Babylonians had done repeatedly before the destruction of Old Jerusalem. When the invading Romans conquered Israel, some would be taken into exile and some would be left behind. Neither the Assyrians nor the Babylonians took every single Israelite into captivity, and neither would the Romans. The book of Jeremiah, in particular, delineates the fate of those who were left behind by the Babylonians (Jer. 39–44).

---

63. See our discussion of the sign of Jonah and Jesus as New Ark, above on pages 87-89.

Jesus is predicting another aspect of the coming Cataclysm. The invading army is portrayed as a new flood of waters in such passages as 2 Samuel 22:5; Psalm 18:4; Isaiah 59:19; Jeremiah 46:7-8; and Daniel 9:26; 11:22. As Noah predicted the Flood, so the prophets predicted new floods of invasion and exile. In all cases, the wicked refused to hear and were caught unawares.

Field and mill speak of men and women. The men grow the wheat, while the women glorify it into flour and bread. It is certainly easier for two men to work a field than for one, and the mills of the ancient world, except for very small, crude ones, required two women to work them.

While we might be tempted to try and distinguish the righteous and the wicked, in terms of who is taken and who is left, Jesus has already warned the righteous to flee to the mountains. In terms of the prophecy, there would not be any of the Godly left in the fields or in the mills when the disaster came. Rather, the idea is that some of the wicked would be taken into captivity, while others would remain behind impoverished and struggling. Both would come under severe judgment.

Indeed, in terms of Biblical imagery, the man who is taken from his own field is a man who is taken into slavery to work the fields of his captors. And, since grinding in a mill is sometimes a sexual metaphor, the woman who is taken from the mill faces "grinding" for her captors (Job 31:10; Isa. 47:2; Jer. 25:10; 1 Sam. 8:13 + 2 Sam. 13:8; and more distantly Ruth 3).

Also involved in this prophecy is the dissolution of covenant bonds. We have three pictures of covenant linkage here: two men working together in a field, two women working a mill, and by implication men and women cooperating to make bread. These social bonds would be torn apart, as an outworking of the rending of their bond with the Lord. When people cut themselves off from God, they wind up cut off from one another also.

Jesus speaks of this event as the "coming of the Lord." This is language appropriate to the imagery. God revealed Himself in the Kingdom period as Yahweh *Adonai,* Yahweh *My Lord.* Thus, in drawing on the language of invasion and exile, events that happened most pointedly at the end of the Kingdom period, Jesus speaks of Himself as the Lord of the people.

The reference to a coming exile also adds a dimension to something Jesus has said earlier, that His servants would be persecuted and betrayed and would have to confront false prophets. It was Jeremiah, more than any other prophet, who predicted exile and who was persecuted, betrayed, and continually opposed by such false prophets as Hananiah. The disciples would have to think of themselves as new Jeremiahs, predicting exile, and would have to be prepared for the same treatment.

Yet, those who listened to Jesus would preserve not only their bonds with Him, but with one another. Friends would flee to God's protective mountain together, as would husbands and wives. They would not be split apart.

C. THE HOUSEBREAKER

The thief digs through the walls of the house, breaking into it, at a time the master cannot predict. As with the Flood and exile analogies, Jesus' imagery is fairly straightforward but carries deeper implications for those who know the Bible well.

The prophet Ezekiel was told, in a vision, to dig through the wall of the court of the temple (Ezek. 8:8). This prophetic "thief" caught the masters of the house busy worshiping other gods, and then proceeded to bring destruction on the temple (Ezek. 9–11; 43:3).

Similarly, in Zechariah 5:1-4, the prophet is shown the word of God's judgments moving into the houses of the wicked and consuming their walls. The immediate allusion is to "house affliction" as it is set forth in Leviticus 14:34-35. We notice that the two sins mentioned in Zechariah 5:4 are theft and false swearing. These are the same two sins Jesus condemned when He inspected the temple for "house affliction" in Matthew 21:12-13. He said that God's house is to be a house of prayer (not false swearing), but they had made it a den of robbers (theft). Jesus' entrance into a house where men swore false allegiance to God, and where they acted as thieves, fulfilled Zechariah 5:4 in a particular and full way. (For more on this, see our discussion in Chapter 2.A. above.)

These passages in the prophets are the background for the several predictions that Jesus comes "like a thief in the night" (1 Thess. 5:2, 4; 2 Pet. 3:10; Rev. 3:3; 16:15). All of these passages concern the Cataclysm of the first century, the end of the Old Creation. Jesus is the True Thief, who comes to rob the wicked of their treasures and give them to the righteous. He comes to spoil the Egyptians and transfer their wealth to the New Creation. He comes to the house, finds the corruption of "affliction" within, pulls the good furniture out, and leaves the house to rot.

This time, Jesus speaks of the event as the coming of the Son of Man. We have seen that the coming of the Son of Man on the clouds refers back to Daniel 7 and points to the ascension of the saints, which took place at this time. Because "on the clouds" is not included in the statement here, it is less likely that Daniel 7 is in view. Rather, as Jesus has just said that "your Lord is coming," we should expect a direct parallel here: The coming of the Son of Man is the coming of the Lord to bring judgment on apostate Jewry.

Why "Son of Man" and not "your Lord" here? Because Ezekiel, the original son of man, is in the background. As Ezekiel invaded the temple as a thief and then destroyed it, so the Greater Son of Man will invade the temple-house and destroy it.

16
TO THE END OF HISTORY
(24:45–25:46)

A. THE TIMES OF THE PARABLES

Jesus now provides us with three parables: the Parable of the Unfaithful Servant (24:45-51), the Parable of the Ten Virgins (25:1-13), and the Parable of the Talents (25:14-30).

The three parables are parallel to one another in their basic story line and emphasis. In each parable, someone is expected to come and bring about a great change of affairs. In each parable, that coming is delayed beyond what it expected, with the result that some people remain faithful and watchful while others fall away.

Naturally, we expect all three of these parables to be dealing with the same events: three pictures of the same period of history. Conventionally, it is assumed that the beginnings of the parables (the *termini a quo*, or "extreme from which") have to do with Jesus' departure from the world, and the judgments at the ends of the parables (the *termini ad quem*, or "extreme toward which") have to do with the end of human history. Some, however, have suggested that the beginning point is the Sinaitic covenant and the time of judgment is the AD 70 Cataclysm.

There is evidence in the parables for taking them sequentially. To introduce this subject: I suggest that the first parable, that of the Unfaithful Servant, begins at Sinai and ends at Cataclysm. The second parable, of the Virgins, begins at Pentecost and ends at Cataclysm. The third parable, of the Talents, begins at either Pentecost or Cataclysm and ends at the Last Judgment.

That the passage continues to progress beyond the Cataclysm to later events should not surprise us. Jesus has presented His discourse in a clear historical sequence thus far. Matthew 24:4-14 concerned events of the Apostolic Era from Jesus' time to the establishment of the Abomination of Desolation. Matthew 24:15-28 concerned the events of the Great Tribulation meted out against the Church. Matthew 24:29-31 concerned the events that happened right after the Great Tribulation: the harvest of the Old Creation. What follow after that are a series of warnings to be on the alert, since the precise time of these soon-coming events is not revealed (24:32–25:13). The disciples had asked for a sign, and Jesus had revealed to them the sign(s) to watch for. When we come to Matthew 25:14-30, however, there are no signs and they are not told to be watchful. It seems that we are moving on beyond the first century events. And after that comes a judgment scene that is so close to the Last Judgment in Revelation 20 that the Church has always assumed the same event is in view.

We know from Revelation 20 that there is a long history, a "millennium," that comes after the Cataclysm and leads to the final judgment. Although that detailed information had not yet been revealed when Jesus gave this discourse, it is implied with certainty from the history of the Bible as a whole. There were originally seventy nations in the world (Gen. 10). Israel was selected out as a microcosm of the kingdom of God, for a set period of time. The end of Israel's history would be the end of this focussed center, this group that represented all the rest of humanity, in world history. As Israel was brought into final judgment in the Cataclysm, so the whole world would eventually be brought into judgment as well. The disciples would surely realize that the earlier judgment was to be a type, a foreshadowing, of a fuller judgment to come. Thus, it would not have surprised them that Jesus would, in His prophecy, move beyond a time of signs to a more general prediction about the course of human history.

Thus, the question before us is whether or not Matthew 25 does in fact move beyond the Cataclysm and predict the course of history down to the Final Judgment.

Notice that in the first parable, the reward is to be put in charge of the master's possessions. The slave is elevated from mere service to viceregency (24:47). Now this is exactly the place where the third parable begins: The master entrusts his possessions to his slaves, obviously higher servants (25:14). It seems that the third parable begins where the first parable ends. The change from mere household service to dominion over all the master's possessions is very much the change from the status of believers under the Law to their status in the Kingdom.

In all of these parables, the master is said to delay his coming (24:48; 25:5; 25:19). In the first and second, it is merely a delay, while in the third, it is a long time. The forty years from Pentecost to Cataclysm is not what one would readily regard as a long time, though of course in the life of an individual it would be. Since, as we shall see in Chapter 18 below, Revelation 19 makes it clear that the marriage takes place in connection with Cataclysm, that is the *terminus ad quem* of the parable. But since the parable is said to be about the kingdom of heaven, which everywhere in Matthew is something that begins with Jesus' ministry, the *terminus a quo* of this parable is the time of Jesus, and Pentecost in particular. Thus, the "delaying" of the bridegroom is roughly a forty year period. That being the case, a delay "for a long time" would seem to imply a much longer period of time for the third parable.

As noted, it seems that the third parable extends all the way to the Last Judgment. This follows from several factors. First, as we have noted above, the parable seems to take up where the first parable ended.

Second, the reward in the third parable is not more dominion in this world, but entry into the joy of the master (25:21, 23). It would seem that history is over at this point.

Third, both the first and second parables take up Jesus' earlier statement about the coming day and hour and the disciples are warned to be watchful (24:50; 25:13), but nothing is said either about watchfulness or about a coming day and hour in the third parable. One might argue that this parable simply has a different emphasis, while referring to the same span of time. Since, however, Jesus has warned them to be watchful in every parable He has given thus far (24:32-33, 36-39, 40-42, 43-44, 50; 25:13), the omission of that warning here is surely significant. A chord we have heard six times in succession is suddenly absent. It seems we are dealing with a different event, one far into the future beyond the days of the disciples.

Fourth, the third parable is said to be "just like" the second (25:14). As we shall see, they are alike in that the extra flask of oil in the second parable corresponds to the doubled talents in the third, and the two parables explain each other. In light of that similarity, however, the contrasts between the two are highlighted: between mere "delay" and "after a long time," between "watching for day and hour" and no watching for any day of hour. They are "just alike" in that they both begin at the same time, with the coming of the kingdom of heaven, but their spans of time stand in contrast to one another.

Fifth, the judgment scene that follows this parable in 25:31-46 is most likely not the Cataclysm but the Last Assize.

B. THE TIME OF THE JUDGMENT SCENE

Some have seen this judgment as part of the events surrounding the destruction of Jerusalem. Let us survey the arguments that might be put forth in this regard.[64]

First, on this occasion all nations are gathered before the throne of God. Matthew 24:14 said that the gospel would be preached to the (Hellenistic) Oikumene before the Cataclysm, as a witness to all nations. The command given in Matthew 28:19 is not merely to take a witness to the nations of the Oikumene, but to transform every nation on earth into a theocracy—marching orders far vaster in extent. Matthew 24:14 says that before the Cataclysm, the gospel would be taken as a witness to all the Oikumene. And it was. The context of Matthew 24:14 is the Oikumene or Guardian Beast Empire set up in Daniel 7, which was

---

64. I know of only one detailed published argument for this position, and so I am interacting with what I have heard by word of mouth and how I think such an argument might best be run. The one published argument is in J. Stuart Russell, *The Parousia: A Critical Inquiry into the New Testament Doctrine of Our Lord's Second Coming* (1887; reprint, Grand Rapids: Baker, 1983). This book argues that all Biblical prophecy relates to the events of AD 70 and that a final coming of Christ is not predicted in the Bible.

presently a Hellenistic imperium ruled by Rome. The context of Matthew 28:19 is the seventy nations of the entire world, from Genesis 10, out of which Israel had been selected as one model nation, a firstfruit theocracy.

So the question is this: What "all nations" are gathered in 25:32? All the nations of the Oikumene or all the nations of the original world, the nations of Genesis 10? Arguably, only the Oikumene nations are in view, and this judgment is part of the events of the Cataclysm. Against this, however, is the statement that during the Apostolic Age, the disciples will be hated by "all nations" of the Oikumene (24:9). That being so, *all* the nations of the Oikumene would be wicked goats; none of them would be righteous sheep. The language of the judgment scene in 25:32, however, certainly implies that some nations are righteous.

On the other hand, the shift from the neuter "nations" to the masculine "them" in this verse (25:32) shows that it is individuals within the nations that are being judged, not the nations themselves. Thus, it can be argued that though all the nations as such persecuted the Church during the Apostolic Age, many within these nations were sheep rather than goats.

The quixotic assertion of J. Stuart Russell, that the word "nations" can mean "tribes" and thus refer to the tribes of Israel, is a complete fantasy.[65] The word is *ethnos*, and almost always refers to those outside Israel. It always means the Gentiles when used in the plural. That fact, however, raises another point: What about the judgment of those within Israel? If we restrict "all nations" to the Gentile nations of the Oikumene, then the Jews are pointedly excluded. If, however, we take the scene in its traditional sense, as the judgment at the end of history, then no one is excluded from the meaning of "all nations," for after the Cataclysm, the Jews are just one nation among all the rest.

Yet, on the other hand, there are passages that speak of the "nation" of the Jews, such as Luke 23:2, John 11:48-52, Acts 10:22, and a few others. Thus, the judgment of "all nations" here might mean the

---

65. Russell, *Parousia,* 104f.

Oikumene and the Jews. Moreover, Matthew 24:14 says that the gospel will be preached in the Oikumene as a witness to all nations, and historically, that included the Jews. The Jews were part of the Oikumene, though usually they are distinguished from it. But the witness to the Gentiles was indeed a witness to the Jews, as Paul sets it forth in Romans 11. Thus, the prophesied gathering of all nations in Matthew 25:32 could very well include the Jews, along with the Gentiles of the Oikumene, and be an event fulfilled in the first century.

Thus far, we have not been able to resolve the question of which event is in primary focus in Matthew 25:31-46. Let us turn to another consideration: The judgment meted out is eternal fire (25:41), which surely is to be linked with the lake of fire in Revelation and is ultimately the consuming fire of God's presence, in which the wicked as well as the righteous will spend eternity (though the wicked will not enjoy it, since God is what they hate more than anything else; see Revelation 14:10): From the book of Revelation we learn that four groups of beings are cast into the lake of fire. According to Revelation 14:8-11, the ungodly Circumcision who oppressed the Church in the Apostolic Age, those who sided with the Beast and his Herod-temple image, are shortly to be cast into the lake of fire. According to Revelation 19:20, the Sea Beast (Satanic Rome) and the two-horned False Prophet (Herods and high priests) are cast into the fire immediately after the Cataclysm. This would seem to mean not just these two as individuals—who would they be?—but all the wicked Gentiles who oppressed the Apostolic Church. These would seem to be the same event: Those who sided with the Beast among the Jews, and the False Prophet (Herods and high priests), and the Beast himself, are cast into the lake of fire at the end of the Cataclysm events. (The Beast and False Prophet are two "anti-witnesses" who correspond to the hosts of those who attacked the Church, just as the two witnesses of Revelation 11 correspond to the 144,000 host of witnesses.)

After the Millennium, which begins after the Cataclysm, the Final Judgment takes place (Rev. 20). This event has not yet happened. We read that just before the Last Judgment, Satan and His demonic army are sent into the lake of fire (Rev. 20:10), and then, finally, all the wicked dead of the all the ages are removed from Sheol and sent into the lake of fire (20:13-15).

So, which of these events squares best with what Matthew 25:31-46 predicts? We can eliminate the destruction of Satan. It remains entirely possible that it is the casting of the wicked of the Circumcision and the Oikumene nations into eternal fire that is in view. And it is possible that the Last Judgment is in view.

There are additional details in Revelation that bear on this question. In Revelation 19:19-21, we find the Beast, the False Prophet, and the Kings of the Land (the religious rulers among the Jews) continuing to make war on the Church immediately after the destruction of Babylon/Jerusalem. The Beast and False Prophet are cast into the lake of fire, while the "rest" (i.e., the Kings of the Land) are killed by the gospel-sword of Jesus and devoured by the birds. This is the curse of the covenant and is a specifically Jewish judgment. In the light of Revelation 14:9-11, however, this same group of ungodly Jews is sentenced to (the lake of) fire.

Accordingly, we have here, portrayed in Revelation's symbolism, the judgment of all the nations of the Oikumene, with those who persecuted the Church being cast into the lake of fire. Once again we find that the language of Matthew 25:31-46 could apply to either the judgment of the Old Creation or the judgment of all of human history.

Let us consider another line of argument. Matthew 25:31 says that the Son of Man will come "in His glory," with His "angels," and will sit on the "throne of His glory." Previous statements about the coming of the Son of Man in this discourse have not included the notion of glory, except as it applied to the coming of the saints to the Ancient of Days in 24:30. Perhaps this language presses us beyond the Cataclysm to the Last Assize. Coming with the angels does not tell us anything, because the word means "messenger" and can refer to the spirit angels who judged the Old Creation in Revelation 6–18 or to the gospel messengers, the saints, who will judge the world with Jesus at the end of history.

At the same time, Jesus was clearly glorified at His ascension, and He sat down to reign at that time. Thus, this passage may well speak of His coming, in His glory, with spirit-angels, to pass judgment on the Old Creation.

Yet it is possible that this language implies the Last Judgment rather than the Cataclysm judgment. If we look back at Matthew 16:27-28, we find Jesus' predicting that the Son of Man will come in His glory with His angels to recompense every man according to his deeds. The language is almost the same as that in Matthew 25:31-46, but we should notice that nothing is said about the throne of His glory. Then Jesus follows by saying that some of His disciples will not taste death until they see the Son of Man coming in His kingdom—not "coming in the glory of His Father," but "coming in His kingdom."

Now, it is clear enough that Jesus' coming in His kingdom was to happen in that generation, and some of the disciples would live to see it. The Transfiguration, which follows immediately after this prophecy in Matthew 17, is a foretaste of that coming event. Is this the same event as His coming in the glory of His Father, or does the change of language between the two sentences signify two different events? It appears that two different events are in view, because in 16:24-26 Jesus has been speaking of personal death and judgment, not of a cosmic or political event. The disciple must take up the cross of martyrdom and be willing to lose his life to save his soul. It is in that context that Jesus predicts that He will come in glory to pass judgment. This would not seem to be the historical judgments of the Cataclysm but the personal judgments of the Last Day.

At the same time, we have seen that some personal judgments were meted out at the Cataclysm, and some people were cast into the lake of fire. Mark 8:34-38 is parallel to Matthew 16:24-38, except that in Mark Jesus is speaking also to the multitudes, not only to the disciples. In Mark's version, Jesus says, "For whoever is ashamed of Me and My words in this adulterous and sinful generation, the Son of Man will also be ashamed of him when He comes in the glory of His Father with His holy angels." In Mark's case, the coming event is would seem to be the Cataclysm, although it could readily mean that at the Last Judgment the Son of Man will be ashamed of those who rejected Him while He was on earth. Because the parallel is so strong, I am not comfortable insisting that Matthew 16:27 must refer to the Last Judgment. It may very well refer to the Cataclysm. In chapter 12.A. I argued that "coming with glory and angels" alludes back to Ezekiel 8–11, and thus that Matthew 16:27 refers to the Cataclysm.

Though Matthew 16:27 speaks of coming in glory with angels, it does not speak of sitting on the throne of glory. Perhaps the addition of the throne to the situation indicates a different event. We turn to a fairly cryptic saying of Jesus in Matthew 19:28-30. There Jesus says to Peter and the disciples that since they have left everything behind, they will sit with Him on the throne of His glory judging the twelve tribes of Israel. What does this mean, and when did it happen? It has to mean that Jesus, at His ascension, came to His throne and enthroned the disciples to rule Israel with Him during the Apostolic Age. This rule was on the earth and by means of witness and eventually martyrdom. Just as Jesus ruled from His cross, so did they. The "regeneration" spoken of in Matthew 19:28, thus, began at Pentecost.

At this point, I feel fairly confident in making the following suggestion. Jesus ascended to sit in glory with the Father at His ascension in AD 30. Glory in the Bible is not just a matter of radiance, but also of community. A person is glorified when he has a community of people around him who respect him, who glorify him. Initially, in AD 30, that glorious community was the angels. In terms of Biblical history, a human glorious community was formed after the Cataclysm, as we see the glorious City descend from heaven in Revelation 21:11. The new community was formed by the work of the apostles, out of believing Jew and believing Gentile. Then it underwent a death and resurrection and glorification. At that point, Jesus came to be enthroned in the New Jerusalem in the glory of His people (Rev. 22:1). His throne at that time became glorious in the sense that He was enthroned among a glorified people, who at that point began to sit on their own heavenly thrones with Him.

If this interpretation of the prophecies is correct, and I believe that it is, then the "throne of Jesus' glory" is language appropriate first for His ascension into the glory of the Father and the angels, and even more appropriate, second, for His enthronement among His glorified people. Jesus came to *that* throne—or better, His throne took on that glory—when the ascended saints joined with Him. Turning back to Matthew 25:31, then, what is described could either be a judgment at the time of the Cataclysm (AD 70) or at the end of history.

We saw above that there are references to Jesus' coming in the glory of His Father, while other passages speak of His coming in the throne of His glory. The Father's glory is bestowed on Jesus from above, while a throne is a support from beneath. In the tabernacle and temple, Yahweh sat on a throne consisting of the wings of angels, enthroned upon the cherubim. Since men now replace angels, Jesus' throne now consists of His people and their praises. Along these same lines, the bride is the glory of her husband, according to 1 Corinthians 11:7. Agreeable to both these lines of thought, we find that the New Jerusalem is both bride and throne, and glorious. While the fullness of the New Jerusalem cannot be manifest before the Last Judgment, it is already present, with gates open to welcome the nations and people invited to come in. Yet, the New Jerusalem is the glorified bride and does not appear until after the death and resurrection of the bride in the events of the Great Tribulation. The glorified Jesus now has a glorified Bride, and that glorified Bride is the "throne of His glory."

According to this line of thinking, the fulness of the throne of Jesus' glory did not exist until after the Cataclysm. Coming as it does after the Parable of the Talents, the judgment scene in Matthew 25 cannot refer to the Cataclysm but must refer, specifically, to the Last Judgment.

What we have seen is that the judgment scene in Matthew 25:31-46 is written in such a way that it can without much of any difficulty apply both to the Cataclysm judgment and to the Last Judgment. This kind of "double fulfillment" or "double manifestation" in prophecy is certainly not new or strange. To take but two well-known examples: In 2 Samuel 7 the son predicted for David is obviously both Solomon (near manifestation) and Jesus (distant fulfillment). In Isaiah 7-9, the prophesied son is both Maher-Shahal-Hash-Baz (near manifestation) and the Wonderful Counselor (distant fulfillment). The language in both prophecies is such that it is clear that both a near manifestation and a full, distant fulfillment are in view. Thus, it is possible that the same thing is to be seen here.

The language of the judgment scene (Matt. 25:31-46) is such that is can readily be applied to the near judgment of the Cataclysm. There are indications in the text, however, that point to a fuller, distant fulfillment, especially as this judgment scene follows the Parable of the Talents, which we have seen extends down to the end of history. The distinction between the two fulfillments is provided in much more detail in the book of Revelation.

In conclusion, the predictions of Matthew 23:1–25:13 concern the coming judgment on the Old Creation in the events of the Cataclysm. The principles involved in these predictions apply in every generation and will apply at the Last Judgment, but there is no double reference implied in any of the language. When we come to 25:14-46, however, the emphasis shifts to the course of history after the Cataclysm down to the end of history. We can say that the principles involved in these prophecies applied in the first century, but that first century events are not directly in view.

17
THE PARABLE OF THE UNFAITHFUL SLAVE (24:45-51)

[45]Who then (*ara*) is the faithful and prudent slave, whom the master has set over his household, that he give to them food at the proper time?
[45]Blessed is that slave, when, having come, his master will find thus doing.
[47]Amen I say to you, that over all his property he will set him.

[48]And/but (*de*) if that evil slave should say in his heart, "Delays my master,"
[49]and (*kai*) should begin to beat the fellow-slaves,
and/but (*de*) eat and (*kai*) drink with the drunkards,
[50]he will come, the master of that slave, in a day that he does not expect,
and (*kai*) in an hour that he does not know,
[51]and (*kai*) will cut him in two,
and (*kai*) his portion with the hypocrites will appoint;
in that place will be the weeping and the gnashing of the teeth.

The first paragraph has a roughly chiastic order:

- A. The master has set
  - B. Over his household
    - C. Give food and drink
      - D. Blessed is that slave
    - C' Thus doing (giving food and drink)
  - B' Over all his property
- A' The master will set him

Also, the word order reversal in A.-B. and A'-B' serves to stress a contrast between merely being over the household and now being over all the master's property.

Though this is a parable, and arguably the first of a set of three, it continues the narrative straight from the preceding statement. The word *ara*, "then," is a particle that serves to draw a consequence from a preceding statement.[66] The "head of the house" in verse 43 is to be identified with the slave set over the master's household. As we have seen, both the larger and the more specific context of these sayings link the head of the house with the temple and its priests. The temple is in view throughout this sermon, and it concerns the fate of the temple and Jerusalem. Thus, it is no surprise that the servant in this parable is directed to dispense food, for the sacrifices were also sacraments, food, given to the people, as at Passover, Booths, and all Peace Offerings. These and similar events are the "proper times" when the food was to have been given out from the Lord's table.

Because of the link to the preceding context, which not only concerns the management of the temple but also alludes to the exile of Israel in the days of Nebuchadnezzar and to the Flood, we are to see the *terminus a quo* (the beginning point) of this story as the time of the former covenants, and in particular the Sinaitic Covenant. That was when Yahweh set up His table and appointed slave-priests to manage it for the benefit of His people. The *terminus ad quem* (the end point) would be the judgment on the Old Creation at the Cataclysm, not the Final Judgment at the end of history. Those faithful with these "small things" are, at that time, set over larger things (all the property of the Lord, v. 47), and it is this event that is the beginning point of the Parable of the Talents (25:14).

When did the Lord set the faithful slaves over all His possessions? I submit that this began to happen at Pentecost and culminated at the beginning of the Millennium. Those who had been faithful previously were given the Kingdom at Pentecost, in principle. In Matthew 5:19 Jesus had already told them that those who kept the Law faithfully would be great in the Kingdom, while those who had not done so, would be small

---

66. Walter Bauer, Frederick W. Danker, W. F. Arndt, and F. W. Gingrich. *Greek-English Lexicon of the New Testament and Other Early Christian Literature*, 3rd ed. (Chicago: University of Chicago Press, 2000).

in that Kingdom. The Kingdom was coming, and everyone would enter it, one way or another. Everyone would come under the rule of the enthroned Christ at His ascension. The faithless would be "small" in that Kingdom and would be in danger of judgment if they did not change their ways. The faithful would be "great" and would, in terms of our present passage, be put over all the Lord's possessions.

The judgment on the bad slaves would be delayed for a short season, however. They would be given another chance, until the Cataclysm arrived, until the "day and hour" that Jesus was prophesying arrived.

A. THE DELAY

We should notice a bit of literary artistry in this parable. The evil slave says, "Delays my master," putting the verb first. Accordingly Jesus says, "He will come, the slave's master," again putting the verb first (vv. 48 & 50). Yes, there is a delay, but just as certainly there is also a coming!

The bad slave notices that the master does not come as soon as he expects him to. What is the time of this delay? In contrast to 25:19, it is not said to be "for a long time." It is not an objective period of time, but a subjective one. The slave says to himself, "He's not coming for a while yet, not as soon as I expected." In the third parable, there is no promise of coming soon, but in the background of the present parable, there seems to be such an expectation.

Was it the case that from Sinai forward the Hebrews-Israelites-Jews expected the Messiah to come soon and thus perceived a delay? No, not from Sinai forward. There is no indication in the Scriptures that the Messiah was to come "soon" after Sinai or soon after David set up the first kingdom. In fact, in the prophecy of Daniel 9, a predicted 490 or so years would take place before the Messiah came on the scene. The Jews could count, however, and they could count the years from Cyrus's decree. The fact that so many false Messiahs showed up around the time of Jesus seems to indicate that a literal 490 years could be counted from Cyrus's decree to three years after the crucifixion (in the middle of the seventieth "week" of years). On the other hand, there can be little doubt but that the 490 years as a whole cannot be taken literally, for it is about eighty years too short. Thus, the appearance of Jesus was "delayed" by about eighty years beyond what Daniel's prophecy, taken literally, would indicate.

Another possibility—and these are not mutually exclusive, since the parable is given in very general, non-allegorical terms—is that the delay is between the time of Jesus' ministry and the Cataclysm. The Jews knew that Jesus had predicted their destruction in an event to come soon; Jesus had said just this to the multitudes in Matthew 23. The unrepentant Jews would see the early Christians acting on this prophecy—selling their property in Jerusalem—but they would also see that the predicted destruction did not happen right away. Thus, while initially they were a bit fearful of the Christians, they would gradually begin to beat them and persecute them, which is just what we see in the early chapters of Acts. As 2 Peter 3:3-4 says, they would begin to mock, asking, "Where is His promised coming?" Indeed, Peter says that these men would "follow their own lusts," language similar to "eat and drink with drunkards" in Matthew 24:48. As the epistle of Jude, 2 Peter 2, and the later letters of Paul make clear, some of the Christian teachers and disciples also fell away and began to mock and live wantonly.

Moreover, if we add the suggested eighty-year delay to the additional forty-year delay between Jesus' ascension and the Cataclysm, we come to about 120 years, the same number of years during which Noah built the ark and warned the people (Gen. 6:3; Matt. 24:37-38). Peter alludes to the "delay" in the days of Noah (2 Pet. 3:5-6). If this supposition is correct, then there was a delay of about 120 years between the time Daniel could be read as indicating that the city would be destroyed and when it actually was.

My interpretive guess is that the Jews did know, from Daniel 9, that the Messiah would come and bring judgment on their city. They expected it to happen around 50 BC. When this did not happen, the faithful religious leaders kept being faithful, like Hannah, who was eighty-four when she saw the baby Jesus (Luke 2:37) and like old Simeon, who had been told he would not die before seeing Him (Luke 2:26), but those who were not inclined to be faithful fell into evil behavior. Jesus condemned them in Matthew 23. Then, when Jesus appeared and raised people from the dead and the sky was darkened for three hours over the city at His crucifixion, they began to walk softly (like Ahab before them, 1 Kings 21:27-28) and look for the judgment to come soon. When that judgment did not come, they went back to their evil behavior, but worse than before (Luke 11:24-26).

The Delay is an important theme in the Bible and an important aspect of how God deals with us. It should make us afraid, very afraid. God promises judgment for a sin and then delays the judgment after we sin. He does this to give us time to repent but also time to harden in our sin. We see this principle immediately in Genesis 3. We know from Genesis 1–3 that only Adam heard God forbid the eating of the fruit of the Tree of the Knowledge of Good and Evil. Eve got her information from Adam, her husband and protector. We know that Adam was standing by silently the whole time the serpent persuaded Eve to eat (Gen. 3:8: "with her"). He did not intervene. Clearly, Adam wanted her to eat the fruit, so he could test God's word. When Eve did not drop dead immediately, Adam went ahead and ate as well. Only then, after the Delay, did God appear to judge Adam.

Similarly, Samuel delayed to come to Saul, arriving after Saul had decided to take matters into his own hands and had stopped trusting the Lord (1 Sam. 13:8-10). Similarly, God did not send Nathan to David immediately after David took Bathsheba, nor after she told him she was pregnant (after a couple of months, probably). God delayed, and David did not repent. David went further and murdered Uriah. Then Nathan came to David.

Be afraid, reader! When you transgress God's law, judgment may not come immediately. The Delay is both a blessing and a curse. God gives you time to repent, but also an opportunity to fall asleep and stop fearing Him. But after the Delay, He surely will come!

B. FOOD

This parable concerns food. The supervision of food takes us all the way back to Genesis 3. Adam was to supervise Eve's eating. That is why God told Adam the rules before Eve was made. Adam was over the Garden, and Eve was part of the Garden he was to serve and guard. Adam was the first priest.

A priest is a royal household servant, a palace servant, and in particular the priests of the Law were concerned with the Lord's Table.[67] As holy chefs they prepared His own meals, the sacrifices, which are called "food offerings" (Lev. 3:11, 16: "bread" for Yahweh). They also dispensed food from His Table to the people, as we have noted. They supervised the eating of the people by maintaining the laws of clean and unclean animals and the law against consuming blood (Lev. 11, 17). In a broader sense, they prepared the people as food for God by teaching them and cleansing them betimes. They were never to grab the food set aside for God or for the people, and they were never to drink wine or strong drink while going about their priestly duties (Lev. 10:9; 1 Sam. 2:15-17).

The wicked priests, however, oppressed the people and ate the food set aside for God and for them (1 Sam. 2:15-17). The wicked priestly house of the Hasmoneans (descendants of the Maccabees) brutally oppressed the people until the Romans rescued them. The evil priest-king Alexander Jannaeus (103–76 BC) slaughtered six thousand of the early (faithful) Pharisees, and on another occasion crucified eight hundred of their leaders during one of his banquets. As we noted, the new priests of God's new Kingdom were beaten by the leader of the Jews throughout the book of Acts.

Did the wicked Jewish priests and religious leaders literally "eat and drink with the drunkards"? Perhaps and perhaps not. Jesus is alluding to the Law and to the history of Israel. Whether they literally did these things or not, in God's eyes they were doing the equivalent.

---

67. See Peter J. Leithart, *The Priesthood of the Plebs: A Theology of Baptism* (Eugene, OR: Wipf & Stock, 2003).

We should not fail to see an allusion to Deuteronomy 21:18-21, which authorizes the death penalty for a *son* who is disobedient and becomes a glutton and a *drunkard*. The wicked Jews had accused the *Son* of Man of this sin (Matt. 11:19), but it was in fact they themselves who were rebellious *sons* and doomed to destruction.

C.   CHOPPED IN TWO

Jesus says that the wicked servants will be cut in two and apportioned with the hypocrites. Several observations should not escape our notice.

First, being apportioned with the hypocrites puts these servants in the same category as the scribes and Pharisees condemned as hypocrites in chapter 23. Thus, Jesus links the Pharisees of His day with these unfaithful slaves.

Second, a hypocrite is literally a person who wears a mask. He has two faces. He is double-minded. Thus, eye for eye and tooth for tooth, his punishment is to be cut in two. His mask will be cut from him.

Third, we should probably link this "dichotomizing" (cutting in two) with the judgment Jesus has already mentioned in which one man is taken and another is left. Just as the unfaithful priest-slave is cut in half, so the nation of priests will be cut in half also.

Finally, being cut in half and then devoured by the birds and beasts is the "curse of the covenant." We have already looked at part of this in Chapter 12.E. above. To review what we wrote there: Every Jewish hearer of Matthew would immediately remember that God had repeatedly pronounced judgment upon Israel in terms of eagles descending upon their corpses (Deut. 28:49; Jer. 4:13; Lam. 4:19; Hos. 8:1; Hab. 1:8). More than that, a basic part of the covenantal curse is to be devoured by birds of the air (Gen. 15:9-12; Deut. 28:26; Prov. 30:17; Jer. 7:33; 15:3; 16:3-4; 19:7; 34:18-20; Ezek. 39:17-20; Rev. 19:17-18). Specifically, the curse was to be hanged up after death on a tree or stake for the birds to eat (Deut. 21:23; 2 Sam. 21:9-10).

When God made the covenant with Abram, He caused the patriarch to divide a set of animals. These animals, made of soil, represented both Abram and the land, which were estranged from one another because of the death-curse of Adam's sin. God's living Shekinah Spirit passed between the dead parts, sealing them back together with His transfiguring fire, uniting Abram to the land in terms of the promise of the covenant (Gen. 15:7-21). Now, in this visionary ritual, the birds tried to devour the divided animal carcasses before God could reunite them, but Abram drove them away (15:11). The meaning is that it is one thing to die, but another to die and be eaten by birds and wild animals. To die and *not* be eaten by the world is to have the prospect of being raised again, but if one *is* eaten by the world after death, then there will be no resurrection to newness of life, only a resurrection to eternal fire. For that reason, the person put to death and hanged up for all to see was not to be left to the wild animals, but to be buried. This rule was fulfilled when Jesus was taken down from the cross and buried, not left for the birds to eat.

Yahweh threatened in Deuteronomy 28:26 that if His people provoked Him too far, they would be slain and left for the birds, "and there will be no one to frighten them away." In other words, they would be abandoned by Abraham. They would not be taken to Abraham's Bosom in death, but would be carried by the birds to Torments in Hades (Luke 16:22-23).

Now, going beyond what we saw in Chapter 12 of the present study, we must build on the fact that Abraham cut the animals in two parts. This is only the first part of death; the animals might be put back together by God's Spirit or left to be eaten by the birds and beasts. Except for Passover, every animal sacrifice was cut into at least two pieces and then put into the fire of God's presence and thereby put back together again, and even in the case of the Passover, the blood was divided from the flesh. It is God who joins things in covenant (1 Sam. 20:42; Gen. 31:49). In circumcision, the human body is cut into two pieces, not in a life-threatening way but in a way that signifies (in part, among other things) what will happen if the covenant is not followed. Dividing them in half and then putting them back together in a new way is what God did as He (covenantally) structured the world in Genesis 1 and when He made Eve out of Adam in Genesis 2. It is how the covenant was made in

Exodus 24:5-8 and how it was affirmed and pronounced over the Land in Deuteronomy 27:12-13. Rending one's garments was a sign of death, and many think that a person rent his garments when he took the curse-oath: "May God do the same thing to me, and more also, if I do not keep this covenant/vow/promise." In other words, "May God tear my body in half, just as I have torn my garment, and also give my flesh to the birds and beasts" (2 Kgs. 6:30-31; compare Ruth 1:17; 1 Sam. 3:17; 14:44; 20:13; 25:22; 2 Sam. 3:9, 35; 19:13; 1 Kgs. 2:23; 20:10).

Thus, Jesus' threat that the unfaithful slave will be cut in two means that he will come under the curse of the covenant. There will be no Abraham (Gen. 15), no Rizpah (2 Sam. 21), to drive the vultures away from his corpse.

D. WEEPING AND GNASHING OF TEETH

In the place where the wicked slave is sent there will be weeping and gnashing of teeth. True weeping is that of sorrow, not of anger. The wicked weep in self-pity and alternate with grinding their teeth in anger at God. Those who hated David, in rebellion against him, gnashed their teeth at him (Pss. 35:16; 37:12). So do the wicked whenever God rewards the righteous (Ps. 112:10), which is just what is happening in this parable. Stephen's sermon set his enemies to gnashing their teeth at him (Acts 7:54).

Six times in Matthew, Jesus foretells that the wicked will spend eternity weeping and gnashing their teeth. In 8:12, He said that the Gentiles would receive the Kingdom gladly, but that the rebellious Jews would weep and gnash their teeth. In 13:42 and 50, the tares and the bad fish would weep and gnash their teeth. So would the man who tried to sneak into the marriage feast without the garments of baptismal repentance (22:13; cf. Acts 2:38). And so will those who are unfaithful with their Kingdom talents (25:30). Apart from Matthew, only Luke records this saying, and only once (Luke 13:28).

Given that this parable is about serving food, we should also see that the gnashing of teeth relates to the removal of God's food from these wicked priests. They abused food; now they will gnash their teeth.

18
THE PARABLE OF THE TEN VIRGINS
(25:1-13)

---

¹At that time the kingdom of heaven will be like ten virgins who, having taken their lamps, went forth to meet the bridegroom.
²And/but (*de*) five of them were foolish and (*kai*) five prudent: ³For they who were foolish, having taken their lamps, did not take oil with themselves, ⁴and/but (*de*) those who were prudent took oil in their vessels with their lamps. ⁵And/but (*de*) with the delaying of the bridegroom, they all became drowsy and slept. ⁶And/but (*de*) in the middle of the night there was a cry, "Behold! The bridegroom comes! Go forth to meet him!" ⁷At that time all those virgins arose and trimmed their lamps.

⁸And/but (*de*) the foolish to the prudent said, "Give us of your oil, because our lamps are going out." ⁹And/but (*de*) the prudent answered, saying, "There may not suffice for us and you. Rather go to the sellers and buy for yourselves." ¹⁰And/but (*de*) as they went away to buy, the bridegroom came, and (*kai*) those ready entered with him to the wedding feast, and (*kai*) the door was shut. ¹¹And/but (*de*) afterwards came also (*kai*) the other virgins, saying, "Master, Master, open to us." ¹²And/but (*de*) he answering said, "Amen I say to you: I do not know you."

¹³Watch, therefore, because you do not know the day or the hour in which the Son of man comes (*erchomai*).

T he parable is arranged as a rough double chiasm. The first
paragraph begins (v. 1) and ends (vv. 6-7) with the going forth of
the virgins with their lamps to meet the bridegroom "at that time."
Between these is a description of the virgins and the delay of the
bridegroom until midnight.

The second paragraph begins (vv. 8-9) and ends (vv. 11-12) with
appeals from the foolish virgins, which are in both cases rejected. At the
center is the arrival of the bridegroom and the beginning of the great
feast.

A. AT THAT TIME

The first paragraph begins and ends with a temporal marker, "at that
time." At what time? In context, the time would be the unknown but
soon-coming "day and hour," and in particular the time just mentioned,
when the master would return and pass judgment on his priestly
servants.

The time, in this parable, is midnight, when the bridegroom arrives.
Verses 1-6 set up the scenario, and then "at that time" is repeated to show
the specific time in view in verse 1, where the parable begins.

This parable concerns the kingdom of heaven, which began in Jesus'
ministry. Thus, it does not stretch all the way back to Mount Sinai in its
purview. The end is the same event as before, however. At the time when
the Old Creation is judged, the kingdom of heaven will pass from a time
of betrothal to a marriage feast. At the time that the priestly servants of
the Old Creation come under full judgment, at that same time all the
believers of the New Creation will also come under a preliminary
judgment. The priestly servants—the Church considered as priestly
servant—will be granted dominion over the Lord's entire world, and at
the same time the virgins—the Church considered as a betrothed
virgin—will enter into the wedding feast with her Betrothed.

The book of Revelation fills out what is stated here. As we have
noted already several times, in Revelation 6 the dead saints of the Old
Creation were told to wait for a short while before joining Jesus in
heaven. During that time, the Apostolic Church saints were sealed and

martyred *en masse* (though not every last one of them). This sacrificed Bride joined with her Groom "outside the city walls" (Heb. 13:13; Rev. 14:20) and then was raised with Him. Now the resurrected Jesus had a resurrected Bride, and the marriage could commence (Rev. 19:7-9).

We have to set aside for a moment our concern with individual human beings and consider the Bride as a corporate body. At Pentecost, and by baptism, the Bride is selected. Then she is prepared by the work of the Spirit (the oil) during the time between Pentecost and the Great Tribulation. Through her overcoming perseverance unto death, she is made fully ready, and the martyred Bride is then clothed in white and enters the time of the wedding feast. The time of the Feast is the Millennial Age. Following this, the Bride is adorned in rainbow colors, beyond the white garments she already has, and the marriage is consummated (Rev. 21:2). These are historical events. We are now living in the time of the Wedding Feast, which will be over when Jesus finally returns at the end of history and will be followed by our everlasting marriage to Him.

On the clothing, recall that the garments of the priests were white underneath, so that they put white holy garments on first, and then colored and glorious garments were put over these. First there was washing (baptism), then investiture with holy (white) undergarments, and finally investiture with colored (glorious) outer garments. In terms of history, the baptismal period is the Apostolic Age, which culminates with the Church's being given white garments. We now live in the time of white garments, moving toward the future time of glorious rainbow garments. (The fact that the New Jerusalem also has a present reality, as people are invited into her, does not change the fact that the primary reference of the image is to the future glory of the Church.)

Jesus has already told us in Matthew 22 that the Wedding Feast phase of history does not start until after the Cataclysm. In the Parable of the Wedding Feast (22:1-13), we find a first group of servants sent out to invite men to a future feast for the Son. These are the Old Creation witnesses. Then, just before the feast begins, new servants are sent forth. These are the New Creation Churchly witnesses. Those invited to the feast, the Jews, as a corporate body reject the invitation, so their city is burned down. That is the Cataclysm. Then the offer is taken to the whole world, because at that point the feast has begun. The feast continues for some time, and at a point during the feast, there is a judgment and those who don't belong there are cast out. This judgment is not said to happen at the end of the feast, but during it. Yet, it points also to the Final Judgment at the end of the feast. In the same way, Jesus' judgments in history, as in Revelation 2–3, anticipate His final judgment at the end of history.

For our purposes here, it is clear that the bridegroom arrives and the wedding feast begins not at Pentecost but at the beginning of the Millennium in AD 70.

B. THE TEMPLE CONTEXT

A Bible-educated Jew of Jesus' day, hearing this parable, would recognize that it alludes to the temple. The wedding feast takes place inside the temple, and the use of lamps and oil as imagery relates to the lampstand in the Holy Place. This connection seems strange to twentieth-century people only because we don't know the Scriptures very well.

While no specific line of the Bible states something like "The temple is where Yahweh married Israel," any Bible student would realize the connection from the following data:

First, the tabernacle/temple was Yahweh's house, and Yahweh took His bride into His house. Note the tabernacle/temple imagery in Ezekiel 16 and Song of Solomon. Ezekiel 16 makes it clear that Yahweh married Israel at Mount Sinai. The tabernacle and later the temple was a symbolic replica of Mount Sinai, a continuing trysting place for God and His bride.[68]

Second, the temple was built on a threshing floor (2 Sam. 24:16-24; 2 Chr. 3:1), a site where several theophanies took place (Judg. 6:37; 2 Sam. 6:5); and Ruth went to Boaz at a threshing floor, which associates

---

68. On the tabernacle as Mount Sinai, see Jordan, *Through New Eyes*, 212f.

the threshing floor with marriage. Hosea 9:1 links sexual fornication with spiritual adultery and a threshing floor.

In some (preliminary) sense, Yahweh was married to Israel at Mount Sinai. The tabernacle/temple was His house and the place where He met with His Bride, Israel. The temple was built on a threshing floor, a place with marital associations. Yet, throughout this period of history only priests were allowed into the temple, and then only into the outer room, the Holy Place. The high priest was allowed to take a step into the inner room, the Holy of Holies, only on the Day of Coverings, and then only to toss blood toward the Ark-throne.

Thus, the temple as Yahweh's house was the place where God and His wife Israel met by proxy (through the representative priests), but it was also a picture of the fact that there was going to be a future, fuller marriage. The veils of the tabernacle and temple correspond, in part, to the veil between groom and bride, mentioned in Genesis 24:65 and 2 Corinthians 3:12-18. In Genesis 24:65, Rebekah veils herself, not because she is going to meet a man—she has been unveiled with the (male) servant of Abraham all this time—but because she is about to meet the man she is going to marry. The rending of the veil at the death of Jesus spoke of the beginning of the wedding event.

Note also the mention of the door in verse 10. In our comments on 24:33 (in chapter 14 above), we pointed out that the doors of the temple were in plain view during Jesus' speech. At this point, we should remember that the doors of the temple, as a permanent building, correspond to the veils of the tabernacle, a temporary building.

As noted above, the saints in Revelation passed from being "under the altar" to being in the heavenly temple at the close of the Apostolic Age. As we shall see in a moment, they are the virgins who enter into the marriage feast at that time.

C. Midnight

The bridegroom arrives "in the middle of the night," or at the center of the night, at midnight. Immediately we think of Passover. When God brought judgment on Egypt, after many warnings, the Angel of Death visited the land during the night and slew the firstborn of those who refused the blood of the Passover lamb. Revelation 11:8 tells us that the judgment on Jerusalem/Babylon is a fulfillment of the judgments on Sodom and Egypt. In both cases, judgment took place at midnight.

At midnight things are settled. After midnight, the day moves toward dawn and daylight. Lot and his family left Sodom during the night, and as the day broke, Sodom was destroyed but they were saved. The Israelites left Egypt as the day broke after the Passover night, while the Egyptians mourned the destruction of their future (their sons). At midnight, Boaz (Jesus) awoke to Ruth (the virgins of the church) (Ruth 3:8). At midnight, King Ahasuerus decided to honor the Jews (Esth. 6). At midnight, God restored Israel in the person of Jeshua the high priest (Zech. 3, at the center of the night visions of Zech. 1–6). At midnight, an earthquake shook the Philippian jailor to his senses (Acts 16:25). At midnight, Paul raised a fallen son to life again and served the Christian Passover meal (Acts 20:7-12). At midnight, Paul challenged the Romans to abandon the ship of Rome and put their trust in Jesus, and served them bread (Acts 27:27-44).

While midnight brings a change, it is also associated with marriage, as in the case of Boaz and Ruth and in the case of Yahweh's claiming Israel at Passover (Ezek. 16).

Midnight is the "hour" of the "the day and the hour." When midnight is reached, it is too late for the Egyptians and for all others who refuse to trust the word of God and come under the blood of Jesus. When midnight is reached, the saints of God are delivered.

D. THE VIRGINS

The Church is a corporate Bride. Jesus marries the Church. The virgins as a group are the Bride; we notice that there is no other "bride" mentioned in the parable.

Virginity is a symbol of natural, unspoiled purity. Eve was the virgin bride of Adam. The high priest was required to marry a virgin (Lev. 21:13). The daughter of a priest who played the harlot in her father's house, spoiling her virginity, might be killed and then her body burned as something unclean (Lev. 21:9). Any girl who married and turned out not to be a virgin also might be put to death if her husband demanded it (Deut. 22:13-21).

Of course, all of us have played the harlot in Adam, and thus none of us are spiritual virgins. How can we be counted as virgins? The only way is if someone takes the penalty we deserve. The proof that a girl was a virgin is the blood on her wedding sheet (Deut. 22:15). If the girl is not a virgin, substitute blood is required. Jesus' blood is our substitute. As our "tokens of virginity," His blood is publicly displayed on the cross. The blood on the doorways at Passover also had this meaning, among other meanings. Those within the houses, who passed through the blooded doors, acquired tokens of virginity and went to marry Yahweh at Mount Sinai. Under the Law, part of the meaning of the circumcision of the man was that his blood would become a token of virginity for his wife; that is why women did not need to be "circumcised" in some fashion. This explains why Zipporah, when she circumcised her son, called him a "bridegroom of blood," for it is on the wedding night that the bridegroom gets blood on himself, and thus the blood of circumcision is related to the blood that proves a woman a virgin (Exod. 4:24-26). Notice that Zipporah smeared the blood on the legs of her sons, displaying it openly, just like Passover.[69]

The virgins in our parable are the 144,000 saints of Revelation. They are the untouched oil and wine, the firstfruits of the harvest, that are sealed by the Spirit before the destruction of the Cataclysm (Rev. 6:6; 7:3ff.). They stand on Mount Sinai, the place of the earlier marriage, as virgins with the Lamb, whose blood provides a legal restoration of their virginity (Rev. 14:1-5). It is they, along with the earlier saints under the altar of Revelation 6, who join Jesus at the Marriage Supper of the Lamb after the Cataclysm (Rev. 19; cf. 2 Cor. 11:1-3).

---

69. For a full discussion of this matter, see my essay "Proleptic Passover" in Jordan, *The Law of the Covenant* (Tyler, TX: Institute for Christian Economics, 1984).

E. THE OIL

In terms of Biblical symbolism, oil is liquid light. The description of the anointing oil in Exodus 30:22-33 occupies the fourth speech in God's commands to make the tabernacle (Exod. 25–31), which consists of seven speeches replicating the seven days of Genesis 1. The oil, thus, corresponds to the heavenly lights. Also, Exodus 25:1–30:10, the First Day/first speech section of the tabernacle commands, has seven sections, and the oil for the lampstand occupies the fourth section (27:20-21).[70] Oil fed the lampstand in the tabernacle and temple, making light. Oil placed on priests and kings made them lights. Thus, the oil in the vessels of the virgins provided light in their time of darkness.

Behind light is the Holy Spirit, who made light on the first day of creation. Thus, oil signifies the Spirit, who makes the lampstand in the tabernacle shine. The lampstand itself is a golden almond tree (in Hebrew, a "watcher tree"). The lights of that overseer tree shine over the twelve loaves of face-bread, signifying the priests (and Yahweh) watching over Israel (Exod. 25:37). Symbolically, we can add, gold is solid light in the Bible, and thus the overseer lampstand was a tree of light.[71]

It is the Spirit who empowers the lampstand to shed light. It is the Spirit who empowered the priests and kings of the Old Creation. It is the Spirit who empowers us as lights in the world today. The Spirit was given in full measure on Pentecost, and He is the oil carried by the virgins of the New Creation Church.

The priests were required to trim the wicks of the sevenfold watcher-lampstand daily and to fill the lamps with oil (Exod. 30:7-8; Lev. 24:3). As the watcher-lampstand oversaw the twelve tribes of face-bread, the watcher-lampstand represented the priests. They were trimming their own wicks and taking oil into themselves, so that they could shine forth

---

70. For a full discussion of Exodus 25–31, see Jordan, *The Tabernacle: A New Creation*, Biblical Horizons Occasional Paper 5 (Niceville, FL: Biblical Horizons, 1993).

71. In Exodus 38:24, the gold adds up to twenty-nine talents, the days of a lunar month, and 730 shekels, twice the days in a solar year—thus, symbolically, the solar and lunar light. Also, Zechariah 4:12 calls the lampstand oil "gold."

God's light faithfully to the people. Since the tabernacle was enclosed completely, it was dark all the time and the lampstand probably burned day and night; but the texts cited above speak only of burning the lamps from evening to morning, during the night. The priest would have to make certain that each lamp had enough oil to last the night. It was during the night, before the lamps had given out of oil, that God called Samuel and condemned Eli—another "midnight" event (1 Sam. 3:3).

Now in the New Creation, all believers are priests. We all are lampstands, shining in this world. We must keep our wicks clean and maintain our oil. That oil is the Spirit. The Spirit does not come to us only once and deposit a lifetime's supply of His power. We have to renew our fellowship with Him periodically and ask Jesus for the Spirit from time to time (Luke 11:13).

The wise virgins kept close to God, renewing their fellowship with Him by asking for the Spirit and receiving a double portion—enough to keep their lamps burning and enough to resupply their lamps. The foolish virgins coasted on their past experiences, and when the crisis came, found that they did not have the Spirit with them any longer.

The foolish virgins were told to go to the sellers and buy more oil. Buying and selling is a frequent metaphor for worship in the Bible, especially in the book of Revelation (Isa. 55:1; Rev. 3:18; 13:17; 18:11-17a; 22:17). Before the Bridegroom comes, it is always possible to go to God and ask for the Spirit—that is what the advice of the wise virgins means. But when the Bridegroom comes, it is too late. Notice in the parable that the foolish virgins went away to buy oil, but it is not said that they were successful. When they come back, nothing is said about their having gotten more oil. The implication is pretty clear: It was too late to buy oil. The shops had closed long before midnight.

F.   THE JUDGMENT

Jesus tells the foolish virgins: "Amen I say to you: I do not know you." This is virtually the same thing He said in Matthew 7:23 to the false prophets. It is a fearful statement.

If we look at the Gospels, Acts, and Epistles, we find those like Judas and Demas who did receive the Spirit but who failed to persevere and eventually fell away. Moreover, the whole company of the Judaizers is in this category. The Epistles warn against grieving the Spirit, and even more to our purpose, quenching the Spirit: putting out His light with water (1 Thess. 5:19). In Galatians, Paul warns his Gentile hearers that they must maintain their walk in the Spirit and not be drawn away (Gal. 3:2-3).

The warning is clear: There definitely are such people as temporary believers, those who do not keep up their walk on the Way. Jesus had spoken of them in the Parable of the Soils in Matthew 13. Hebrews 6 speaks of them, and so do many other passages of Scripture.

The warning had a particular historical urgency in the first century, since Jesus was shortly going to manifest His rule in the Cataclysm. But it applies in all times, for none of us knows the hour of his death. When we die and our souls come to the doorway into the ongoing heavenly marriage feast, we must be ready with oil in our lamps.

The wise virgins of the parable entered into the feast when they died. Revelation 14 speaks of the massacre of the 144,000 virgins. Their blood covered the land and called up the Avenger of Blood, who came and destroyed Babylon/Jerusalem and the Beasts. In Revelation 15, they are shown in heaven, and shortly they enter into the marriage feast. The same is true of us when we die. We enter into the continual feast, joining the heavenly saints in waiting for the feast to end and the full marriage to begin. To be sure, we have a foretaste of that feast each Sunday when we come to the Lord's Table, but in heaven the feast will be continual.

THE PROGRESS OF THE CELESTIAL MARRIAGE

1. **The Betrothal Period:**
   A. From Abraham to Passover (Israel's typological history).
   B. From Adam to the Cross (history of humanity).

2. **The Restoration of Virginity before the Marriage:**
   A. Passover: the blood of the Lamb.
   B. The Cross: the blood of Jesus.

3. **The Beginning of the Wedding Ceremony:**
   A. Moses enters the cloud: veil lifted.
   B. Veil of the temple is rent: veil lifted.

4. **The Wedding Ceremony:**
   A. The events at Mount Sinai: formation of the bride.
   B. From Pentecost to the Cataclysm: formation of the bride.

5. **The Marriage Feast after the Ceremony:**
   A. The festivals of the Law.
   B. The Marriage Supper of the Lamb.

6. **The Divorce:**
   A. The Destruction of Babylon/Jerusalem (Deut. 24:1).
   B. The Last Judgment.

7. **The Married Life: From the Last Judgment forever and ever.**

19
THE PARABLE OF THE TALENTS
(25:14-30)

¹⁴For [it is] just like [this:]

a.　A man going on a *journey*

　　b.　called his own *slaves,*

　　　　c.　and (*kai*) delivered to them his property;

　　　　c'　¹⁵and (*kai*) to one he gave five talents, and to another two, and to another one,

　　b'　*each* according to his own ability;

a'　and went on the *journey.*

Immediately ¹⁶he who received the five talents worked with them and gained another five talents. ¹⁷In like manner he of the two gained also another two, ¹⁸and/but (*de*) he who received the one, having gone away, dug earth and hid the money of his master.

¹⁹And/but (*de*) after a long time comes the master of those slaves and settles account with them. ²⁰And (*kai*) having come forward, he who had received the five talents brought another five talents, saying, "Master, five talents to me you delivered. Behold, another five talents have I gained besides them." ²¹His master said to him, "Well done, good and faithful slave. Over a few things you were faithful; over many things will I set you. Enter into the joy of your master."
²²And/but also (*de kai*) having come forward, he of the two talents said, "Master, two talents to me you delivered. Behold, another two talents have I gained besides them."

²³His master said to him, "Well done, good and faithful slave. Over a few things you were faithful; over many things will I set you. Enter into the joy of your master."

²⁴And/but also (*de kai*) having come forward, he who had received [and still retained] the one talent said, "Master, I knew [full well] that you [of all people] are a hard man, reaping where you did not sow and gathering whence you did not scatter, ²⁵And (*kai*) being afraid, having gone away I hid your talent in the earth. Behold, you have your own."

²⁶And/but (*de*) answering, his master said to him, "Wicked slave, and slothful! Did you know [have information] that I reap where I sowed not and gather whence I scattered not? ²⁷You were obligated therefore to put my money with the bankers, and (*kai*) coming I should have received my own with interest.

²⁸"Take therefore from him the talent, and (*kai*) give to him who has the ten talents. ²⁹For to everyone one who has will be given, and he will be in abundance, and/but (*de*) the one who has not, even what he has will be taken from him. ³⁰And (*kai*) the useless slave, cast out into the outer darkness. In that place will be the weeping and the gnashing of the teeth."

The parable has three sections: The departure of the master, the work of the slaves, and the judgment of the slaves. The opening paragraph, vv. 14-15, has a roughly chiastic structure. This paragraph also sets up the structure of the remainder of the parable, which consistently progresses from the five-talent slave to the two-talent slave and then to the one-talent slave.

A. THE TALENTS

A talent weighs about seventy-five pounds. We are not told whether these were silver or gold talents, but since silver was worth only slightly less than gold in the ancient world, it does not make much difference. The talent was the largest weight in the ancient world, and thus the largest weight of money. William Hendriksen writes that "an Attic [Greek] talent, the kind probably meant here [Matt. 18:24], amounted to no less than six thousand denarii or denars. At the rate of six denars a week (a denar for each working day, cf. 20:1, 13), it would take a laborer a thousand weeks to earn just one talent."[72] In other words, a talent was roughly equivalent to twenty years' pay for a day laborer. Accordingly, we are dealing with a very large amount of money in this parable.

While food is the responsibility of priests, as we saw in the first parable (24:45-51), money, especially in large amounts, is the provenance of kings. The word "talent" in particular is associated with kings. First it is associated with the tabernacle, the palace of King Yahweh, in Exodus 25:39; 37:24 (the weight of the golden lampstand); 38:24-29 (the weights of gold, silver, and bronze used in the palace); and with the temple, also Yahweh's palace (1 Chr. 22:14; 29:4, 7; 2 Chr. 3:8; Ezra 8:26). Otherwise, it is associated with earthly kings (2 Sam. 12:30; 1 Kgs. 9:14, 28; 10:10, 14; 16:24; 20:39; 2 Kgs. 5:5, 22-23; 15:19; 18:24; 23:33; 1 Chr. 19:6; 20:2; 2 Chr. 8:18; 9:9, 13; 25:6, 9; 27:5; 36:3; Ezra 8:22; Esth. 3:9). Interestingly, apart from Revelation 16:21, the equivalent Greek word occurs only in Matthew 18:24 and in our parable.

Thus, we move from priestly to kingly in the progression of the parables. Those who were faithful as priests are now elevated to kings. This is a move from the Old Creation to the New, as we have seen. In the first parable, the master is not said to depart. Though later on he comes and judges the slaves, this does not mean he has been wholly absent from the scene. Applying this to covenant history, we see Yahweh set up His palace at Sinai and assign His palace servants (priests) to administer His food to His people. His coming in judgment corresponds to the events of the Cataclysm. In the present parable, the servants are given charge of the entire estate and the master departs for a distant land, returning only after a long time. This corresponds to Jesus' ascension and His bequest of His kingdom to His people, especially to those who have the keys of the kingdom (the pastors). The parable, thus, begins in AD 30 with Jesus' departure and really gets going in the events of the Cataclysm, when the saints ascend to reign with Him. It ends at the second coming.

---

72. William Hendriksen, *The Gospel of Matthew* (Grand Rapids: Baker, 1973), 705.

The talents are often associated with our native abilities and capacities. This cannot be correct, since the talents are given to the slaves according to the abilities they already possessed. The talents are something added, something intimately related to the Kingdom of God. We need to note that this parable is "just like" the preceding parable. Thus the talents correspond to the oil of the Spirit in the Parable of the Virgins. In the book of Revelation, financial transactions symbolize liturgical transactions, and Jesus' statement in Matthew 6:24 that "you cannot serve God and mammon" builds on the fact that *mamon* is related to *amen* (cp. Luke 16:11).[73] Thus, ultimately the talent that God gives to us is our personal relationship with Him; that is, God gives us Himself. In historical context, the talent, like the oil, is the gift of the Spirit that Jesus leaves behind when He departs.

The way of the Kingdom is that it grows through faithfulness in the midst of tribulation. The saints in Revelation "overcome" through suffering and martyrdom. The talents have everything to do with this call to faithful endurance, as we shall see.

B. DOUBLING THE TALENTS

Thus, to build on our talents is to build up our relationship with God. The wise virgins had double the needed amount of oil. In the same way, the wise believer doubles his original relationship with God. Just as the foolish virgins failed to take double the amount of oil they would need, so the wicked slave fails to double his talent. At the end, those with only the original deposit are lost.

The person who is only baptized, or only converted, will not be saved. That is the meaning of the parable. We must grow in our relationship with God, whether that relationship begins at our baptism, or when we are infants, or when we are converted later in life. If there is no growth, then there was no true conversion. The talent given at baptism or

---

73. See James B. Jordan, "The Financial Metaphor in Revelation," *Special Studies in the Book of Revelation*, Biblical Horizons Occasional Paper 40 (Niceville, FL: Biblical Horizons, 2011).

conversion, the oil received at that time, will prove useless unless we grow with it.

The same teaching is found throughout the book of Hebrews, as well as in Jesus' Parable of the Vine in John 15. The Parable of the Vine teaches us that if we abide in Jesus we will bear fruit, but that if we don't abide with Him, we shall be cut off. The Parable of the Talents does not contradict this, as if the Master's departure means that we are on our own. Rather, the talent is the Spirit, and the Spirit connects us to our absent Savior, making Him Spiritually present with us. Thus, to use our talent is to use the Spirit to keep in touch with Jesus, to abide in Him, so that we grow.

Hence, the praise of the Master is that the good slaves are "faithful." They had lived by faith in Him. Their faith was not a one-time act but a life of faithfulness. They were trustworthy and loyal. It is as we remain faithful, trusting God day by day, accepting His gift day by day, that our talents transform and multiply, even if we don't see it and others don't see it. It is not a matter of works, but a matter of remaining faithful, of coming to God day by day and asking for the Spirit, trusting Him.

By way of contrast, the wicked slave was "afraid," "slothful," and "useless." He did not trust God day by day but claims that he was afraid of Him—something that was not true, as we shall see. Being slothful, he assumed that having the initial deposit of the talent was enough. He is like the man who is baptized and assumes he will go to heaven because of that alone, or like the woman who has a conversion experience and assumes that this initial deposit is enough for final salvation. Being slothful and not moving on into a life of faithfulness, he becomes useless.

It does not matter how many talents we have. The talents are given to each slave according to his or her God-given capacity. Thus, to reiterate, our original gifts and abilities are not the talents in view in this parable. The talents are added to them. Again, then, the talents are the Spirit, who is given to enable us to transform and enlarge our original capacities. Those who have many native gifts are given more of the Spirit, because their greater capacities and abilities require more.

We must be aware that God does not measure ability and does not give out talents along the lines we might think. The humble, uneducated peasant woman might be the person of large capacity who is given five talents, while the deep and Godly theologian might in fact be the person of lesser capacity who is given fewer talents. Who of us is to say?

The talents are intimately related to *suffering*, our participation in the tribulation and death of Jesus. Like the apostles in Acts, we rejoice that we are awarded the privilege of suffering for Jesus' name (Acts 5:41). This has been a theme of the entire discourse, especially in Matthew 24:21-22. Those who suffer in union with Jesus, through the Spirit, will be rewarded in union with Him.

The parable makes a fairly direct allusion to Job, who was given double what he lost (Job 41:10). Job did not "earn" anything; he simply suffered in faith. He remained faithful. The talent given him was suffering. That suffering bore fruit in a transformed person, whose capacities were enlarged as a result of it. At the end of his suffering, Job had become a man who was able to manage twice as much as he had been able to govern before. The talents are the Spirit, who enables us to be faithful in the midst of tribulation and to be transformed by it.

Job, in fact, lost his first set of talents. They were destroyed and he was left alone. His talents were ploughed under and arose as a doubled set. As we shall see, this burying of the initial talents is an integral part of the deep structure of the parable. (Recall that parables are not simple stories, but mysteries that contain great depths.)

The book of Job is part of the "wisdom literature" of Israel produced in the days of David and Solomon. Job is a true Solomon. If we look at Solomon, we see the wicked slave. Solomon was given great talents but chose to hoard them rather than use them. He built up his own glory and as a result lost control of his kingdom. King Job (Job 29:25) parallels King Solomon as "the richest man in the east."

If we look at the priestly period in the Bible (from Sinai to Saul), we do not see men going through this calling of suffering with great rewards at the end. That is because priests (children) are not given talents in the sense kings (adults) are. The people of the first period of history are called to guard and administer God's palace, not to administer something given to them. Kings, however, are given an estate to manage. The passage from priestly childhood, where God feeds us and shelters us, to the time of kingly adulthood, where God calls on us to suffer with Jesus, is the passage not only from Aaron to Saul, but from Israel to the Church. Thus, to reiterate a point made earlier, the Parable of the Talents contrasts with the Parable of the Unfaithful Slave in Matthew 24:45-51. The unfaithful slave was called to feed God's people; the slaves in the Parable of the Talents are called to suffer.

Kings are called to manage an estate given them, the outward form of their talents. But how must they manage it? Not by grasping it and holding onto it, but by freely giving it out. They must be like God, who with infinite generosity gives Himself and His gifts to others. By enslaving the people and making them labor at public works, Solomon proved a wicked king. Job, however, was always generous. He used his riches to care for the poor and the widow and the fatherless. The bounty of his table was open to all who needed it. Job, in other words, put his talents to use.

Then God took them all away from Job. Job did not bury his talents, but God buried them! Job was left alone. Like Abraham, Jacob, Joseph, and Moses before him, Job was challenged to forsake everything God had given him, trusting God to return to him in time.[74] Passing through this period of desertion, when the Spirit (the fullness of the talents) seemed to leave him and his sense of God's presence evaporated, Job was transformed into a man able to manage double what he had managed before. It was just the opposite with Solomon: Half his kingdom was taken from him. Solomon's talents were halved while Job's were doubled.

---

74. See my essays "Patriarchal Dominion," *Biblical Horizons* 108 (August 1998) and "Crisis Time: Patriarchal Prologue," *Biblical Horizons* 109-113 (September 1998–January 1999).

C. THE REWARD

Whether we have small or large abilities and whether we receive few or many talents of the Spirit, the reward for faithfulness is the same: Commendation, exaltation, and eternal joy with the Master. No Christian will resent the fact that others seem to have more, because all will be suffused with joy and will rejoice in what others have.

The fact that the talent of the wicked slave is given to the man with ten talents calls for two comments. First, we see that nothing God gives is ever wasted. While this parable points to the last judgment, it also applies in history. If God gives men abilities that are not transformed by the Spirit, those abilities will be given to others and thereby will be incorporated into the developing and maturing of His people.

Second, it may seem "unfair" that the man with ten talents is given an eleventh, while the man who was just as faithful, but who has only four, is not given a fifth. Perhaps, though, we should think that the man with ten talents is in the best position to make use of the extra one. On the other hand, the way the parable is worded indicates to me that both men are given access to the additional talent in the common Kingdom.

Notice that verse 17, dealing with the two-talent man, is a much-condensed version of verse 16 but begins "in like manner." Similarly, verse 22 is a condensed version of verse 20. If they were precisely identical, then the gift of the extra talent to the first man would stand in contrast with the estate of the second. Jesus' choice of phrases, however, indicates that the second man did exactly what the first man did. There is a hint that he was taking his cue from the first man.

If I am right, the first man is the leader and the other two are called to be followers, in some sense. The second man acts "in like manner" to the first, while the third man separates from them, "having gone away." This phrase, "having gone away" is repeated (vv. 17, 25) and thus is important. The third man did not bury his talent near where the other two were working but separated from them. By implication, the second man stayed with the first and thus shares in the extra talent given to the first.

Along these lines, we can consider an alternative parable, in which there are only two servants, one faithful and one wicked. Jesus might have told the parable that way, and we might expect it in light of many other passages of the Bible (Cain and Abel, Jacob and Esau, the two men in the temple, etc.) but He did not. The fact that there are three man and two of them are faithful indicates that community is in view. The first two slaves form a community, from which the third isolates himself. Thus, the gift of the extra talent to the first man means that it is given to the whole community, including the second.

D. The Sin

The Spirit works in community, not in isolation. We are commanded not to forsake assembling together but to remain in the community of the Church that we might be stimulated to love and good works (Heb. 10:24-25). This is precisely what the third man did not do. Forsaking the community of the laboring and suffering faithful is equivalent to burying his talent. It is because he received no stimulation to love and good works that his talent was not doubled and he was condemned.

Verse 18 says that the third man "dug earth" and hid the money of his master. It does not say that he dug a hole in the earth, but that he dug earth. This strikingly condensed phrase points us to the nature of his action, which is more than merely practical. The judgment on humanity is to return to the earth in death (Gen. 3:19), and being buried in the earth is a symbolic picture of death, as when Joseph and later Jeremiah are lowered into pits. Thus, the third man killed his talent, consigning it to death. The meaning would be the same, of course, even if Jesus had said that he "dug a hole in the earth," but the terse wording calls our attention to the nature of the sin more pointedly.

Verse 24 uses the present participle of "receive," literally reading "he who is receiving the one talent," to indicate that he still had the talent given him. The contrast is with verse 20, which says that the first slave "had received" his talents. The fact that the third slave still had his original talent tells us that the other two slaves did not have their original talents. Theirs had been ploughed into use and had become double. Until the day of judgment, however, it was still possible for the third slave to retrieve his and begin to make use of it.

He never did so, however, because he "knew" the master was harsh. Again, the book of Job provides light on the matter. Like Job, the first two slaves underwent trials. Like Job, they may have felt harshly treated, but like Job they never charged God foolishly. The loss of the talents, which again are ultimately the Spirit, is seen in Job as Job loses any sense of God's nearness. Job maintains faithfulness, however, even through this "dark night of the soul," with the result that his Spirit-talents are doubled. Seeing what the first two slaves were undergoing in their lives, the third slave rejected the life of faith. He buried his talent and walked away. He did not persevere through tribulation. He did not remain in the community of the faithful and receive stimulation to love and good works, help through his trial. Instead, he charged God foolishly.

When called before the master, the third slave accuses him of harshness and unfairness. The word "know" (*ginosko*) in verse 24 means "full knowledge" or "heart knowledge" and contrasts with the word for "know" (*oida*) in verse 26, which means "information knowledge." Moreover, the slave includes the pronoun "you" when speaking to the master, something that is unnecessary in Greek and indicates emphasis: "you of all people."

Thus, the third slave was convinced in his heart that the master had evil intentions toward him and toward people in general. He accuses the master of reaping where he did not sow and of gathering whence he did not scatter seed. This is a false accusation. Not only does nothing indicate that the master is like this, but since the master is God, it is preposterous. As the Creator, God sowed and scattered every seed that has even grown up in history. Since God sowed everywhere, He is fully entitled to reap everywhere. With this view of the master, and of God, the servant was afraid, and in his fear refused to use his talent.

Whence came these notions? From Satan in the Garden of Eden. Satan's word to Adam and Eve boils down to this: "God does not have good intentions toward you. God wants you to be deprived. You cannot trust Him. And because God is evil, you need to be afraid of Him." In other words, God is a monster.

The third slave thinks exactly this way, which is the way all sinners think, inheriting this attitude from Adam. Because we are sinfully afraid of what God is doing to us, Jesus repeatedly commands us, "Fear not!" Over and over again the Bible shows us God doing good things for those who do not deserve it. We are assured repeatedly that God has good and loving intentions toward us, and indeed toward all mankind and toward every particular individual. Before God calls us to suffer as kings, He feeds us and cares for us as priestly children. The slaves had been cared for by the master for years before he left and put them in charge. Thus, we have no reason to fear God's intentions, but every reason to fear His judgment.

The third slave did not fear God's judgment until it was too late, and even then he asserted his pride and charged God falsely. It is either the one or the other: Either we are suspicious and fearful about God's intentions toward us, in which case we are not really fearing His day of reckoning, or else we are fearful of the day of reckoning, in which case we shall obey Him and put away our fear. Again we see this in Job, who kept in mind that at the last day he would stand in his flesh before God and who endured in faithfulness because of that belief.

When bad things happen to us, we naturally think, "Why is God doing this to me?" Following Satan's word, and like Adam, we suspect that God wants to hurt us. In fact, however, the bad things that happen to us are intended for our good, to prune us and to transform us. In the same way, God's prohibition on the Tree of the Knowledge of Good and Evil was for Adam's good. The sinner, however, thinks that God's "thou shalt nots" are intended to keep us from good things, from happiness.

If the third slave had really feared God in the right way, he would never have forsaken the companionship of the other two. They would have stimulated him to love and good works, and he would have grown in faith and confidence and his talent would have doubled. For this reason, even his assertion that he was afraid is suspect.

E. THE JUDGMENT

The master repeats the wicked slave's accusation with sarcasm: "So you received information that I am unfair, did you?" Sarcasm is indicated not only by the fact that it is phrased as a question, but also by the change in the verb for "know," discussed above. In essence, the master accuses the slave of having received an evil report. As we have seen, this evil report originated with the Slanderer.

Then the master points out the absurdity of the evil slave's charge: "If you were really afraid of me, and you knew that I expected a return on my money, you would at least have invested it." By saying this, the master rejects the slave's claim to have been afraid. The slave may have felt fear, but it was the fear of personal discomfort, not any fear of the master. If he had feared the master, he would not have buried the master's talent.

The judgment on the wicked slave fits his crime. The slave had "gone away" from the community of the other slaves, and now he is sent away for good. He wanted to be separate, and now he will be separated forever.

This judgment is a fearful warning to those who separate from the Church and become merely "private Christians." It stands against ordinary people who don't bother to come to Church on Sunday. It stands against those monks of the early Church, some of them anyway, who lived alone in the desert. It stands against those who reject God's calling to tribulation, who fear pain more than judgment.

And since what applies to individuals also applies to groups, this judgment stands against communities of "Christians" who isolate themselves from the larger Church and from God's work in history, such as many groups of Mennonites, the Amish, and the like. The Amish have been given talents by the Spirit, but instead of developing them in time and history, they have separated themselves and to too large an extent buried their talents, isolating them from God's call to disciple the nations.

20
THE FINAL JUDGMENT
(25:31-46)

---

³¹And/but (*de*) when the Son of man comes (*erchomai*) in His glory,
and (*kai*) all the angels with Him,
{1} at that time will He sit on the throne of His glory,
³²and before Him will be gathered all the nations.
And (*kai*) He will separate them from one another,
as the shepherd separates the sheep from the goats.
³³And (*kai*) He will set the sheep at His right hand,
and/but (*de*) the goats at the left.

{2} ³⁴At that time will the King say to them at His right hand,
"Come, blessed ones of My Father,
inherit the kingdom prepared for you from the foundation of the world:
³⁵for I hungered, and you gave Me to eat;
I thirsted, and you gave Me drink;
a stranger I was, and you took Me in;
³⁶naked, and you clothed Me;
I became ill, and you looked after Me;
in prison I was, and you came to Me."

{3} ³⁷At that time will the righteous answer Him, saying,
"Lord, when did we see You hungry, and fed You?
or thirsty, and gave You drink?
³⁸And/but (*de*) when did we see You a stranger, and took You in?
or naked, and clothed You?
³⁹And/but (*de*) when did we see You ill, or in prison, and came to You?"
⁴⁰And (*kai*) answering the King will say to them,

"Amen I say to you,

Inasmuch as you did it to one of these least of My brothers,

you did it to Me."

{4} [41]At that time will He say also (*kai*) to them at the left hand,

"Depart from Me, cursed ones,

into the everlasting fire which is prepared for the devil and his angels:

[42]for I hungered, and you did not give Me to eat;

I thirsted, and you gave Me no drink;

[43]a stranger I was, and you took Me not in;

naked, and you clothed Me not;

ill, and in prison, and you did not look after Me."

{5} [44]At that time they also will answer, saying,

"Lord, when did we see You

hungry,

or athirst,

or a stranger,

or naked,

or ill,

or in prison,

and did not minister to You?"

{6} [45]At that time will He answer them, saying,

"Amen I say to you,

inasmuch as you did it not to one of these least,

you did it not to Me."

[46]And (*kai*) these will go away into everlasting punishment,

but (*de*) the righteous into everlasting life.

This passage consists of six paragraphs, the first of which begins with "at the time when" and the next five of which begin "at that time." The four lists have a certain balance in that the second and fifth paragraphs list six items using the same basic grammatical form, while the third and fourth paragraphs condense the list of six into five by linking illness and imprisonment.[75]

In chapter 16 of these studies we have seen that this scene prophesies the events of the final judgment at the end of history, not the judgment upon Jewry and the Oikumene that came in AD 70. Since the two events are analogous, of course, this prophecy certainly received a preliminary fulfillment in the complex of events around AD 70, but in context, and given the "all nations" language as well as the "throne" language, we have seen that the final coming is principally in view.

We can also notice that the saints are given a kingdom here that is everlasting (vv. 34, 46). This is not the Millennial kingdom, which began in AD 70 and which will come to an end. Thus, the judgment scene in this passage is the same as the Great White Throne judgment in Revelation 20:11.

In terms of the chiasm of Matthew 23–25, this passage fits with the beginning of Matthew 23. There the scribes and Pharisees sat on the seat of Moses to pass judgments; here the Son of Man sits on the glorious throne provided by His Father. The disciples were told to hearken to the judgments of the scribes and Pharisees for the time being, but at the end, all will hearken to the judgment of the Son.

---

75. That this list is carefully repeated four times may be important thematically to the passage as a whole. The number four in Scripture is often used symbolically or with symbolic overtones to indicate the extent of dominion, as in the four corners (literally sides) of the earth, the four corners of the altar, the four rivers that flow from the garden of Eden, and so forth. In Matthew 23–25, a number of significant words appear either four times or in multiples of four, and in contrast to this we do not find any terms repeated six or seven times. Hence, the number four seems to be linked with the passage as a whole as a kind of deep structure indicating in another way the fulness and extent of the judgments prophesied. To wit:

Jesus 4x
scribes and Pharisees 8x
prophet 8x
manifestation (*parousia*) 4x
come (*erchomai*) 8x
Son of Man 8x
day 12x
hour 4x
angel/messenger 4x
mislead 4x

In Matthew 23:1-12, Jesus said that those who humbled themselves would be exalted, and here we see what this means: Those who serve the poor, the hungry, the ill, the imprisoned, and so forth, will be exalted. Those who refuse to humble themselves will be abased.

In Matthew 23:1-12, Jesus had said that there was one Father over all, and one Teacher and Leader, Himself. He had said that His followers were all brothers. These themes now recur in this section at the end of His discourse.

Though the nations are gathered, it is not the nations as such that are judged but individuals. This is indicated by the fact that "nations" is neuter, while the "them" that are separated is masculine. The same kind of shift is found in the Great Commission of Matthew 28:19: Go to all nations (neuter), baptizing them (masculine). Thus, the sheep and goats are not nations, but individual people within all the nations.

A. THE SON OF MAN AS SHEPHERD

As we have seen throughout this study, "the son of man" can be a reference to the entire community of the saints or to their Head, Jesus Christ. Here it is clear that the individual person of Jesus is in view, because it is the saints who are judged along with the rest of humanity.

We have seen that Jesus as "Son of Man" is a Greater Ezekiel. Ezekiel passed judgment not only upon Jerusalem (Ezek. 43:3; 11:1-13), but also upon the nations as well (Ezek. 25–32). Ezekiel did these things as a priest, not as a king, and in a sense, Jesus' work of judgment in AD 70 is of the same sort. He judged Jerusalem and the nations around her, the nations of the Oikumene, but He did so before His throne was formed by the ascension of the saints.

Now, however, Jesus comes as priest-king (Matt. 25:34, 40), as Melchizedek, as a priest who also sits on a throne. If AD 70 was a priestly judgment of the priestly nation and its surroundings, the Final Judgment is a kingly judgment of all humanity, all nations, all history.

Is a priest a shepherd? In the Bible, the shepherd is the king, not the priest. David is the premier example, and before him, Jacob. In a very important sense, however, the priest is also a shepherd, since he offers the sheep to God. The difference is that the king provides life to the sheep, while the priest kills them.

But the order is also very important. The priest comes first and then the king. Abraham must be priest and offer Isaac before Jacob can be king and rule flocks and many sons. Israel had a human high priest for centuries before she was also given a human king. Symbolically, this indicates that the herd (oxen) and flocks (goats and sheep) of Israel must undergo death and transformation through God's altar-fire before they are ready to be ruled by Him as their Shepherd and King. The same, of course, holds true for us as Christian believers.

The priestly judgment of the flock of sheep and goats comes at the beginning and sets up the people of God. Then for a period of time those flocks are ruled by the kingly shepherd. At the end, the kingly shepherd will separate them as he prepares to make use of them, since they are not the same. That priestly judgment is what is described in Revelation 14–18, as the kingdom begins. Then follows the Millennium, during which Jesus rules as King. Finally comes the Last Judgment and the everlasting kingdom.

B. SHEEP AND GOATS

Christians are so accustomed to this story that we do not realize right away that Jesus is altering traditional symbolism. In the Levitical system, both sheep and goats were used as sacrifices. Either might be used at Passover (Exod. 12:5). The offering of the Feast of Firstfruits required a lamb (Lev. 23:12; Rev. 5:6, 12), but on the Day of Coverings the sacrifice consisted of two goats (Lev. 16). Of these two goats, one was exiled from the camp while the other was sent up to God. Thus, on that occasion the division was between two goats, representing the faithful and the wicked within Israel.

We might expect the same imagery here: two goats. But that is not what we find, and again this points us beyond AD 70. In the book of Revelation, the offering of the 144,000 and the destruction of Babylon are the Day of Coverings (Rev. 14, 17). The events of AD 70 fulfill the Day of Coverings as an historical type and prophecy. Since Matthew 25 is about a different event, the final judgment, we have sheep and goats, instead of two goats.

Thus, we can ask if there is any root for Jesus' distinction between sheep and goats as righteous and wicked. If, as Augustine wrote, "the New is in the Old concealed; the Old is in the New revealed," then where does the "Old Testament" conceal this kind of distinction?

There is some foundation for this kind of distinction in Ezekiel 34, where we find an oracle of judgment against the shepherds of Israel. As we have noted, shepherds are the political leaders of the nation. As the oracle progresses, God speaks of the wicked leaders not as shepherds but as bad goats and bad sheep (Ezek. 34:17-23). We have to note that the distinction is not between sheep and goats as a whole, but between good and bad in both groups.

Similarly, Daniel 8 provides a vision in which the kings of Persia are pictured as a ram (sheep) and Alexander the Great as a goat. Out of the goat arises a horn that tramples down the people of God and blasphemes against God Most High. If we bear in mind that the Persian kings Cyrus and Darius were both favorable to God's people and probably converts to the true religion, while the goat-horn personage was a great and terrible oppressor of the faithful, we can see a shadow of the kind of distinction Jesus makes here as He prophesies the Last Judgment.[76]

Neither of these is, however, very close to what Jesus actually says. I suggest that the distinction arises as an application by Jesus of a distinction found in Leviticus 4. There we find that the bull represents the high priest and also the nation as a whole; the he-goat represents the leaders of the nation; and the she-goat and sheep represent the ordinary faithful person. Jesus has characterized the leaders of Israel as vain and lacking in humility. In terms of Levitical symbolism (given by Jesus Himself as Yahweh), the scribes and Pharisees are bad goats. By way of contrast, Jesus says that His followers will be humble, and the sheep

---

76. The goat-horn personage is usually linked with Antiochus IV Epiphanes. I believe that the reference is to the Herods. For a full discussion, see my commentary on Daniel, *The Handwriting on the Wall*.

represents the ordinary person. In terms of Matthew 23–25 as a whole, and taking its chiastic structure into account, the scribes and Pharisees are like the proud goats who are put at the King's left hand and are condemned. The faithful are like humble sheep, delivered by the Good Shepherd.

We need only distinguish the sociological and the moral possibilities in this symbolic system. Morally and spiritually, we are all to be sheep, for we are all to be humble. In purely religious terms, the man who tries to be a goat is proud and will come under judgment. Within this society of humble sheep, some will be goats and some will be bulls, as political and religious leaders within the Kingdom of God. Yet such leaders, such goats and bulls, must always be sheep first and foremost; they must rule and lead with humility and service, not lording it over others (Matt. 20:25-28). In terms of the law Yahweh-Jesus gave to Israel, the leaders (bulls) must come up from among the people (sheep) (Deut. 17:15).

Behind the Levitical symbolism lies the history recorded in Genesis. It is there that an even deeper layer of symbolism lies. To begin with, recall that when Abraham brought Isaac to God to offer him as a sacrifice, God provided a ram, a male sheep, as a substitute (Gen. 22:13). Earlier, in Genesis 21:28, Abraham had sent seven ewe lambs, female sheep, to Abimelech as part of the covenant established between the two. I submit that when Isaac later on moves to Abimelech's territory in Genesis 26, he is carrying forth the meaning of Abraham's sending the sheep to Abimelech. These stories serve to show us that the sheep is the primary sacrifice in the sacrificial system set up in Genesis 15. For minor sins, all the animals except a male sheep might be offered (Lev. 4), but for the major sins, only a male sheep might be offered (Lev. 5:14–6:7).[77]

When we move to the story of Esau and Jacob, however, we find that the goat comes into prominence. Esau is represented by the goat, and Jacob is disguised by Rebekah with the hairy skins of goats when he

---

77. On the centrality of the ram in the sacrificial system, see James B. Jordan, "The Lamb of God," *Biblical Horizons* 39 and 40 (July & August 1992).

deceives Isaac (Gen. 27). Moreover, the meal served to Isaac on this occasion consists of two goat kids combined into one dish.

Isaac's failure to carry forth the covenant, and indeed his intention to destroy the covenant by giving it to Esau, serves to disqualify him as a true "lamb" of God. He is replaced by Jacob, whose name means "replacement." We are so accustomed to thinking of Jacob as a replacement for Esau that we overlook the fact that more importantly he is a replacement for Isaac. When God appears to Jacob, He calls Abraham Jacob's father (Gen. 28:13).[78]

Thus, Jacob is the sheep and Esau is the goat.

Now, one other layer of symbolic meaning must be added, and that is that the best sheep are white, while the best goats are black. The symbolic opposition of black and white, of darkness and light, is pervasive in the Bible and familiar enough not to require comment here. It is important, however, to realize that *within history no sheep are pure white and no goats are pure black*. This is set forth in the flocks of Jacob, which we recall consisted of goats with white speckles, spots, or stripes on them and of sheep that were not pure white (Gen. 30:32-42). The mixed flock of Jacob signifies the people of Jacob. With Jacob, Israel becomes a nation of many sons, and simultaneously Jacob becomes a man of many flocks. Genesis 27:9 is the tenth mention of "flock" in Genesis. In the ensuing story, Jacob is associated with a "flock" thirty-eight times. Totaling all the words for sheep, goat, he-goat, ewe, lamb, flock, etc., we find fifty-five occurrences. In the Joseph narrative (ch. 37–50), "flock" occurs fifteen times.

In summary, then, we can lay out the distinction between sheep and goats as follows:

1. Sheep are white; goats are black. At the end of history, all the black is gone from the sheep and all the white from goats.
2. Sheep are humble; goats may become proud.
3. Sheep are associated with Jacob, goats with Esau.

---

78. For a fuller discussion of Jacob and Esau, and Jacob as Isaac's replacement, see my book *Primeval Saints*.

C. AT THE RIGHT HAND

As Jesus sits at His Father's right hand, so now the sheep are positioned at Jesus' right hand. There are several dimensions of this that need addressing.

First, the right hand is the hand of power (Matt. 22:44; 26:64), a symbol that is understandable when we recall that most people are right-handed. The right thumb, ear, and toe of the priest were bloodied and anointed as part of his ordination for service (Lev. 8:23-24; cf. 14:14, 17, 25, 28). True power, Biblically, is seen through service.

Second, what Jesus actually says alludes to Psalm 45:6-9, which refers to the throne of King and concludes with, "At Your right hand stands the queen in gold from Ophir." The psalm follows by saying that Daughter Zion, the Queen, will enter the King's palace. Perhaps we should also notice that the Queen is told to forget her old father's house, and this is similar to what Jesus said when He pointed to the Father as the only real Father for His people (Matt. 23:9). Here in 25:34, when the King speaks to the Bride-sheep at His right hand, He refers to His Father, who is also their Father.

Third, once again there is a contrast of imagery between what is said here and the Millennial rule of Revelation 20. There the saints sit on thrones around the throne of the King, and these are the thrones vacated by the angels who had sat on them in Revelation 4. We have seen in chapter 18 that the Millennium is the Marriage Feast, but that the full consummation waits for the Everlasting Kingdom. Thus, the invitation to join Jesus at His right hand is an exaltation beyond the thrones of the Millennium and signifies the full entrance into the eternal marriage.

Fourth, the use of right and left here, with Jesus as King, can profitably be linked with the kingship of Yahweh in the temple of Jerusalem. Yahweh was enthroned in the westernmost room of the temple, the Holy of Holies, so that He faced east. You enter the temple from the east, heading west. First you come to the altar, then to the holy place, then to the holy of holies, which is the farthest west. And that means Yahweh is facing *east.* If you're facing *east,* then your right hand is south. To His right was the south of Israel and to His left was the north.

I submit that a Jew, steeped in the history of Israel, would catch an allusion to the apostate kingdom of Ephraim in the north, which lay to the King's left, and to the more faithful kingdom of Judah in the south, which lay to His right. The right hand, thus, is the side of Judah, which is definitely to be preferred.

D. GOOD WORKS

There can be no doubt but that the Final Judgment will be meted out in terms of good works, but what are good works? Good works consist of faith-filled obedience. When we obey, trusting God in spite of everything and believing His promises of deliverance and reward, we are obeying in faith. Faith all by itself does not really exist, in a sense, because human beings are always doing something. Faith is the attitude that accompanies our actions. We can distinguish faith and action (works), but we cannot separate them. Faith and works are two sides of one coin. True faith is faithfulness and manifests in good works. True good works are always done in faith.

If we believe God, we will do what He says and ask for forgiveness when we disobey. If Adam had really believed God and what He said, Adam would never have eaten the forbidden fruit. What Jesus says here is along the same lines. The whole revelation of the Last Judgment tells us that we can afford to be the kind of humble people Jesus told us to be back at the beginning of the discourse (Matt. 23:1-12), because we are promised that we shall be rewarded with everlasting happiness if we do so.

It has been said that though we are saved by faith alone, yet the kind of faith that saves is never found alone. In other words, you cannot trust God and then *never* do what He says, because the fear of God is the beginning of wisdom and life. Saving faith is *faithful* faith. We are saved wholly by Jesus' work and thus by nothing that we have done, but when we have been saved we will begin to do the kinds of things Jesus did.

Jesus returns here to what He had said in the Sermon on the Mount (Matt. 7:15-23). He tells us there that His people do good works, but that there are those who do counterfeit "good works." Such counterfeit people can be identified by the fact that, over the course of time, it becomes apparent that they do their good deeds for the wrong reasons and that they also do some very wicked deeds, which they seek to justify. Notice that the counterfeiters address Jesus as "Lord" in both Matthew 7:21 and here in 25:44. God is not interested in being acknowledged in a merely ceremonial fashion.

True good works occur unspectacularly as a result of the quiet and invisible influence of the Holy Spirit. In Matthew 7:17-19, Jesus compared such good works with the fruit naturally born by a good tree over the course of time. Paul picks up on this when he speaks of the "fruit" of the Spirit in Galatians 5:22, which he contrasts with the "deeds" of the flesh (Gal. 5:19).

Thus, good works are not heroic. They stand in contrast with what the fleshly world thinks good works are. Those who are great in God's eyes are not necessarily those who fight great battles or who campaign for needed political reform, but those who do simple things in ordinary life. The person who lives by faith in God and is moved by the Spirit knows what to do when he encounters a hungry person: He gives him food. He does not turn away and mollify his conscience by working to pass social legislation (though such legislation might be important at times, depending on what it actually enacts); rather, he gives from what he has to the one who is in need.

E.   WHY THESE PARTICULAR WORKS?

Jesus provides six good works that are characteristic of those who are sheep. We might expect seven, signifying fullness and completeness, but Jesus gives only six. Actually, though, these are grouped in pairs to produce a list of three. This grouping in pairs emerges from looking at how the list is actually stated.

"I hungered" and "I thirsted" are both verbs (v. 35ab). Not only so, but they are clearly linked conceptually. Moreover, they are put together in one sentence in the question asked in verse 37.

"A stranger I was" is a noun and a verb, and "naked" has no verb with it, linking it to the preceding phrase grammatically (vv. 35c-36a). They are put together in one question in verse 38.

"I became ill" is a verb and "in prison I was" is a noun with a verb. But these are put together in one phrase in verses 39 and 43c.

We might say that by listing these simple good works, Jesus means to include all good works, and that is enough by itself. It is perfectly true. But there is likely a greater depth to be plumbed here, and I suggest that these three works relate to the three temptations Satan put before Jesus in the wilderness. Matthew 4:1-11 and Luke 4:1-12 set out the temptations in different orders, each having the same first temptation but reversing the order of the second and third. Clearly each writer has his own Spirit-directed literary-theological purpose, but that does not mean one or the other is not strictly and chronologically true. It is possible that Satan approached Jesus more than once with these temptations.

First, when Jesus became hungry, Satan tempted Him to turn stones into bread (Matt. 4:3-4). We can obviously link this with Jesus' statement here that He was hungry and thirsty. Satan offered Him the wrong bread, but the good sheep offer Him good bread and drink. What He rejects from Satan, He is pleased to accept from us. Priests provide food. Jesus asks us to be priests to Him.

Second, Satan challenged Jesus to put Himself at risk (Matt. 4:5-6), saying that surely angels would catch Him if He leaped off the temple's pinnacle. I suggest that this links with the third pair of good works here, for ill and imprisoned people are at risk and near to death (especially in the pre-modern world). Jesus refused to put Himself at risk to please Satan, but here He says that He does put Himself at risk so that we can be angels and catch Him. Kings have power and majesty. Jesus comes to us as the opposite of a king, as someone ill or imprisoned, and asks us to be kings to Him.

Third, Satan promises Jesus the whole world if He will only bow down and render homage to him (Matt. 4:8-10). To understand this, remember that Jesus, as the only perfectly righteous man ever to walk the earth, was estranged from the world. He was the stranger, and He would be made naked on the cross when the world rejected Him. Satan offers an alternative: worship Satan, and thereby admit that the creature and the Creator are the same, and Jesus will be accepted by all. Jesus refuses to come before Satan as a naked stranger, asking to be let into Satan's world. But what Jesus refuses to do before Satan He does do before us. He humbles Himself and asks to be let in. Prophets judge the whole world, as members of God's council, glorifying (robing) some and debasing (stripping) others. Jesus comes to us naked, as an exile from this world, and asks us to be prophets toward Him.

Jesus comes to us thirsty and hungry and asks us to feed Him. He comes to us naked and a stranger and asks us to let Him in. He comes to us near to death and asks us to give life to Him.

This is an amazing reversal of what we expect the Kingdom to be like. Clearly, we are the ones who are hungry, naked, and near death, and we must come to Jesus for the Spirit of salvation. True enough. But when we have come to Him, He sends us His Spirit and asks us to do the same for Him! He makes Himself "least" so that we may minister to Him, as He ministered to us first.

F. WHO ARE THE BROTHERS (V. 40)?

To begin with, the word means "brothers" and is masculine. It does not mean "brothers and sisters" in an ordinary sense. Biblical theology uses daughter and bride language to speak of the Church corporately as a whole, and it uses son and brother language to speak of the individuals in the Church. Thus, we are all brothers, regardless of sex, and we are all part of the Bride of Christ, regardless of sex. Recent translations, which seek to render "brothers" as "brothers and sisters," nullify this important theological point.

As Christians, we are so used to thinking of the brethren as fellow Christians that we might miss what is actually said here. It is true, of course, that we are to do good first of all to the household of the faith, but we are also to do good to all mankind (Gal. 6:10).

So then, is Jesus speaking only of how we treat other believers or of how we treat all people? The answer is the latter. The reason we can be certain of this is the inclusion of "stranger" in the list, because in the Law the stranger was the person outside of the covenant people of Israel, the "least" in Israel.

It can be replied that in Matthew 10, the disciples are sent out as sheep among wolves. Such disciples will appear as strangers, but those who receive them will be rewarded (10:11-15). The disciples will be imprisoned (10:17-19). Those who give cups of water to "little ones" will be rewarded (10:42). Thus, it can be argued that the brethren in Matthew 25 are the disciples and believers in general.

All this is quite valid, in the sense that we are to do good first of all to the household of faith. But "stranger" has a long and potent meaning in Biblical revelation, and it will not do to link it to Matthew 10, where the word is not actually used, while overlooking that larger context. When we turn to Acts 10–11, we see that Peter would not visit the house of even a converted and God-fearing "stranger," and God had to rebuke him. Thus, we should not restrict the "brethren" only to those who are already converted into the Kingdom, or to the special servants of the Kingdom (the missionary disciples).

Rather, we must bear in mind that this is the last judgment of all. It is not a preliminary judgment coming in the midst of human history. It covers all of human history, all of humanity. All human beings are images of God, and thus are images of the Second Person of God. The Bible nowhere teaches or hints that the image of God is "lost" or "marred" by sin and the fall of Adam. Rather, the image of God is simply what human beings are, for better or worse. Sinners are images of God who sin.

This means that we can and should see Jesus in the face of every human being, whether or not that particular person acknowledges that he or she bears the image of God. Jesus cared for us when we hated Him, and that is how we are to be as well. What we can learn from this is that when we do good to people who ultimately despise and reject us and who reject the gospel that we bring them, we are still doing good to Jesus, to the "least" of the King's brothers, and it will be counted as such by Him at the Last Day.

Once again, we need to see the contrast with the scribes and Pharisees of Matthew 23. These men abused the food laws of the covenant, adding to them in such ways that the hungry were not fed. They abused the stranger by inventing new rules for avoiding non-Jews (Acts 10–11). The ill and imprisoned they viewed as being under God's curse and avoided them (John 9:2). Most interesting, Jesus condemns them for saying that if they had lived in the days of the prophets, they would have honored them (Matt. 23:30). That is precisely the outlook of the goats in this passage: "If we had actually encountered You, Lord, we would have cared for You!" Like the Pharisees, the goats fail to see Jesus where He actually is to be seen: in the face of all human beings, all of whom are made in His image.

G. THE FINAL SEPARATION

At the fall of Satan, the angelic realm separated definitively and once and for all into two parties. They are both mentioned here (vv. 31, 41). There is no salvation for fallen angels, though they have not yet been consigned to the everlasting fire that burns as an altar before the throne of God (Rev. 14:10).

The final separation of humanity means that the wicked receive the same judgment as the fallen angels, while the saints receive the same blessedness as the holy angels. In the book of Revelation we see that the holy angels, as they finish their work, give up their thrones to the saints. They enter into everlasting rest and bliss. At the end of history, the saints will also give up those thrones, at the end of the Millennium, and enter into their own everlasting rest and bliss. With Jesus, they will retire from being kings, in a sense, when the Kingdom is returned to the Father (1 Cor. 15:28).

We should notice that when Jesus speaks to the sheep, He calls Himself the King (vv. 34, 40), while He does not call Himself King when He speaks to the wicked (vv. 41, 45). Jesus is their Judge, precisely because they would not have Him as their King.

Additionally, the sheep are called "blessed" while the goats are called "cursed." This separation runs back to Leviticus 26 and Deuteronomy 27–28, of course, but also to the Sermon on the Mount. Recall that the eight Blessings of that Sermon are matched with the eight Woes of Matthew 23. Once again, we see that the goats judged at the end of history are like the Pharisees condemned at the beginning of the Gospel Age.

Finally, notice also that the Kingdom was prepared for the sheep from the foundation of the world, while the everlasting fires were not prepared for humanity at all, but for the devil and his angels. While "satan" means "accuser," "devil" means "slanderer." The serpent slandered God in the beginning, saying that God did not have good intentions for Adam and Eve. By putting their faith and trust in the serpent's words, Adam and Eve joined with the devil, the slanderer. Human beings who don't repent of this sin and who keep slandering God, as the one-talent sinner of the Parable of the Talents does (Matt. 25:24), will continue to abide with the devil forever and ever. God's original intention, however, was for all human beings to abide with Him, and there was a Kingdom prepared for them from the beginning.